East–West Exchange
and Late Modernism

East–West Exchange

AND

Late Modernism

Williams, Moore, Pound

Zhaoming Qian

University of Virginia Press

CHARLOTTESVILLE AND LONDON

University of Virginia Press
© 2017 by the Rector and Visitors of the University of Virginia
All rights reserved
Printed in the United States of America on acid-free paper

First published 2017

9 8 7 6 5 4 3 2 1

LIBRARY OF CONGRESS CATALOGING-IN-PUBLICATION DATA

Names: Qian, Zhaoming, author.
Title: East-West exchange and late modernism : Williams, Moore, Pound / Zhaoming
    Qian.
Description: Charlottesville : University of Virginia Press, 2017. | Includes
    bibliographical references and index.
Identifiers: LCCN 2017021807 | ISBN 9780813940663 (cloth : acid-free paper) |
    ISBN 9780813940670 (pbk. : acid-free paper) | ISBN 9780813940687 (e-book)
Subjects: LCSH: Modernism (Literature) | East and West in literature.
Classification: LCC PN56.M54 Q34 2017 | DDC 809/.9112—dc23
LC record available at https://lccn.loc.gov/2017021807

Cover art: A Breath of Spring, Zou Fulei, mid-fourteenth century. (Freer Gallery of Art,
Smithsonian Institution; purchase, Charles Lang Freer Endowment)

For May
and for
Lilyan Qian Hernandez

Contents

Illustrations

Preface

THIS BOOK HAS ITS ORIGIN in my research for *Ezra Pound's Chinese Friends: Stories in Letters* (2008). In studying Pound's exchange with Paul Pao-hsien Fang, a Naxi (Na-khi) man of southwestern China, it occurred to me that roughly during the same period William Carlos Williams was working with the Chinese poet David Wang on Tang dynasty poems and Marianne Moore was corresponding with the Chinese painter-writer Mai-mai Sze about Taoist aesthetic. My investigation of the three American poets' late-life exchanges with China led to my inquiry into the impact of these encounters on their last books—Williams's *Pictures from Brueghel* (1962), Moore's *Tell Me, Tell Me* (1966), and Pound's *Drafts and Fragments of Cantos CX–CXVII* (1969). The three modernists in question are among the most written about figures in literary criticism. Their last volumes of verse, however, remain relatively overlooked. A study of late Williams, late Moore, late Pound, and East–West exchange will fill a gap in modernist studies.

Two books, *21st-Century Modernism* by Marjorie Perloff (2002) and *Illustration* by J. Hillis Miller (1992), have proven wonderful guides for this project. For some critics, modernism belongs to the pre-1945 era. In *21st-Century Modernism*, Perloff made a pioneering effort to verify a resurgence of modernism at the millennium. It paved the way for my attempt to justify the three American poets' renewal of modernism in the 1960s, the "postmodernist era." Previous critics in discussing cross-cultural literary works largely focused on textual and visual influences. In *Illustration*, Miller established the interlocutor from the target culture as the most authentic and compelling source of cross-cultural exchange. Without Miller's sophisticated conceptions of cultural studies, it would be difficult to untangle the complex matters in these three poets' interpersonal East-West exchanges through which they learned ways to guard against the realism that often came to replace the more abstract modernism of the early twentieth century.

The three modernists under scrutiny have appeared in my earlier books—Pound and Williams in *Orientalism and Modernism* (1995) and Pound and Moore in *The Modernist Response to Chinese Art* (2003). Is there any overlap? *Orientalism and Modernism* explored Pound, Williams, and Chinese poetry from 1913 to 1923. *The Modernist Response to Chinese Art* examined Pound's, Moore's, and Wallace Stevens's visual exchanges with China from the beginning of their careers up to the 1950s. The late modernist works—Williams's *Pictures from Brueghel,* Moore's *Tell Me, Tell Me,* and Pound's *Drafts and Fragments*—are not discussed in either of my earlier books. In addition to the difference in the periods covered, there is a shift in focus from exchange via text and image to exchange via personal interaction. The aim of the present study is to further the latest trends of crossing cultures and uniting intertextuality practice with cultural studies and to reinforce the view of twentieth-century poetic development—that late modernism is a continuation of the aesthetic of the early twentieth century and that it fulfils the avant-garde project.

Although all three of the modernist poets chosen are Americans, "modernism" in this project does not exclusively mean American modernism. Indeed, my first example is French artist Claude Monet's "Japanese inspired" *Water Lilies,* a precursor to abstract expressionism of the 1950s. The book also includes a brief discussion of Irish poet and playwright W. B. Yeats's *At the Hawk's Well,* modeled on the Noh of Japan, and references to the East Asian connections of late modernists Lee Harwood (Britain) and Steve McCaffery (Canada). Admittedly, my central focus is on poetic modernism, but my illustrations cross the disciplines of visual art, theater, dance, and architecture.

The research for this book began with a Yale Comparative Literature Fellowship in 2005 and continued with a chancellor's research grant from the University of New Orleans (2009–12) and a Yongqian Tang endowment grant from Zhejiang University (2008–10). A grant from the Chinese Academy of Social Sciences combined with a smaller grant from Hangzhou Normal University (2013–16) permitted me to complete the book. For all this support I am grateful.

Without the assistance of the heirs of the three modernist poets and their Chinese friends, this project could not have been completed in its present form. Ezra Pound's daughter Mary de Rachewiltz helped locate materials. Mai-mai Sze's sister Alice Sze Wang responded to my queries. Paul Fang's widow, Josephine Fang, and I. M. Pei's son Chien Chung Pei respectively reviewed the Pound-Fang chapters and the Pei section for accuracy.

An earlier version of chapter 1 appeared in *Modern Philology* 108.2 (2010) under the title "William Carlos Williams, David Raphael Wang, and the Dynamic of East/West Collaboration," copyright 2010 by The University of Chicago. The substance of chapter 3 is adapted from "Mai-mai Sze, the Tao, and Late Moore" in my edited volume *Modernism and the Orient* (New Orleans: University of New Orleans Press, 2012). A version of the Arthur Miller discussion in the coda appeared in the *Arthur Miller Journal* 12.1 (2017) under the title "Miller, BPAT, and the Dynamic of East-West Collaboration," copyright 2017 by The Pennsylvania State University Press, used by the permission of The Pennsylvania State University Press. I thank the editors and publishers for their permission to reprint.

I enjoyed delivering a paper, "Williams, Wang, and the Visualization of Classic Chinese Poetry," at the 2006 MLA convention in Philadelphia. I thank Zhang Jian and Sun Hong for inviting me to give a keynote speech, "Ezra Pound, Paul Fang, and Naxi Culture," at China's first Ezra Pound conference held in Beijing in June 2008. It was my pleasure and honor to direct the Third International Conference on Modernism and the Orient in Hangzhou in June 2010 where I gave a keynote address, "Moore's 'Lost' Essay on the Tao and Her Final Achievement." I thank Michael O'Sullivan and Li Ou for inviting me to present a paper, "Monet's *Water Lilies* and Moore's Final Version of 'Poetry,'" for a seminar at the Chinese University of Hong Kong in June 2012.

This book has benefited from my conversations with the following persons: Barry Ahearn, Charles Altieri, Massimo Bacigalupo, George Bornstein, Ronald Bush, Xiaomei Chen, Wendy Stallard Flory, Ben Friedlander, Christine Froula, Simon Haines, Gregory Harvey, Christian Kloeckner, Linda Leavell, Li Ou, Tony Lopez, Anne Luyat, Christopher MacGowan, Glen MacLeod, Stephen Marino, Cristanne Miller, David Moody, Ira Nadel, Michael O'Sullivan, Ou Hong, Josephine Park, Richard Parker, Marjorie Perloff, Roxana Preda, Ran Yi, Claude Rawson, Lisa Ruddick, Haun Saussy, Peter Schmidt, Sabine Sielke, Emily Mitchell Wallace, Ban Wang, and Patricia Willis.

Barry Ahearn, Xiaomei Chen, Joseph Dahm, Ben Friedlander, John Gery, Glen MacLeod, Lisa Ruddick, and Charles Wu read early versions of different chapters. I am grateful for their input. My greatest appreciation goes to the readers for the University of Virginia Press. Their alacrity, encouragement, and advice are a marvel.

For their assistance I would like to thank the directors, curators, archivists, and librarians of the following institutions: Gina Bedoya at Pei Partnership Architects, Janice Braun at the F. W. Olin Library, Mills College, Michaelyn Burnette at the Bancroft Library, University of California, Berkeley, Sheila Connor at the Arnold Arboretum Horticultural Library in Boston, Elizabeth Fuller and Jobi Zink at the Rosenbach Museum and Library in Philadelphia, Nancy Kuhl and Adrienne Sharpe at the Beinecke Rare Book and Manuscript Library, Yale University, Connie Phelps at the Earl K. Long Library, University of New Orleans, Betsy Rose at the National Poetry Foundation, University of Maine, Jay Satterfield at the Rauner Special Collections Library, Dartmouth College, Erin Schreiner at the New York Society Library, Michael Thomas at the Joseph F. Rock Herbarium, University of Hawaii, and J. Dustin Williams at the Hunt Institute for Botanical Documentation, Carnegie Mellon University.

For their friendship and support I thank Linda Blanton, Mackie Blanton, John Gery, John Hazlett, Kris Lackey, Patricia Roger, Peter Schock, and Robert Shenk at the University of New Orleans; Fan Jieping, Gao Fen, He Lianzhen, Lu Qiaodan, and Shen Hong at Zhejiang University; and Chen Lizhen, Deng Tianzhong, Feng Xin, Guan Nanyi, Li Gongzhao, Ou Rong, Ye Lei, Yin Qiping, and Ying Ying at Hangzhou Normal University.

Mary Bamburg, Douglas Barry, Rich Goode, and Liu Xiaofang have been my superb student assistants. Mary Bamburg helped transcribe the recording of Marianne Moore's lecture "Tedium and Integrity in Poetry." Douglas Barry assisted my research on Moore and Sze.

At the University of Virginia Press Eric Brandt, Bonnie Susan Gill, Morgan Myers, Ellen Satrom, and Cecilia Sorochin make up a wonderful team. It has been a pleasure to work with them and with Siobhan Drummond, my copy editor.

As always my wife, May, actively participated in this project. She assisted my research at Yale (2005, 2013), Mills College (2010), MoMA (2013), Stanford (2014), Lijiang (2014), and the Suzhou Museum (2015). This book is dedicated to her as well as to our granddaughter Lilyan Qian Hernandez, who just celebrated her third birthday.

Grateful acknowledgment is made to the following publishers, estates, and individuals for permission to use copyrighted materials:

New Directions Publishing Corporation for the excerpt from *End to Torment: A Memoir of Ezra Pound* by H.D., edited by Norman Holmes Pearson and Michael King, © 1979 by New Directions Publishing Corporation.

New Directions Publishing Corporation for Cantos XCVIII, CI, CX, CXII, and CXVI from *The Cantos of Ezra Pound,* © 1973, 1986, 1993 by the Trustees of the Ezra Pound Literary Property Trust.

New Directions Publishing Corporation for "Complete Destruction," "Nantucket," "Portrait of the Author," "The Red Wheelbarrow," "Spring," and "To the Shade of Po Chü-i" from *The Collected Poems of William Carlos Williams, Volume I, 1909–1939,* edited by A. Walton Litz and Christopher MacGowan, © 1986 by William Eric Williams and Paul H. Williams.

New Directions Publishing Corporation for "The Blue Jay," "The Chrysanthemum," "The Corn Harvest," "The Dance" (When the snow falls), "Iris," "Landscape with the Fall of Icarus," "The Newlywed's Cuisine," "The Peerless Lady," "Poem" (The rose fades), "The Rewaking," "Self-Portrait," "Short Poem," and "Spring Song" (A young lass) from *The Collected Poems of William Carlos Williams, Volume II, 1939–1962,* edited by Christopher MacGowan, © 1988 by William Eric Williams and Paul H. Williams.

New Directions Publishing Corporation for the excerpt from *I Wanted to Write a Poem: The Autobiography of the Works of a Poet,* by William Carlos Williams, reported and edited by Edith Heal, © 1977 by the Estate of Florence H. Williams; © 1976 by Edith Heal.

New Directions Publishing Corporation for the excerpt from *Paterson,* Book II, by William Carlos Williams, edited by Christopher MacGowan, © 1992 by William Eric Williams and Paul H. Williams.

Viking Books, an imprint of Penguin Publishing Group, a division of Penguin Random House LLC, for "Arthur Mitchell," "Blue Bug," "An Expedient—Leonardo da Vinci's—and a Query," "Granite and Steel," "Old Amusement Park," "Poetry" (final version), "Tell Me, Tell Me," "To a Giraffe," and "W. S. Landor" from *The Poems of Marianne Moore* by Marianne Moore, edited by Grace Schulman, © 2003 by Marianne Craig Moore, Literary Executor of the Estate of Marianne Moore.

Josephine Riss Fang for previously unpublished material by Paul Pao-hsien Fang, © 2017.

Elizabeth Pound for a previously unpublished letter by Dorothy Pound, © 2017 by the Estate of Omar S. Pound.

Mary de Rachewiltz and Elizabeth Pound for previously unpublished material by Ezra Pound, © 2017 by Mary de Rachewiltz and the Estate of Omar S. Pound.

Irene Tseng for previously unpublished material by Mai-mai Sze, © 2017.

The William Carlos Williams Estate in care of the Jean V. Naggar Literary Agency, Inc., for previously unpublished material by William Carlos Williams, © 2017 by the William Carlos Williams Estate.

Despite my diligence, not all copyright holders have been located. My publisher and I would be grateful to be notified of corrections or omissions that should be incorporated in the next printing or edition of this book. In the rare cases when the copyright holder has not responded within six months, I have concluded that there is no objection to citing the source.

Illustrations were provided through the courtesy of Art Resource, Inc., the Beinecke Rare Book and Manuscript Library at Yale University, the Dartmouth College Library, the Imogen Cunningham Trust, the Freer Gallery of Art, the Metropolitan Museum of Art, Pei Partnership Architects, Josephine Riss Fang, and Mary de Rachewiltz.

Marianne Moore's "Tedium and Integrity in Poetry" appears courtesy of Special Collections, F.W. Olin Library, Mills College.

Abbreviations

East-West Exchange
and Late Modernism

East–West Exchange

and the Renewal

of Modernism

Far from being irrelevant and obsolete, the aesthetic of early modernism has provided the seeds of the materialist poetic which is increasingly our own. —Marjorie Perloff, *21st-Century Modernism*

Paradoxically, modernism may seem postmodern after all, not surprisingly since the charges that postmodernism levels at modernism often replay those that modernism itself leveled at Victorianism. —George Bornstein, *Material Modernism*

The various new aesthetics of early twentieth-century Europe register not just breaks and continuities but global historical processes ... to the point that there hardly exists a purely European or western aesthetics. —Christine Froula, "Proust's China"

I BEGIN WITH the above three quotations because they will help answer questions the reader may have about my title. What is late modernism? What has it to do with East–West exchange? *Late modernism* is a contested term. Tyrus Miller uses it to mean modernism between the world wars.[1] Anthony Mellors uses it to designate "the continuation of modernist writing into the war years and until at least the end of the 1970s."[2] Neither definition has been accepted as standard. For me modernism as a literary and artistic culture not only survived the Second World War but has continued through the second half of the twentieth century into the present century. Accordingly, I am using the term *late modernism* to refer to the post-1945 renewals of early twentieth-century modernism, an avant-garde project distinguished by anti-tradition, anti-mimesis, and radical formal innovation. In *21st-Century Modernism* (2002) Marjorie Perloff defines modernism not as "an epoch fast receding into the cultural past" but as an early twentieth-century "avant-garde project" disrupted by the disaster of the world wars and subsequent political disturbances only to be rejuvenated in due course.[3] Taking my cue from Perloff, I shall contend in this study that contrary to assumptions of the past century there was a revitalization of modernism in the 1960s, the "postmodern era."

Modernism may seem to have nothing to do with the West's exchange with East Asia, but as an avant-garde project it favors transnationalism and interculturalism, or as Christine Froula claims, it approves of "cross-fertilization, assimilation, creative adaptation, indigenization, translation, and making-new, within and across locally differentiated traditions."[4] There were many factors contributing to the development of late modernism. In the cases of three American modernist forerunners, William Carlos Williams (1883–1963), Marianne Moore (1887–1972), and Ezra Pound (1885–1972), one of the factors that assisted their renewal of modernism was interaction with East Asian sources and interlocutors.[5]

The West's exchange with East Asia, or China and Japan, has sometimes been a spur to late-life creativity, as the example of Claude Monet (1840–1926) illustrates. A look at Monet's case will prepare for my exploration of the American modernists' late-life exchange with China and renewal of modernism. Visitors to Monet's home at Giverny marvel at his collection of 231 Japanese prints.[6] Whichever room one enters one is surrounded by ukiyo-e paintings. Kunisada's *Abalone Fishing* in the sitting room is said to have served as a model for Monet's *The Pink Skiff* (1890).[7] Hiroshige's *Inside Kameido Tenjin Shrine* in the hall presumably inspired Monet to have a Japanese footbridge built in his garden, which in turn stimulated him to create his own Japanese bridge series in 1899–1900.[8]

Monet's love affair with Japanese art began before 1867. In order to make a scientific collection of Japanese prints, Monet befriended French-speaking Japanese art dealer Tadamasa Hayashi (1853–1906) at the 1878 World's Fair in Paris. In Monet's collection are a dozen or so Japanese prints bearing Hayashi's seal, and Hayashi owned Monet's paintings of the 1880s. This suggests that Monet traded his paintings for Hayashi's Japanese prints.[9] Hayashi became general commissioner for Japan at the 1900 Paris World's Fair. Among his books in French are *Histoire de l'Art du Japon* (1901) and *Objets d'art du Japon et de la Chine* (1902).[10]

Monet's infatuation with Japanese art stirred him to experiment with new ways of treating the figure in nature. From *Women in the Garden* (1866) which portrays four women relaxing in the shade of a tree he moved on to *The Cliff Walk at Pourville* (1882) which depicts two women on a cliff gazing at the sea. *Cliff Walk* is said to be modeled on Hiroshige's *Yui, Satta Pass,* which was in Monet's collection.[11] While the figures in both Hiroshige's *Yui, Satta Pass* and Monet's *Cliff Walk* turn away from the viewer toward the sea, the sea in the former is pushed to the lower right corner and the sea in the latter is thrust to the lower left corner. Both Hiroshige's *Yui, Satta Pass* and Monet's *Cliff Walk* follow the so-called one-corner composition of Southern Song painter Ma Yuan (ca. 1160–1225), in which the central figures turn away from the viewer toward water and mountains shoved to a corner.[12]

Monet owned nine views from Hokusai's *Thirty-six Views of Mount Fuji.* By the end of the nineteenth century Monet became so fascinated by Hokusai's late-life views of Fuji reproduced in *One Hundred Views of Mount Fuji* that he imagined Mount Fuji covered with snow when he caught sight of a distant mountain on a trip to Norway in 1895.[13] In a letter to his daughter-in-law Blanche-Hoschedé, he wrote: "I have here a delicious motif . . . a mountain in the background. One would say it's Japan. It is like Japan, which is, moreover, frequent in this country. I had in the train a view of Sandviken which resembles a Japanese village, and I also did a mountain which one can see from everywhere, and which makes me dream of Fuji-Yama."[14]

At age seventy-one (1911) Monet lost his second wife, Alice Hoschedé-Monet. Misfortunes never come singly. The death of Alice was followed by his losing battle against cataracts, the outbreak of the First World War, and the death of his eldest son, Jean. Monet's career had come to a crisis when he was rescued by his passion for contemplation of nature. After a brief hiatus he resumed painting and began creating his own series of views, not of a mountain but of the water lily pond in his garden. As Monet pursued this series year after year from 1914 to 1926, his colors turned simpler, his brushwork became more rhythmical, and his canvas appeared less full. The overall effects of his final works turned out to be comparable to those of Japanese or Chinese artists whose strengths rest on simple colors, rhythmical brushwork, and fragmentary treatment of nature.[15] With Japanese models constantly in his presence, Monet remade his pond scenes over and over again for twelve years, leaving to the world more than 250 paintings of water lilies.

Ironically, for thirty years the art world was so absorbed by the modernists—Picasso, Matisse, Cézanne, and Mondrian—that few art lovers

Figure 1. *Water Lilies,* Claude Monet, 1914–26. (Museum of Modern Art, New York; photograph by John Wronn; digital image © the Museum of Modern Art, licensed by SCALA/Art Resource, New York)

paid any attention to Monet's culminating achievement of a lifetime. It was not until the mid-1950s, with the rising impact of the New York School of abstract expressionism, that the French impressionist master was rediscovered. All of a sudden his water lilies became a much sought-after treasure. In 1955, the New York City Museum of Modern Art (MoMA) acquired a *Water Lilies* painting gathering dust in Monet's Giverny studio. When the large canvas was exhibited for the first time, art critic Ronnie Landfield observed that it "took on new and prophetic significance."[16] In 1957 the MoMA acquired a second *Water Lilies* painting by Monet. Unfortunately, a 1958 fire destroyed both of MoMA's *Water Lilies* works, compelling it to purchase in 1959 the *Water Lilies* triptych now installed on its fifth floor (figure 1).[17]

In February 2010 Madrid's Thyssen-Bornemisza Museum launched an exhibition entitled *Monet and Abstract Art.* Brought together were more than one hundred paintings of late Monet and abstract expressionist artists Jackson Pollock, Mark Rothko, and Willem de Kooning. Monet spent the last decades of his life developing his own artistic style, far removed from what was happening in Paris. "That's why he was always seen as old-fashioned," said the exhibition curator, Paloma Alarco. "But the arrival of abstract art after the Second World War turned the spotlight again on Monet, because the abstract artists saw something more in his use of colors, his unique style of painting and techniques."[18]

Did Monet pioneer abstract art? Abstract art was in full swing during the last two decades of Monet's life. Preoccupied with Japanese art and his own series, Monet paid little attention to the abstract art of Piet

Mondrian and others. True, Monet's water lilies and Mondrian's abstract landscapes such as *View from the Dunes with Beach and Piers* (1909) share some affinities. Both paintings explore nature in their own ways, and both seek to simplify and abstract colors and shapes. But nothing besides such accidental affinities is evident.

Was late Monet an inspiration for American abstract expressionists? American abstract expressionists acknowledged their debt to Kandinsky for abstraction theory, dada for emphasis on chance, and surrealism for enthusiasm for dreamlike effects. With their goal of expressing emotion through "spontaneous action," they were not admirers of Monet, who focused on contemplating nature's changes and translating their effects into art.

Since there is neither evidence of Monet's taste for abstract art, nor evidence of American abstract expressionists' penchant for Monet, why should Clement Greenberg's claim that late Monet "belong[s] to our age in a way Cézanne's own attempts at summations (in his two large *Bathers*) no longer do" appeal to so many art critics?[19] Why should the 2010 Madrid exhibition *Monet and Abstract Art* appear as a real shock of recognition to large crowds of art lovers? For one thing, Monet learned from the Japanese to elaborate on art's physicality, which turns out to distinguish him as a forerunner of the formalistic grounds for abstract expressionism. For another, he acquired from the Japanese a purer and more concentrated manner of painting, resulting in a dreamlike and edgeless quality in his late work, which happens to anticipate surrealism's emphasis on dreamy effects and abstract expressionism's choice of "all-over painting."

Late Monet as a precursor to modernism testifies to the validity of Christine Froula's argument that "the various new aesthetics of early twentieth-century Europe register not just breaks and continuities but global historical processes—cross-fertilization, assimilation, creative adaptation, indigenization, translation, and making-new, within and across locally differentiated traditions, through centuries of uneven modernities—to the point that there hardly exists a purely European or western aesthetics."[20]

My summary of Monet's case opens issues central to this project's claims. What does old age mean to creative artists? Is the breaking of style catastrophic to established artists? Would parleys with age-old East Asian aesthetics pull them out of step with the times? Probing into the empirical and theoretical aspects of these questions will pave the way for my discussion of the three American modernists in the mid-twentieth century—the energy/creativity crisis they faced and their respective East-West encounters which jolted them back to early twentieth-century modernism, what Perloff refers to as the "avant-garde phase of modernism," a course disrupted by the Second World War and its subsequent turmoil.[21]

Why do some artists bring out only mediocre works in old age while others sustain creativity and sometimes even achieve greater successes later in life? This is an endlessly fascinating question addressed by Edward Said in *On Late Style* (2006) and Nicholas Delbanco in *Lastingness: The Art of Old Age* (2011).[22] For Said work in contrariety is a good many artists' secret to greater successes in old age. What Dylan Thomas urges as "rage, rage against the dying of the light," in Said's analysis characterizes the late achievement of German composer Richard Strauss (1864–1949), "the keeper of the flame and of 'the art of our fathers.'"[23] Delbanco backs up Said's position with many more examples. The creative artists he has examined include, besides Claude Monet, the Spanish cellist and conductor Pablo Casals (1876–1973), whose motto was "Each day I am reborn"; the English novelist Thomas Hardy (1840–1928), who gave up the novel at age fifty-five to become a thriving poet; and the American painter Georgia O'Keeffe (1887–1986), who ceased painting the non-vegetal at age sixty-two to concentrate on flora.[24] According to UCLA neurobiologist and professor of psychiatry George Bartzokis, for older creative people, "the key is finding work that calls on you to remain nimble, adaptive, even visionary, to invent ideas and solve problems on the fly rather than just responding to the same questions with the same answers again and again."[25] Bartzokis has given away the secret of how Delbanco's subjects manage to live long and remain productive. While O'Keeffe replaced her human and animal subjects with flora to keep herself interested, Hardy switched from fiction to poetry so as not to respond to "the same questions with the same answers again and again." The way Monet and the American modernists under scrutiny challenged their brains in their later years was to engage in exchange with less familiar territories such as Japan and China for technological and conceptual innovations. Like O'Keeffe and Hardy, they all continued to flourish in old age.

For the American modernists, as for Monet, East Asia's attraction was not its progress in the twentieth century but its legacy of age-old art and literature. Why should their exchange with past East Asian concepts and forms help revitalize modernist sensibilities? This is an issue I have addressed in my previous studies. Charles Altieri reminds us that modernism aspires to use "formal energies to reject mimetic structures and [to] still retain extraordinary semantic force."[26] Traditional East Asian aesthetic shares this aspiration. It does not follow the rules prescribed by Aristotle. Southern Song Chinese painting, a precursor to Japanese painting, for example, is distinguished by its disregard for formal likeness in favor of inner spirit and by its emphasis on spontaneity, reflected in the style of Liang Kai and Muqi. These two thirteenth-century artists' "splash ink," aiming "to capture their subject's essential nature," as Tung Wu has shown, had an impact on generation after generation of Chinese and Japanese painters.[27] According to Cristanne Miller, in their attempts to deviate from the Aristotelian mimetic tradition the American modernists discerned in traditional East Asian aesthetic "crucial authentication," sustaining and empowering their "continued experimentation with new forms in English."[28] In *Orientalism and Modernism* (1995), I argue that we may find in Heidegger's hermeneutics theoretical justification for identifying Japan and China as "crystallizing examples of the Modernists' realizing Self."[29] Hans-Georg Gadamer, a leading proponent of hermeneutics, observes that "interpretation begins with fore-conceptions that are replaced by more suitable ones."[30]

For Theodor Adorno, modernist art typically refuses "to duplicate the façade of reality"; it customarily "makes an uncompromising reprint of reality while at the same time avoiding being contaminated by it."[31] What Adorno says of modernist art also holds well for modernist poetry and drama. Traditional East Asian art and literature appear to modernists exactly like that. In Moore's description, they center "much less on seeing the real world than on making of it another world" (see the appendix "Tedium and Integrity in Poetry"). For the American modernists, to go traditional East Asian is to go nonmimetic and radically modernist. Modernist art and literature must be abstract. According to Adorno, modernist art becomes "abstract by virtue of its relation to what is past."[32] Traditional East Asian aesthetic discourages artists from reproducing the appearance of their subject; it boosts expressing emotion by spontaneously catching the spirit of their subject. Spontaneously catching the spirit of their subject sounds as good as Kandinsky's idea of conveying emotion offhand "by means of an arrangement of shapes, or planes, or colours."[33] Pound is not exaggerating when he claims that "from Whistler and the Japanese, or Chinese, the 'world,' that is to say, the fragment of the English-speaking world that spreads itself into print, learned to enjoy 'arrangements' of colours and masses."[34] Modernist art and literature must be physically novel. Traditional East Asian art has a visual language quite different from that of Western art. Traditional East Asian poetry has physical properties foreign to Westerners. "Asian discourse," in Cristanne Miller's characterization, "extend[s] the boundaries of tolerance, supporting [the modernists'] cosmopolitan and international poetics rather than marking its exclusions."[35] To turn to traditional East Asian aesthetic is to learn novel physical features, features such as rhythmical brushstroke, splash ink, one-corner composition, syllable count, minimalist design, and superposition. It is to interact across time with East Asian innovative projects to make Western things new.

Monet's East-West dialogue bears directly on my discussion of Williams's, Moore's, and Pound's creativity crisis/solution in the mid-twentieth century. One aim of this project is to argue for the revaluation of these three American modernists' late works. While Williams, Moore, and Pound have long secured their positions in the literary canon, their last books remain comparatively overlooked. Part of the problem is the widespread bias against creative talents' so-called swan songs, and part of the problem is the assumption, guided by textbooks and university courses, that modernism flourished in the early decades of the twentieth century and not after the Second World War.

It is worth noting that University of California, Davis psychologist Dean Keith Simonton, after studying with a group of musicologists 1,919 compositions written by 172 classical composers, found that pieces written later in the composers' lives "tended to be briefer, with cleaner, simpler melody lines, and yet scored higher in aesthetic significance, according to the experts."[36] Around 1960, when Charles Olson, Allen Ginsberg, and other postmodernists were turning out long poems, the three veteran modernists were doing the opposite. After a decadelong commitment to a five-volume epic poem, Williams suddenly returned to his minimalist, spatial design. Correspondingly, Pound reduced the length of his cantos from hundreds of lines to thirty lines ("From CXII"), twenty-one lines ("From CXV"), and ten lines ("Fragment [1966]"), and Moore cut down her masterpiece "Poetry" from five six-line stanzas to three lines. The three first-generation modernists all went for East Asian simplicity and economy due to a common drive to regain their formalist ground. Are the shorter poems that form Williams's last book, *Pictures from Brueghel* (1962), less avant-garde than his *Paterson* in five books (1946–58)? Has Moore loosened up experimental modernism by abbreviating "Poetry"? Asked about creative talents' final works, Berkeley psychologist Robert Levenson responds: "In the past the thinking was that the swan song was all about terror management, trying to stay busy and deny death. But it's also about leaving a legacy, generating something lasting to mark your time here."[37]

In *21st-Century Modernism,* Marjorie Perloff acknowledges that the avant-garde phase of modernism was short-lived. "Indeed, between the two world wars (and well beyond the second one)," observes Perloff, "it almost seems as if poems and art works made a conscious effort to repress the technological and formal inventions of modernism at its origins."[38] Thus Williams's minimalist, spatial design, a hallmark of poetic modernism, gives way to the endless triads of *Journey to Love* and *Paterson.* "With the publication of *Paterson* I," according to Perloff, "the analogy of Williams' poetry to avant-garde painting—whether Cubist, Dada, or Surrealist—breaks down."[39] Similarly, just as Moore's "counted formalisms" of "The Fish" relax, so Pound's vorticism, found in his poems from *Lustra* (1916) to *A Draft of XXX Cantos* (1930), is replaced by the lengthy political discourse of Cantos LII–LXXI and *Rock-Drill.*[40]

Everything has its highs and lows. The decline of experimental modernism in literature and art before, during, and after the Second World War does not signify its termination, however. It simply suggests hiatus or deferral. In *21st-Century Modernism* Perloff has convincingly documented a powerful resurgence of experimental modernism at the millennium. In this study I shall argue that three or four decades prior to that resurgence was an earlier resurgence of modernism in poetry remaining to be recognized.

There is no need to deny that the 1960s was a decade of triumphs for the postmodernists—the Black Mountain artists, the Beats, and the confessional school of poets. The decade began with Robert Lowell winning the National Book Award for his confessional signature collection *Life Studies* (1959) and Black Mountain professor Charles Olson launching *The Maximus Poems*. These were followed by the publication of Beat poet Allen Ginsberg's *Kaddish and Other Poems* (1961) and the airing of a BBC interview with confessional poet Sylvia Plath and her husband, Ted Hughes (1961). The year 1965 saw confessional poet John Berryman winning the Pulitzer Prize for *77 Dream Songs* (1964). And 1967 witnessed another confessional poet, Anne Sexton, garnering the same honor for *Live or Die* (1966).

From the 1960s to the 1980s postmodern critics and anthologists made so much noise about modernism coming to an end that some would imagine modernists had fallen out of luck with national book awards. But in the 1960s the Pulitzer Prize and other honors went to modernists too. Williams posthumously won the 1963 Pulitzer for *Pictures from Brueghel* (1962), and second-generation modernist George Oppen received the 1969 Pulitzer for *Of Being Numerous* (1968). The 1960s was a remarkable decade for many other second-generation modernists. In that decade American modernist composer and writer John Cage rose to fame partly due to the success of *Silence* (1961), a collection that included his "Lecture on Nothing," and partly due to the sensation of his chance-controlled compositions written with the oldest of the Chinese classics *Yi jing* (*I Ching*) as a tool. American modernist poet Louis Zukofsky brought out his epic poem *"A"*-14 (1964), made up of haiku-like tercets; British modernist poet Basil Bunting established his reputation by publishing *Briggflatts* (1966) with short musical lines; and Irish modernist playwright and novelist Samuel Beckett moved from the compactness of the 1950s to the minimalism of the 1960s, represented by his stage work *Breath* (1969).

How did the three first-generation modernists respond to postmodern poetry? Wasn't Williams a mentor of Ginsberg and several other postmodernists? In a letter to Cid Corman dated September 15, 1959, the doctor-poet expressed his true feeling about them: "When I see how unenlightened, technically unenlightened, many of our prizewinning poets are, I do not feel discouraged though my time is running out. Once in a while I can still do it." To Williams, Zukofsky was still "miles ahead" of them all.[41] Whereas Williams privately made these comments, Moore, in poems such as "Blessed Is the Man" (1956) and lectures such as "Idiosyncrasy and Technique" (October 1956) and "Tedium and Integrity in Poetry" (October 1957), openly criticized the Beats. Didn't Pound become silent after his release from St. Elizabeths Hospital and return to Italy? His silence was not complete after all. On July 9, 1962, he wrote a three-page letter to E. E. Cummings, acknowledging Cummings's 1933 travelogue *EIMI,* Ernest Hemingway's "few good poems," T. S. Eliot, and Robert Frost, and wondering "do yu evuh read contemporaries? I mean are there any fit for me to read."[42] The question betrayed his lack of interest in Lowell and Ginsberg even though both younger poets had paid tribute to him and sent him their new poems for advice.[43] In 1966, a year after the passing of Eliot, he appeared in *The Sewanee Review,* encouraging graduate students to explore his and Eliot's "burning topic" of 1920 or '21 and urging them, "with the urgency of 50 years ago," to "READ HIM."[44]

Was Williams serious when he asserted, "Once in a while I can still do it"? Did Moore just chastise the Beat generation and not fight back with some stunning work to crown a lifetime creative achievement? Did Pound advise younger poets to read Eliot and not demonstrate how some of his and Eliot's modernist innovations could be reinvented? Williams, Moore, and Pound did not wait for future generations of experimental modernism to carry on the course they had set. Partly boosted by the escalating postmodern challenge, the three old guards' enthusiasm for experimentation was rejuvenated. Admittedly, not all their poems of the early 1960s excel, but many do make new what they started as avant-gardes. Similar to the instance of their younger colleague Zukofsky, a key factor among factors that nourished the renewal of modernism was their interaction with East Asia.[45]

Does the West rely only on text and image to learn about the East? In Monet's case we have encountered two of three types of East-West exchange: East-West exchange via image, East-West exchange via text, and East-West exchange via personal interaction/collaboration. How do East-West exchange via image and East-West exchange via text compare with East-West exchange via personal interaction/collaboration? According to J. Hillis Miller, "cultural studies tend to assume that a work of art, popular culture, literature or philosophy ... has its best value or purchase on the world if it remains understood in relation to some specific and local people, a people defined by language, place, history and tradition."[46] Williams, Moore, and Pound, if not Monet, would certainly see eye to eye with Miller, who favors exchange via interaction with interlocutors from the target culture informed of its language, place, history, and tradition. For a Western artist, the best way to study an East Asian artist is not to read books *about* that artist but to study his or her art *with* him or her. When working with an East Asian artist is out of the question, the Western artist will do well to opt for studying as many artworks by that artist as possible, which was precisely what Monet did.

Monet's knowledge of Hokusai or any other Japanese artist was far from being satisfactory. His lesson bears critically on the claims of this project. During or shortly after the First World War, Pound, Williams, and Moore were attracted to traditional Chinese art and literature. Their initial exchange with China contributed more than topical and thematic ideas to their early modernist work. In the same way that Monet depended on image to parley with Japan, the three American poets in their early and middle years relied almost solely on image and text to learn about China. It was not that the three American modernists were not aware of the limitations of image and text but that until their final decades they rarely had a chance of encountering any well-informed Chinese interpreters. It was especially frustrating that virtually all the texts about Chinese literature and art then available were by Western orientalists. In 1915 Pound had reason to dissociate himself from his mentor in East Asian culture, Laurence Binyon, ridiculing him for "constantly hark[ing] back to some folly of nineteenth century Europe, constantly trying to justify Chinese intelligence by dragging it a little nearer to some Western precedent."[47] He was similarly critical of the English missionary translator James Legge, whose texts he relied on in the 1930s and '40s for his Confucian studies. "The trouble with Legge's versions," he told Georgetown University student William McNaughton in 1955, "is whenever Confucius disagrees with St Paul, Legge puts in a footnote to say that Confucius must be wrong."[48] Moore and Williams certainly shared Pound's resentment about Western orientalists' Eurocentrism. In her review of a book about Chinese painting, *Guide-Posts to Chinese Painting* (1927), Moore articulated her dissatisfaction with author Louise Wallace Hackney, whose "writing" and "thinking" were "occidentally 'prompt,'" and whose handling of the delighted subject appeared "less than delightful."[49]

As Christopher Bush has argued, "the West's relationship to and interest in China during the modernist period was far more extensive and real than is generally credited."[50] When I stated that the three American poets relied *almost solely* on text and image to learn about China, I had in mind an instance in which Pound got real help from a local interpreter in his attempt to use an old book from East Asia. This refers to a source of Canto XLIX also known as the "Seven Lakes" canto. The eight scenes introduced by Canto XLIX's opening line, "For the seven lakes, and by no man these verses," are said to be based on the pictures and poems of a screen-book Pound received from his parents in 1928.[51] A relic from Japan, the screen-book consists of eight ink paintings, eight poems in Chinese, and eight poems in Japanese, mutually representing eight classic scenes of the Xiao and Xiang Rivers in Hunan province, south central China. Without the assistance of a local interpreter, Pound would not have been able to decipher the poems in the screen-book. It happened that shortly after Easter 1928 a lady from the Xiao-Xiang region, Baosun Zeng (Pao Swen Tseng, 1893–1978), founding president of Yifang Girls' Academy in Hunan, was visiting a friend in Rapallo, Italy, where Pound resided from 1924 to 1945.[52] Pound's wife, Dorothy, arranged a meeting between Pound and Miss Zeng. At the meeting Zeng offered an impromptu translation of the screen-book's eight Chinese poems.[53] In *The Modernist Response to Chinese Art* (2003), I improperly considered the making of Canto XLIX's first thirty lines merely as Pound's split response to the image and text of the screen-book, overlooking Zeng's extratextual contribution.[54] What is involved and must be recognized as equally important is Pound's response to the offhand comments made by Zeng, a local expert "defined by language, place, history and tradition."

Indeed, had Pound's interpreter been a native Chinese speaker from another part of China less informed about classic Chinese poetry set in the Xiao-Xiang region, he or she would not have referred to the eight scenes as the "seven lakes." "Seven lakes," *qi ze* or 七澤 in Chinese, is an example of what Miller would call an auratic reference "possessed only by those within the culture."[55] When first used in "*Fu* of Sir Vacuous" by Sima Xiangru (ca. 179–117 BC) "seven lakes" refers to lakes both in the Xiao-Xiang region and north of it.[56] The expression occurs juxtaposed with Xiao-Xiang in a famous poem by Li Bai (Li Po, 701–762). After him "seven lakes" tends to go with Xiao-Xiang, thus securing its association with that region. In a version of the eight views of Xiao-Xiang by the Ming emperor Zhu Zhanji (1399–1435) "seven

lakes" occurs three times to allude to Xiao-Xiang: first in "Night Rain,"
then in "Snowfall on the River," and finally in "Sailboats Returning."[57]
As a poet knowing most if not all those poems, Zeng would probably
refer to the eight views not by their common name "Xiao-Xiang"
but by the literary epithet "seven lakes." She is likely to have spoken
of the eight scenes as "seven lakes," leading Pound to do the same in
Canto XLIX.

The Seven Lakes canto is a collage of eight Chinese scenic poems,
two ancient Chinese songs, and the poet's interposed voice. Some hidden link between the scenic poems and the ancient songs is commonly
lost to readers. The rustlings the speaker hears from the bamboos in
"Night Rain," the first scenic poem, allude to the sobs of E-huang and
Nü-ying, daughters of Yao ("YAO like the sun and rain" of Canto LIII)
and consorts of Yao's successor Shun ("Chun to the spirit Chang Ti" of
Canto LIII), mourning the sudden death of Shun on a tour of inspection to the Xiao and Xiang Rivers. Legend says that having reached
Xiao-Xiang the two consorts' copious tears stained the bamboos there
with purple spots. Without Zeng's enlightening, Pound would not have
produced a line so approximate to the original in effect: "and the bamboos speak as if weeping" (C, 244). Nor would he have closed the canto
with the folk songs of Shun's and Yao's times ("KEI MEN RAN KEI /
KIU MAN MAN KEI / JITSU GETSU KO KWA / TAN FUKU TAN KAI" and
"Sun up; work / sundown; to rest / dig well and drink of the water /
dig field; eat of the grain" [C, 245]), which echo the opening scene's
nostalgia for the lost ancient leaders.

What distinguishes Zeng as an influence from the influences of the
screen-book's text and image is her capability of actively interacting
with Pound, looking into his eyes while explicating the eight poems in
Chinese. Not only are her utterances directly heard but her facial expressions and gestures are simultaneously perceived. From the speech-
act theorists' perspective, facial expressions and gestures are indispens-
able components of speech acts.[58] Furthermore, she can be interrupted
for questions and comments. Her kind of influence, the direct influence
of an interlocutor from the target language and culture, might be called
cross-cultural interpersonal influence. Interaction between a Western
artist and an Eastern interlocutor includes but is not limited to conversation, discussion, debate, teamwork, sports, music, dance, and body
language communication, all unwritten, unrecorded, through virtual
reality. Insight into cross-cultural interpersonal influence can illumi-
nate certain culturally charged values that would otherwise be obscured.

Creative works are necessarily shaped by both the material and the human infrastructures. Unlike visual and textual influences that are associated with the material infrastructure, cross-cultural interpersonal influence points to the human infrastructure, that is, interlocutors from the target culture "defined by language, history, place and tradition." While visual and textual influences might be examined in terms of intertextuality, cross-cultural interpersonal influence belongs primarily to cultural studies. Pound in his endeavor to represent eight classical Chinese scenes in Canto XLIX had Miss Zeng serving in that capacity. The potential power of a cross-cultural human presence to instruct, guide, and manipulate is both obvious and easily neglected. Examination of the three modernists' East-West exchanges and their effects in chapters 1–5 will enable us to consider more purposefully (in the concluding section of chapter 5) this long-overlooked cultural discourse. One of this project's goals is indeed to draw attention to cross-cultural interpersonal influence and absorb new insights into our reassessment of modernism in the 1960s.

For Thomas Inge, "anytime another hand enters into an effort, a kind of collaboration occurs."[59] Richard Badenhausen, in *T. S. Eliot and the Art of Collaboration,* relies on this notion to examine Eliot's teamwork and personal interaction with Ezra Pound, John Hayward, Martin Browne, and Vivienne Eliot, revealing the complexities of Eliot's theory and practice of collaboration.[60] In this project I shall follow Badenhausen and proportionately stress the roles primary and secondary collaborators play in creative talents' East-West exchange and renewal of modernism. Any personal interaction that leaves a mark on the nominal author's work is considered as collaboration. This broad definition of *collaboration* makes sense especially in modernist studies because modernists themselves prize any individual who contributes anything in any way to their creative work. For T. S. Eliot, as for Pound, "no writer is completely self-sufficient."[61] In his account of the abbreviation of "In a Station of the Metro" from thirty lines to a haiku-like one-image poem, Pound retold what Victor Plarr told him—how a cat's footprints over snow inspired a Japanese navy officer to make a haiku. "I found it useful," he wrote, "in getting out of the impasse in which I had been left by my metro emotion."[62] This way he acknowledged the nameless Japanese navy officer as an educator, a secondary collaborator, who taught him through Plarr superposition, the technological form with which he made his best-known imagist poem.

In *The Modernist Response to Chinese Art* (2003), I point out that the art objects from China, like their verbal (or textual) counterparts, "tended to mislead as well as enlighten, make visible as well as hide."[63] Williams, Moore, and Pound in their middle years gradually grew fed up with such sources. That partly explains why they were so thrilled when finally enabled to learn about China directly from Chinese interlocutors knowledgeable of specific languages (Chinese or Naxi), places, histories, and traditions.

Just how Williams was enraptured by Chinese poet David Wang's proposal to collaborate with him on a group of Chinese appropriations is evidenced by a letter he wrote Wang on September 28, 1957: "I am fascinated by the prospect of working with you on the Chinese translation . . . I am anxious that a book should come of it."[64] Whereas Pound spent no more than an afternoon with Miss Zeng going over his screen-book's Chinese poems and learning about the "eight views" tradition, Williams worked on the re-creation project with Wang intermittently for three and a half years. The partnership permitted Williams to hear Tang poets read aloud in Chinese and watch their poetic lines written out in characters forming rectangular shapes on the page. With regard to the way that chosen classic Chinese poems were appropriated, however, David Wang sometimes found it hard to accept the doctor-poet's arbitrary exclusion of cultural overtones in order to implement certain formal experiments. Looking back on this collaborative project, a compromise in favor of Williams's "make it new" commitment, what is most noteworthy is not the collaborative project itself (published under the title "The Cassia Tree" three years after Williams's death). Rather, it is the older poet's much-desired reinitiation of his minimalist, spatial design which the project helped bring about. Since the mid-1950s Williams had been regrettably stuck in the overused triadic pattern of *Paterson,* Books II–V, and *Journey to Love* (1955). Without the formal experiments empowered by the collaborative enterprise, Williams would not have been able to accomplish so quickly his renewal of avant-garde strategy in his last book of verse, *Pictures from Brueghel* (1962).

Not all collaborators actually work with the nominal author on a specific project. Some contribute more generally an outlook or a motif that nevertheless becomes "essentially and inextricably a part of the authorship."[65] Unlike Williams, who collaborated closely with David Wang for three and a half years, Marianne Moore had a less professional relationship with a Chinese friend, a fellow New Yorker. For twelve years, from 1957 through 1968, Mai-mai Sze (1909–92), author of *The*

Tao of Painting (1956), shared with Moore *Times Literary Supplement* reviews, responded to her questions about Taoist aesthetic, and offered from time to time emotional support for her formal innovations. In this manner, Sze left an influence no less remarkable than a primary collaborator's on Moore's late works—*O to Be a Dragon* (1959), *Tell Me, Tell Me* (1966), and *The Complete Poems* (1967). Moore's gratitude to Mai-mai Sze is explicit in a letter she wrote Sze on November 20, 1963: "giver and sharer of so much else; in the *Tao of Painting*—of which I never tire, permanent gifts, they have been, that I have for *all time*. Possessions that I carry with me in my mind—along with some incurable ignorances."[66]

During his years of incarceration at Washington's St. Elizabeths Hospital Pound had among his regular visitors a Catholic University of America researcher in physics originally from Lijiang, southwest China. The young researcher, Paul Fang (1922–2011), turned out to be an ethnic Naxi man, fluent in Naxi, a surviving pictographic language, and familiar with the Naxi rites that blend local ethnic religion with Buddhism and Taoism. In the years 1954–58, Pound studied the Naxi language and religious rites with Fang, using American botanist and anthropologist Joseph Rock's monographs on Naxi as texts. The conversation between the two continued after Pound's return to Italy, as is manifest in a letter Pound wrote Fang on August 25, 1959: "I have at last got hold of Rock's 'Ancient [Na-khi] Kingdom [of Southwest China]' with its fine photographs. Have you his Vienna address?"[67] As a result of this cross-cultural exchange, Pound in his final cantos (*Drafts and Fragments,* 1969) extolled Lijiang as an earthly paradise in East Asia, permitted Naxi pictographs to rhyme in phonetics with Latin and English, and set Naxi love tragedy on top of its Western counterparts, at once recalling and challenging his early modernist technological innovations.

Although the focus of this study is the renewal of American modernism in the 1960s, I shall in the book's coda go beyond it to cite four previously discussed cases and consider two unvisited ones. By doing so, I want to suggest that my claims about East-West exchange and the renewal of modernism are not restricted to Williams, Moore, and Pound, or, so to speak, midcentury poetic modernism in the United States. Indeed, in 1983, playwright-director Arthur Miller (1915–2005) collaborated with the theatre artists of the Beijing People's Art Theatre on a Chinese production of his 1949 play *Death of a Salesman*. Its theatrical innovations, documented in Miller's *Salesman in Beijing* (1984), as contributed by his BPAT collaborators found their way into subsequent revivals of *Death of a Salesman*. In 2002, I. M. Pei (b. 1917), designer of the John F. Kennedy Library in Massachusetts, the Grand Louvre in Paris, and other internationally recognizable modernist landmarks, returned to his ancestral home, Suzhou, a beautiful historic city northeast of Shanghai, to design the New Suzhou Museum. It was, in Pei's own words, "in a small way to pay a debt to the culture from which I came."[68] The Chinese American architect's last monument in China signals a new direction in modernist architecture. An inspection of the museum, completed in 2006, brings to light not only features derived from his exchanges with Chinese architects and urban planners but also motifs appertaining to a local opera he watched and studied before his final revision of the project plan.

What follows, then, traces little-known East-West dialogues in the 1950s and '60s, the 1980s, and at the millennium. How did five iconic figures of American modernism—three poets, a playwright, and an architect—interact with Chinese interlocutors, learning, disputing, and working their way to an understanding of East Asian aesthetic concepts—"less is more," "forgetting self," "wholeness of Heaven and Earth," balance of Yin/Yang, and so on? What effects did vigorous interactions with intellectuals from China or in China produce on the creative artists' late-life renewal of experimental modernism? Drawing on cultural studies and intertextuality practice, this project strives to bring new insights to our understanding of late modernism—its heightened attention to meaning in space, increased obsession with imaginative sensibility, and augmented respect for harmony between humanity and nature. These insights will help open up a new way of looking at the relationship of East Asia to modernism (or transnationalism to American literature and culture) and a productive way of interpreting some of the finest late modernist works in poetry and beyond. The American modernists' experiences of sudden renewal in old age might add fresh perspective to Said's immeasurably provocative claim about late-life creativity. This book, crossing several disciplines in modernist studies, I hope will enliven scholars' and students' discussion of the broader cultural issues—language/culture, modernism/modernity, transpacific intertextuality/East-West collaboration, and textual-visual influence/cross-cultural interpersonal influence.

ONE

Williams, Wang, and "The Cassia Tree"

BREAKING STYLE THROUGH translation or adaptation was not new to William Carlos Williams when he made an attempt at it in the late 1950s. Four decades earlier, he had witnessed how *Cathay* "FOR THE MOST PART FROM THE CHINESE OF RIHAKU" (1915) paved the way for his college friend Ezra Pound's sudden shift to an ideal idiom for high modernism.[1] Ford Madox Ford, who had ridiculed Pound's archaism in *Canzoni* (1911), was so dazzled by the freshness, simplicity, and beauty of *Cathay* that he applauded: "If these are original verses, then, Mr. Pound is the greatest poet of this day."[2] Williams was no less extravagant in admiration for *Cathay*. "Pound's translation from the Chinese," he wrote in a letter on April 13, 1915, to *Poetry* magazine editor Harriet Monroe, "is something of great worth well handled. Superb! . . . the Chinese things are perhaps a few of the greatest poems written. The first part of the Anglo Saxon thing ['The Seafarer'] shows splendidly in contrast with the oriental stuff."[3]

Cathay appeared precisely at a moment when Williams was restless and miserable about being a novice poet with no way to get past an impasse. How he envied Pound for having the good fortune to obtain "all old Fenollosa's treasures in *mss*," easy access to both the looks and the senses of classic Chinese verses![4] Without anything similar, he had to rely on Herbert A. Giles's and Arthur Waley's translations to explore Chinese poetry.[5] Before long he found himself speaking, in "Portrait of the Author" (1920), to the "Drunken Beauty" Lady Yang in Giles's version of Bai Juyi's "The Everlasting Wrong":

In the spring I would drink! In the spring
I would be drunk and lie forgetting all things.

Your face! Give me your face, Yang Kue Fei!
your hands, your lips to drink!
Give me your wrists to drink—
I drag you, I am drowned in you, you
overwhelm me! Drink![6]

Waley's versions of Bai Juyi's occasional poems, along with Giles's description of a Chinese poetic pattern called "stop-short," moreover inspired Williams to imitate the Tang poet in that form, testing shorter
lines, more colorful images, and a balanced outlook. Williams's early
exchange with Tang dynasty China culminated in "To the Shade of
Po Chü-i," a draft poem circa 1920 discovered among the *Little Review*
files at the Golda Meir Library, University of Wisconsin-Milwaukee,
and included in *The Collected Poems of William Carlos Williams, Volume I,
1909–1939* (1986):[7]

The work is heavy. I see
bare branches laden with snow.
I try to comfort myself
with thought of your old age.
A girl passes, in a red tam,
the coat above her quick ankles
snow smeared from running and falling—
Of what shall I think now
save of death the bright dancer? (133)

Williams is widely praised for a minimalist, spatial design developed
in *Sour Grapes* (1921) and perfected in *Spring and All* (1923). As I argue
in *Orientalism and Modernism,* it was the cubist artists who coached Williams to disregard syntax in breaking poetic lines, and it was the Tang
dynasty Chinese poets who influenced him to rearrange severed lines
in square-looking stanzas on the page.[8]

It must be pointed out that Williams deviated from his minimalist, spatial design after the Second World War. In Marjorie Perloff's
opinion, the man-city identity in his epic poem *Paterson,* Book I, and
similar figurative patterns in *Paterson,* Books III and IV, "hark back to
the Symbolism of an earlier generation," and *Paterson,* Book V, like his
"Asphodel, that Greeny Flower" (1955), is "an autobiographical lyric in
the Romantic tradition."[9] Williams's invention of the triadic stanza, a
long line split into three staggered segments, marks the beginning of his

departure from modernist minimalism. An early example of this pattern can be found in *Paterson,* Book II (1948):

The descent beckons
         as the ascent beckoned
                 Memory is a kind
of accomplishment
         a sort of renewal
                 even
an initiation, since the spaces it opens are new places
         inhabited by hordes
                 heretofore unrealized,
of new kinds—
         since their movements
                 are towards new objectives[10]

Said to match the rhythm of American speech, it is rehearsed in *Journey to Love* (1955):

carrying a bunch of marigolds
         wrapped
                 in an old newspaper[11]

In a letter from June 1955 to John Thirlwall, Williams called this design running throughout *The Desert Music* (1954) and *Journey to Love* his "solution of the problem of modern verse."[12] But five months later, in November 1955, he confided to Cid Corman that he had found this pattern "overdone, artificial, archaic—smacking of Spencer [*sic*] and his final Alexandrine."[13] Despite his growing dissatisfaction with it, nonetheless, he continued to use the triadic stanza in *Paterson,* Book V. It was not that he changed his mind about this instrument but that he did not know how to get out of it and where to turn for a substitute.

It was at this moment of perplexity that Williams came across eight short poems translated from the Chinese. Writing to Pound at Washington's St. Elizabeths Hospital, Williams praised these poems printed in the February 1957 issue of *Edge:* "I do enjoy EDGE—the last translations from the chink by/of David Rafael Wang are worth the trip half way round the world to have encountered" (Beinecke). The letter prompted Pound to encourage the translator, David Raphael Wang (figure 2), to contact his old friend in Rutherford, New Jersey, for whatever professional help he himself was not able to give.

Figure 2. David Raphael Wang, 1955. (Courtesy of Dartmouth College Library)

David Raphael Wang (Wang Shenfu 王燊甫, 1931–77), also known as David Hsin-fu Wand, was born in Hangzhou, China, on December 28, 1931. His grandfather Wang Fenggao (王豐鎬) served the Qing imperial court as a diplomat. He is now remembered as a founder of Guanghua University in Shanghai. On May 30, 1925, the Shanghai Municipal Police opened fire on Chinese labor and anti-imperialist protesters. By forbidding the support for a rally against the massacre, Shanghai St. Johns University, an American missionary university, pushed its 553 students and nineteen faculty members to walk out and establish an autonomous university called Guanghua. In its first year Guanghua depended on rental space for its classes. To help solve its campus problem Wang Fenggao donated six hundred acres of his private land in Shanghai.[14] In 1949 Wang immigrated to the United States with his widowed mother. He attended La Scuola Italiana in Middlebury, Vermont, before enrolling in Dartmouth College, where he earned a bachelor of arts degree in English in 1955. After writing poetry for the *Dartmouth Quarterly* for several years, he was attracted to Pound at St. Elizabeths Hospital.[15] It was at Pound's suggestion that Wang submitted his Chinese translations to *Edge* (Melbourne), edited by Noel Stock. In 1973, with a PhD in comparative literature from the University of Southern California, the young poet-translator got a job as visiting assistant professor at the University of New Mexico in Albuquerque. While in New Mexico he published one of the first anthologies of Asian American literature, *Asian-American Heritage: An Anthology of Prose and Poetry* (1974).[16] In 1976 David Wang landed a tenure-track position at the University of Texas at Dallas. On April 8, 1977, he was found dead on a lower-level ledge outside a Manhattan hotel. No one was certain whether he had committed suicide or there had been foul play. He was survived by his wife, Yuet-fun, and their eleven-month-old daughter, Angelina Mei-yi.[17]

Encouraged by Pound, David Wang wrote to Williams at 9 Ridge Road, Rutherford, New Jersey, in March 1957. Williams's enthusiasm for the then novice poet is evident in his reply on March 16, 1957:

> For heaven's sake! I've been looking for you everywhere since I read those Chinese translations in the last EDGE. Pound wrote me one of his unnecessarily cryptic cards telling me you were in New York. I thought you were merely passing through the city. Now I find out that you are a friend of Gil Sorrentino. Of course come out and see us. It will have to be after the middle of next week—if you will be free. Come in the afternoon unless you are not free then when you can make it Saturday or Sunday. I'm not much good evenings. Let me hear from you. I'm awfully glad you wrote. (Dartmouth)

Williams, in Rutherford, New Jersey, and Wang, in New York City, did not meet until two weeks later. On April 7, 1957, Wang reported to Pound: "Finally saw Williams as you had suggested. He wanted to write a preface to my grandfather poems and suggested that I should send them to Henry Rago of Poetry, Chicago. He won't be any more help to me on my fellowship applications" (Beinecke). He planned to pay Williams a second visit in late April, but Williams wrote on April 29, 1957: "It is impossible for me to see you now. We are going to Brandeis University—and other places so that I'll be engaged for the whole month of May until June 9th" (Dartmouth). Five months later, Wang brought up the idea of working with the doctor-poet on a group of Chinese poems. "When a poet puts off an old style," Helen Vendler asserts, "he or she perpetrates an act of violence, so to speak, on the self."[18] Translation was the right tool Williams would need to facilitate such an act of violence on his overworked three-step lines of *Journey to Love* and *Paterson,* Book V. Wang's offer was after his own heart. Not surprisingly, in a letter dated September 28, 1957, he heartily accepted the young poet's proposal: "I am fascinated by the prospect of working with you on the Chinese translation—and we will of course do it together and soon but not now." In that letter he also suggested making a book out of the collaboration: "I am anxious that a book should come of it . . .

Talk to David McDowell of McDowell, Obolensky, Inc., 219 E 61, I have engaged myself to let him publish any book I shall write from this point forward" (Dartmouth).

Poems from the collaboration did appear in print three years after Williams's death, although not from McDowell, Obolensky, Inc. The sequence entitled "The Cassia Tree" was included in *New Directions* 19 (1966).

David Wang, of course, had his own motivations for the collaborative project. First, the undertaking would provide an once-in-a-lifetime opportunity to study creative writing with a leading modernist poet. Second, whatever result came of it was likely to send him on the way to an illustrious career. But why should Williams (figure 3), in his old age and with other commitments, have been interested in taking up the enterprise?

Chinese poetry had always been one of Williams's preoccupations. In April 1915 he was among the first to praise Pound's *Cathay*. Under its impact, he engaged in an extended dialogue with Chinese poets through translations, whose effects are manifest in "The Nightingales," "Complete Destruction," "The Red Wheelbarrow," and "The Locust Tree in Flower." Nearly forty years after these early experiments, Williams was eager to better his "acquaintance with the great poets of China through one of their direct descendants" (Williams to Wang, September 28, 1957; Dartmouth). For him this was another chance to use "China" for poetic restructuring and renewal, a chance to fulfil his dream of overtaking Pound, his lifelong friend and competitor. While Fenollosa provided Pound with classic Chinese verses' looks and senses, Wang would allow Williams also to hear them chanted in authentic Chinese. If Williams's Chinese engagement during the late 1910s and early 1920s had facilitated his shift to modernist minimalism, his partnership with Wang would enable him to move away from the three-step line he's been using in his poetry since 1948. The Chinese poems he was to work on contrasted sharply with the triad, a long line made up of three shorter, step-down units.

On January 17, 1958, David Wang "spent whole afternoon and most of evening at Doc Williams'," setting up their collaborative project.[19] The first Chinese poet they chose to work on was Wang Wei (699–759), in Pound's 1916 description, an "eighth century Jules Laforgue Chinois."[20] As Williams recalled in a letter on February 25, 1958 (Dartmouth), Wang chanted to him the Chinese of two of the Tang poet's four-

Figure 3. William Carlos Williams in the 1950s. (© 2017 the William Carlos Williams Estate; used by permission of the William Carlos Williams Estate in care of the Jean V. Naggar Literary Agency, Inc.; courtesy of the Beinecke Rare Book and Manuscript Library, Yale University)

liners and then jotted them down line by line, writing beneath them the meaning of the separate characters:

[Untitled]

空	山	不	见	人
empty	hill or mountain	not	see	man
但	闻	人	语	响
But	hear	man's	voice	sound
返	影	入	深	林
follow	reflected light	into	deep	woods
复	照	青	苔	上
return (to)	shine	green	moss	on

送　別
Farewell

山	中	相	送	罷
mountain	(in the)	see	farewell	end
日	暮	掩	柴	扉
the sun	near evening	close	wooden	gate
春	草	明	年	綠
spring	grass	next	year	green
王	孫	归	不	归?
young	patrician	return	(or) not	return. (Beinecke)

The form in which the two poems were composed was not new to Williams. Kept at his elbow was his personal copy of Herbert A. Giles's *A History of Chinese Literature* (1901) bearing his 1916 autograph: "For Mammie, from her son, Willie, for the gentleness of the ancient Chinese poet, knowing how you love all gentle things."[21] From it he surely had learned something about this form. Giles, who calls the Chinese four-line form "stop-short," illustrates its syllable counts and tone variations in a paradigm:

Sharp	*sharp*	*flat*	*flat*	*sharp*
Flat	*flat*	*sharp*	*sharp*	*flat*
Flat	*flat*	*flat*	*sharp*	*sharp*
Sharp	*sharp*	*sharp*	*flat*	*flat*

"Although consisting of only twenty or twenty-eight words," according to Giles, the stop-short is "just long enough for the poet to introduce, to develop, to embellish, and to conclude his theme in accordance with certain established laws of composition." "The third line," he stresses, "is considered the most troublesome to produce, some poets even writing it first; the last line should contain a 'surprise' or *dénouement*."[22]

In 1956 Williams told Edith Heal that during his early avant-garde phase he was often thrilled by restructuring previously written poems in quatrains, tercets, and couplets. "From the beginning I knew that the American language must shape the pattern; later I rejected the word language and spoke of the American idiom—" "I remembered," he elaborated,

> writing several poems as quatrains at first, then in the normal pro-
> cess of concentrating the poem, getting rid of redundancies in

the line—and in the attempt to make it go faster—the quatrain changed into a three line stanza, or a five line stanza became a quatrain, as in:

The Nightingales

Original version	*Revised version*
My shoes as I lean	My shoes as I lean
unlacing them	unlacing them
stand out upon	stand out upon
flat worsted flowers	flat worsted flowers.
under my feet.	
Nimbly the shadows	Nimbly the shadows
of my fingers play	of my fingers play
unlacing	unlacing
over shoes and flowers.	over shoes and flowers.[23]

Marjorie Perloff is not the only reader who finds Williams's account "confusing and contradictory."[24] What excited Williams evidently was not the sound or the natural American idiom of his new pattern, but its sight, or look. As in the case of the *Sour Grapes* poem "The Nightingales," its "two quatrains, [appear] almost square in shape."[25] Did Williams have a model in mind as he reassembled the lines? One such model would be the Chinese stop-short as shown in Giles's paradigm.

If cubism gave Williams the technique of fragmentation essential to such exercises, the Chinese provided a pithy verse form to follow. As I have demonstrated in *Orientalism and Modernism,* another *Sour Grapes* poem, "Complete Destruction" (*CP1,* 159), also consists of two quatrains, each resembling a stop-short with a square appearance on the page. Even "The Red Wheelbarrow" (*CP1,* 224) with its typical American motif and idiom matches the configuration of a stop-short with a slight deviation. Its eight lines can be seen as four lines, each with a tag of a two-syllable word. Like a stop-short, the first line, "so much depends / upon" introduces; the second line, "a red wheel / barrow" develops; the third line, "glazed with rain / water" embellishes; and the fourth line, "beside the white / chickens" concludes with a surprise.

On January 17, 1958, Williams was supposedly brought back to some of the formal concerns of his early phase of modernism in which he had played with the stop-short in terms of its minimalist, spatial appearance. The versions he "stay[ed] up that late" to produce (Williams to Wang, January 18, 1958; Dartmouth) manifest in their own ways the physical properties of Wang Wei's four-liners:

Empty now the hill's green
but the voice of a man refracted
from the deep woods livens
the green of the moss there.

Farewell
Farewell, the mountain watches
as at evening I close the rustic gate
spring grass will be green again
tho' the young patrician return or no. (Dartmouth)

The rectangular shapes of his versions distinctly take after the origi-
nals. The way the lines are divided, nevertheless, is reminiscent of Williams's practice from the mid-1910s to the 1930s. The re-creation of
Wang Wei's first stop-short, in particular, brings to mind the opening
of "Good Night," a 1916 lyric, which Marjorie Perloff identifies as Williams's early "experiment with the visual placement of words in lines."[26]

In brilliant gas light
I turn the kitchen spigot
and watch the water plash
into the clean white sink. (*CP1,* 85)

Both attempts are in three- and four-stress lines of predominantly
monosyllabic words. Both contain lines broken in syntactically unnatural places. Just as in "Good Night," the third line is cut after the verb
"plash" and before the prepositional phrase "into the clean white sink,"
so in Williams's version of Wang Wei's first stop-short the second line
is severed after the past participle "refracted" and before its prepositional
phrase "from the deep woods," and the third line is enjambed to separate the verb "livens" from its object "the green of the moss there." Such
odd divisions of poetic lines, according to Perloff, are intended to make
the visual objects "stand out, one by one, as in a series of film shots," or
as in Picabia's drawings or Picasso's collages.[27]

Personal interactions proved both to assist and to complicate the
translation or appropriation project. From the outset, Williams's prior-
ity collided with Wang's. The old master privileged formal experiments
over semantic accuracy, whereas the novice found it hard to accept arbitrary exclusion of Chinese expressive syntax features and cultural overtones. Admittedly, Williams's versions have faithfully reproduced in English Wang Wei's perceived objects—"empty hills," "deep woods," and
"green moss" in the first instance, and "mountain," "rustic gate," and

"spring grass" in the second instance, but that is not all in the Chinese original. As Wai-lim Yip notes, "Wang Wei is prized for his ability to turn language into miming gestures of the perceiving act." In the first poem, he indicates, "we notice the *emptiness,* the *openness* first before we are aware of the other state of being ['not see man']."[28] The perceiving *act* of this poem—an impression of an empty mountain followed by an impression of not seeing man—is regrettably lost in Williams's version. Besides, Wang Wei's stop-short poems also contain subtle Taoist/Zen Buddhist overtones. David Wang tried to clarify the no man/voice and deep wood/light contrasts by means of the yin/yang balance principle. That attempt obviously did not work in the collaborators' January 1958 session. It was not until four months later that Wang's commentary finally began to make sense to the doctor-poet, resulting in his belated acknowledgment of its value in a letter: "Ying [yin], the female principle, and Yang, as you have pointed it out to me, have done more than anything I have ever encountered to make me realize what the poets are talking about" (Williams to Wang, May 20, 1958; Dartmouth).[29] In January to February 1958, however, Williams's chief concern was his experiment with the stop-short look. His version of Wang Wei's first stop-short has omitted "not see man" and "light," thus eclipsing the odd pairings of no man/voice and deep woods/light in the original. The odd pairings are meant to signify Zen illumination, with the unexpected human voice and the piercing sunlight symbolizing the sudden leap to enlightenment.

Wang Wei's "Farewell" recaptures a moment when an everyday sight (sunset) strikes a chord in the speaker's heart, reminding him of his sorrow over a friend's departure at sunrise. It similarly contains a minor shock: the certainty of spring grass growing back contrasting with the uncertainty of ever having the company of his friend again. Williams does a better job of appropriating this poem. By juxtaposing "spring grass will be green again" and "the young patrician return or no," he roughly, if not wonderfully, reproduces that effect.

The role Williams played so far in the collaborative project is comparable to the role Pound played in the *Cathay* enterprise. He reworked Wang's draft versions as aggressively as Pound did Fenollosa's Chinese poetry notes. Nevertheless, Williams's and Pound's partners were not of the same kind. While Fenollosa remained a passive textual source, Wang was an active participant in the re-creation, a primary collaborator. As such, he interacted with Williams in multiple ways. When face to face he chanted to Williams the Wang Wei poems in Chinese, jotted them down character by character, and presumably also explained the yin/yang balance in key phrases; and when back in New York City, he sent Williams his feedback on the latter's draft versions. On January 24, 1958, Wang actually criticized the doctor-poet's version of the first Wang Wei poem: "I am afraid that you have changed the meaning too much" (Beinecke). A literal translation he enclosed drew attention to the suppressed details—"no trace of men" (yin) and "reflected light" (yang). Not surprisingly, Wang's criticism met resistance. Williams's revised version (sent to Wang on February 26, 1958) was another formal experiment at the cost of Chinese overtones:

> Across the empty hills
> in the deep woods
> comes a man's voice
> the green moss there (Dartmouth)

To this new version Williams added a note saying, "You can't translate it and give its brevity and overtones that are given in the original language" (Dartmouth).

From the two abandoned, art-making re-creations, David Wang should have no trouble figuring out the configuration of Williams's restructuring interest. He was to copy the older poet's appropriation strategies. His goal was, after all, to study poetry writing with an old master. It would be necessary to surrender some Chinese ingredients. His tactic for minimizing the sacrifice was to cater to Williams's tastes in the selection of Chinese poems. There would have to be a bit of give-and-take on both sides. Williams in turn gave Wang a freer hand. To carry on the cross-cultural collaboration for experimental purposes, he had to keep his Chinese partner on board.

The next piece selected for appropriation was "The Lady of Lo-Yang," an early Wang Wei poem in the ballad mode, with few unfamiliar cultural overtones. When presenting it to Williams on January 27, 1958, Wang chose to withhold the original text and send only a draft version. In doing so he virtually took the manipulation of the form in hand. For this Chinese ballad in twenty seven-character lines with a rhyme scheme of *aaba,* he substituted an unrhymed version in quatrains with five to seven stresses to a line. As the English ballad stanza also consists of four lines, the choice of the quatrain, rectangular in shape, is appropriate.

The lady of Lo-Yang lives across the street.
By her looks she's about fifteen years of age.
Fitted with jade and silk her husband's horse is ready for parade.
In golden plates she is served sliced herring and caviar.

Her painted screen and roseate stairs rival in their hues.
The peach blossoms and willow shades spread outside her room.
Through gauze curtain she glides into her perfumed sedan chair.
'Midst feathery fans she enters her sequined mosquito net.

Her husband is a budding young, haughty millionaire;
His extravagance puts Mark Anthony even to shame.
Pitying her maids she teaches them the classic Chinese dance.
Tired of gifts she freely gives her corals and pearls away.

By her crystal screen she blows the light off her velvety lamp.
The green smoke rises like petals bourne upon the waves.
Filled with fun and laughter she has no regrets
With her hair done up in a roll she sits by the candle case.

In her circle of friends are men of pedigree and wealth.
She visits only the king and aristocrats.
Can she recall the girl who was pure as ivory
And used to wash her clothings by the creek not very far away?
    (*CP2*, 501–2)

This portrait of an eighth-century Chinese wife no doubt had an appeal for Williams, the poet of "The Young Housewife" (*CP1*, 57). Once he read Wang's draft version in an apt spatial form, he could not resist the temptation of rewriting it in more elegant English. The poem is an interested male's monologue about his affluent neighbor's young wife. In David Wang's draft the speaker has just a hint of a compassionate, conversational tone. Under Williams's care this quality is brought out:

Look, there goes the young lady across the street
She looks about fifteen, doesn't she?
Her husband is riding the piebald horse
Her maids are scraping chopped fish from a gold plate. (*CP2*, 364)

The interjection "Look," the rhetorical question, and the piled statements in present continuous tense all help to underscore the immediacy of the speaker's tribute to the Lady of Lo-Yang.

The revised version continues in this fashion with more colloquial phrases, exclamations, midline pauses, and assertions in present continuous tense:

> Her picture gallery and red pavilion stand face to face
> The willow and the peach trees shadow her eaves
> Look, she's coming thru the gauze curtains to get into her chaise:
> Her attendants have started winnowing the fans.
>
> Her husband got rich early in his life
> A more arrogant man you never find around!
> She keeps busy by teaching her maids to dance
> She never regrets giving jewels away.
>
> There goes the light by her window screen
> The green smoke's rising like petals on wave
> The day is done and what does she do?
> Her hair tied up, she watches the incense fade.

And it concludes with the shocking revelation about the wife's family background:

> None but the bigwigs visit her house
> Only the Chaos and the Lees get by her guards
> But do you realize this pretty girl
> Used to beat her clothes at the river's head? (*CP2,* 364)

Without any knowledge of the Chinese language Williams could not have detected certain misrepresentations in David Wang's version of the poem. For instance, where Wang Wei's speaker says, "Day and night she mixes only with illustrious people such as the Chaos and the Lees," Williams, prompted by Wang, has the speaker observe instead, "Only the Chaos and the Lees get by her guards" (line 18). Also, some of Wang Wei's sensual details reproduced in Wang's draft—for example, the "jade" that decorates the husband's horse (line 3) and the "perfume" that fills the wife's chaise (line 7)—are omitted in the final version. But the overall picture and mood of Wang Wei's poem are recaptured. Whereas stanzas 1–3 closely follow David Wang's literal version—thus also the original—in delineating what the speaker has actually observed, in particular, the extravagant lifestyle of his neighbor's household, stanza 4 does so in bringing out what he has imagined, specifically, the young wife's paradoxical emptiness of heart. As to Wang Wei's speaker's self-characterization, his contempt for the husband can be discerned in line

10: "A more arrogant man you never find around!" and his sympathy for the wife can be found in lines 19–20: "But do you realize this pretty girl / Used to beat her clothes at the river's head?"

From the revised version Wang no doubt learned one more facet of Williams's poetics, his rendering of American speech. Wang Wei's monologue "The Lady of Lo-Yang," or "The Peerless Lady," should certainly be rendered in present-day American speech. Without Williams's changes, there would not be such an accessible and palatable final text. Notice that the colloquial phrase "The day is done" has replaced the conceptualized "Filled with fun and laughter" (line 15), and that the slang term "bigwigs" has filled in for the literal "men of pedigree and wealth" (line 17). Stephen Field, in a review of Williams's and Wang's Chinese translations, singles out "bigwigs" as an example of the collaborators' use of the American idiom.[30] It is Williams who has supplied the word, and he deserves credit for many more such colloquial phrases.

In late February 1958 Williams felt that his health was again beginning to fluctuate. After a heart attack in 1948 and three strokes in 1951, 1952, and 1955, he knew that he really should not put too much stress on himself. On February 25, 1958, therefore, he returned all of Wang's draft translations, thanking him for "hav[ing] come out to read ... the wonderful old language" and owning up to his incompetence: "I have struggled with the poems but I cannot get a replica of the ancient language" (Dartmouth).

Wang, though, had not yet completed his lessons with Williams. He was understandably eager to carry on his conversation with Williams. In the next three years, despite Williams's half-heartedness, he continued to send him version after version of Chinese poems. Along with these he also presented some original poems, including cantos 1–4 of his epic poem, "The Grandfather Cycle."[31] Williams reviewed most, if not all, of Wang's offerings, but only occasionally did he make comments or suggest revisions.

Speaking of a poem Wang had composed for the *New Yorker* ("To My Only One"), Williams advised him on April 14, 1958: "I do not think that a poem which does not have a single visual image in it would be of much interest to a *New Yorker* reader. If you are going to write that sort of poem it should have at least the structural interest of a mathematical theorem" (Dartmouth). In reference to Wang's draft versions of more Tang poems, he recommended on May 12, 1958: "It is always a translation into the modern idiom of the old language. The edges must remain clear in the phrases you elect to use, never sentimental" (Dartmouth). Williams's emphases on the "structural interest" and the "modern idiom" set Wang on the right track for the collaborative project.

By midsummer 1958, Wang had moved to the West Coast to serve as a translator and reporter for the San Francisco–based bilingual newspaper the *Chinese World*. On July 10, 1958, he wrote Williams, telling him that he had attended Louis Zukofsky's poetry reading at the art museum. Enclosed was a version of a Li Bai poem entitled "Spring Song":

A young lass
Plucks mulberry leaves by the stream.

Her white hand
Reaches toward the green.

Her rosy cheeks
Shine under the sun.

The hungry silkworms
Are waiting for her.

Oh, young horseman,
Why do you tarry? Get going! (*CP2*, 502)

The version with images such as "a young lass," "mulberry leaves," and "silkworms" should have reminded Williams of the *Cathay* piece "A Ballad of the Mulberry Road."[32] The original is Li Bai's re-creation of the early Chinese ballad that had given rise to Pound's "The Mulberry Road." What is more likely to have impressed Williams, however, was the version's structural interest. Its arrangement of the verse in five uneven couplets brings to mind Williams's poems of the 1930s such as "Nantucket":

Flowers through the window
lavender and yellow

changed by white curtains—
Smell of cleanliness—

Sunshine of late afternoon—
On the glass tray

a glass pitcher, the tumbler
turned down, by which

a key is lying—And the
immaculate white bed (*CP1*, 372)

Its short, oddly divided lines, like those of Williams's abandoned versions of Wang Wei, anticipate the plain (instead of step down) quatrains, tercets, and couplets of *Pictures from Brueghel* (1962)—as in "The
Blue Jay":

It crouched
just before the take-off

caught
in the cinematograph-

ic motion
of the mind wings

just set to spread a
flash a

blue curse
a memory of you

my friend
shrieked at me

—serving art
as usual (*CP2*, 420)

"Blue Jay" was artist Sheri Martinelli's nickname. Martinelli's letters
to Williams along with Pound's letters must have inspired the poem
that echoes the line "Blue jay, my blue jay" in Pound's Canto XCIV
(*C*, 653).[33]

Li Bai's original lyric certainly does not resemble any of these Williams poems. A regulated classic Chinese verse, it consists not of five
couplets but of six lines with no stanza break or midline pause. From his
mentor-collaborator, Wang had learned a way to force the reader's eye
to key noun phrases and verb phrases by splitting one line into several
and isolating them in a stanza. This he did with "Spring Song." After
detaching Li Bai's first two lines in a couplet, he cut each of the next
four in two and arranged them in additional couplets. In dividing lines
in this way, Williams would often violate American speech patterns in
favor of the visual shape. So would David Wang. Take Li Bai's line 3, literally meaning "her white hand on green leaves." In Wang's hands this

line is turned into "Her white hand / Reaches toward the green" (*CP2*, 502). The line, now enjambed, breaks "Her white hand" and its movement "toward the green" into two distinct impressions. Consider also Li Bai's last line, alluding to an arrogant official in a five-horse carriage who lightheartedly proposed to the mulberry girl. The allusion central to the original's theme—a tribute to the girl's self-respect, fearlessness, and intelligence—is given up for minimalist, spatial design. Further, what might be rendered as "Five horses, do not linger" is altered and expanded to "Oh, young horseman, / Why do you tarry? Get going!" (ibid.). The shift from a voice directing a team of five horses to move to a voice urging a horseman to go, along with the enjambment and the strong caesura, clearly copied from Williams.

The emulation must have amused Williams, for he revised three lines and retyped the version for Wang. Inconspicuous as these revisions may appear, their effects are dramatic. If Williams's change of "by the stream" to "by the river" and modification of "toward the green" to "among the green" simply make lines 2 and 4 read better, his revision of "Her rosy cheeks" to "Her flushed cheeks" in line 5 at once avoids a cliché and strengthens an emotional coloring. Incidentally, Li Bai's phrase, if literally rendered (as "rouged cheeks"), lacks this emotional resonance.

Williams's endorsement encouraged Wang to carry on his bold manipulation of line divisions in refashioning classic Chinese lyrics. On August 12, 1958, he sent Williams the result of another exercise, a version of a stop-short by Wang Chien (Wang Jian, 751–830) entitled "The Newlywed's Cuisine":

> The third night after wedding
>   I get near the stove.
>
> Rolling up my sleeves
>   I make a fancy broth.
>
> Not knowing the taste
>   of my mother-in-law,
>
> I try it first upon her
>   youngest girl. (*CP2*, 373)

Notice the version's visual shape: four staggered couplets derived from the original's four short lines. Is this modeled on "The Red Wheelbarrow"? Notice also the separation of "of my mother-in-law" from "the taste" in stanza 3, which underscores a shock: three nights into her marriage, the bride is already left alone with her in-laws, trying to impress them instead of her groom. Williams, the inventor of such strategies, made no comment on this version. Nor did he meddle with Wang's other re-creations with peculiar line divisions.

In the fall of 1959 Wang began working toward a master's degree in creative writing at San Francisco State College. That winter he produced a version of a poem by Du Fu (712–70). Through Kenneth Rexroth's *One Hundred Poems from the Chinese* (1956), Williams had already sampled the brilliance of this poet. In a review of Rexroth's two new books for *Poetry* (the other book being *In Defense of the Earth*), he singled out three poems for praise, two of which were from the Chinese of Du Fu. The Du Fu poem he received from Wang on Christmas Eve 1959, "Portrait of a Lady," was about a woman from a good family who lost everything during the Tang civil war. Wang had done nothing drastic to Du Fu's original composition except to break his twenty-four lines into six quatrains. Avoidable repetition, awkward insertion, and separation of the subject from its predicate are visible in the opening quatrains:

A pretty, pretty girl
Come from a celebrated family
Lives in the empty mountain
Alone with her fagots,

In the civil war
All her brothers were killed.
Why talk of pedigree,
When she couldn't collect their bones?

World feeling rises against the decline,
Following the rotating candle.
Husband has a new interest:
A beauty subtle as jade. (Beinecke)

This poem by Du Fu recalls Wang Wei's "The Peerless Lady," Li Bai's "Spring Song," and Wang Jian's "The Newlywed's Cuisine," all sketches of eighth-century Chinese women that had appeal for Williams. In his edited version Williams renamed the poem "Profile of a Lady" (to avoid a too obvious borrowing from himself or T. S. Eliot), revised the opening stanza, and polished a line in the third stanza. In the revised opening stanza, he reversed the order of lines 2 and 3, changed "Come" in what is now line 3 to "Came," and added "Now" before "alone with her fagots" in the final line (*CP2*, 370). These revisions combine to underscore the contrast between the lady's pre–civil war life and post–civil war life, a contrast obscured in Wang's draft.

After a long silence in 1960, Wang wrote to Williams on January 27, 1961: "I would appreciate if I only get a card from you" (Beinecke). He was perhaps too polite to ask whether Mrs. Williams had ever read to Dr. Williams his letter of February 16, 1960, and an enclosed version of a Li Bai poem entitled "A Letter," in which he had experimented with *Journey to Love*'s triad:

> My love,
> > When you were here there was
> > > a hall of flowers. (*CP2*, 364)

What Wang presented in this letter of January 27, 1961, was a version of another Li Bai poem, "The Knight," which eventually appeared in "The Cassia Tree" collection without further revision. Similar to his earlier efforts, the twenty-six-line poem is broken into seven stanzas, with an opening quatrain distinguished by alliterations of *w*'s and *b*'s:

> In March the dust of Tartary has swept over the capital.
> Inside the city wall the people sigh and complain.
> Under the bridge the water trickles with warm blood
> And bales of white bones lean against one another. (*CP2*, 367)

Wang was surely anxious to know what his mentor might think of the physical appearance of his version, in which quatrains mixed with sestets and couplets, and italicized lines blended with indented ones. No word came from the doctor-poet in February or March of 1961, nor in April or May of that year when David Wang was completing his thesis for a master's degree at San Francisco State College.

Williams's last letter to David Wang is dated August 5, 1961. In it he expressed surprise at Wang's acceptance of an instructor's job at the University of Hawaii, which news Wang must have conveyed in a lost letter to him. Williams asked Wang to give his departure date, for he wanted to send "2 newly published books." In a postscript he instructed: "By all means let them see the translations" (Dartmouth). There is no way to find out where Wang was planning to send their Chinese translations at that point.

Sometime in 1962, David Wang obviously requested a letter of recommendation from Williams. On August 12, 1962, Mrs. Williams responded: "I have taken care of the application—hope it is O.K. Bill is not in very good condition—is no longer writing and has great difficulty talking" (Dartmouth). Seven months later Dr. Williams peacefully passed away in his Rutherford home. His letter of August 5, 1961, had virtually concluded his partnership with David Wang, though its fruit remained unpublished until 1966.

TWO

Modernist
Minimalism
Reinitiated in
Rutherford

HAVING HIGHLIGHTED the master/apprentice relationship between Williams and Wang, I want to stress the mutual inspiration of this dynamic cross-cultural collaboration. From Williams's revisionary suggestions, Wang surely learned a great deal about the handling of poetic re-creation in an effort to make it new and make it modernist. By the early 1970s, he quickly developed into a full-fledged Asian American poet and anthologist. Correspondingly, Williams also learned a lot from Wang. For three and a half years, the younger poet served as Williams's primary collaborator. When face to face, as Williams testified in his letters of February 25 and May 12, 1958 (Dartmouth), Wang chanted to him the old language, put poems on paper character by character, and provided their denotative and connotative meanings. Together the two poets forged an English line of economy, understatement, and power in Chinese re-creations. More importantly, this collaboration inspired Williams to relearn the minimalist, painterly qualities of classic Chinese poetry, easing and speeding his return to modernist minimalism in his final lyrics. Without this cross-cultural textual and interpersonal exchange, Williams would have wrestled much longer to move away from his overused triadic line.

As I have noted, in 1966 David Wang published Williams's and his Chinese translations under the title "The Cassia Tree" in *New Directions*. The thirty-nine poems in the series included the eight Tang poems Wang had published in *Edge* before his partnership with Williams and excluded the first two Wang Wei poems Williams translated and re-translated in early 1958. Ironically, the two abandoned versions of Wang Wei had aesthetic consequences. They unexpectedly paved the way for

Williams's breakaway from the triadic pattern of *Paterson,* Books II–V, and return to his early minimalist, spatial design.

The seventy-six poems that make up *Pictures from Brueghel and Other Poems* (1962) were composed during Williams's collaboration with David Wang. Unsurprisingly, only two of the doctor-poet's final lyrics, "The Gift" and "The Turtle," adhere to the triadic pattern. The rest are all short poems in plain couplets, tercets, or quatrains. Peter Schmidt was among the first to call attention to Williams's recovery of his style of the 1920s with "lines and stanzas . . . taut and curt, in direct contrast to the sinuous, loquacious texture of the poems written using the triadic line."[1] To illustrate this claim, Schmidt compares the *Brueghel* poem "Iris" with the *Spring and All* poem "The Pot of Flowers" (*CP1,* 184) that shares "the Precisionist strain" of Charles Demuth's still lifes.[2] "Iris," a poem Jonathan Mayhew refers to as "a study of perception," opens with a tercet that immediately draws the reader's attention to "a burst of iris" in the speaker's consciousness when he awakes in the morning: "a burst of iris so that / come down for / breakfast."[3] Terse stanza breaks similar to those in "The Pot of Flowers" are used to build suspension. The poem's agent and action are deferred till the second tercet: "we search through the / rooms for / that," where the search goes on and its outcome continues to be held back: "sweetest odor and at / first could not / find its // source then a blue as / of the sea / struck." The triumphant discovery of the source of the fragrance is not announced until the very last stanza: "startling us from among / those trumpeting / petals" (*CP2,* 406). Written during Williams's translation project, this flower poem seems an indirect commentary on his search for and discovery of a refreshing style in classic Chinese poetry, an escape from the triadic line.

"Iris" brings a breath of fresh air into Williams's late lyrics. "It's really a fine poem, really good for reasons that I privately must respect," wrote the poet, battling death stroke after stroke. "It gave me a thrill even to see it again."[4] Nevertheless, in *Pictures from Brueghel* the poems bearing apparent influence of the Chinese are those written in short-line quatrains. Williams first learned the Chinese stop-short form from Giles around 1916. Observing David Wang authentically put on paper Wang Wei's poems in stop-short must have stimulated him to renew experimentation with that form in pieces such as "Short Poem":

You slapped my face
oh but so gently

I smiled
at the caress (*CP2*, 416)

Its choices of words such as "gently" and "caress" and repetitions of the *s* and *l* sounds call to mind "The Gentle Man," Williams's exercise of the stop-short form around 1920: "I feel the caress . . . / of the kind women I have known" (*CP1*, 158).

Does the pronoun "you" in "Short Poem" allude to one of "the kind women" in "The Gentle Man" or to the Chinese stop-short form that has jolted the poet back to his abandoned minimalist, spatial design? According to Giles, a Chinese stop-short poem concludes with a surprise, and "Short Poem" does end with a surprise. However, with a two-syllable third line ("I smiled") "Short Poem" seems an effort to make new and odd the stop-short look on the page.

"The Chrysanthemum" in Williams's last book of verse appears to be a happy return to his initial exercise of the Chinese double stop-short or *lüshi* form:

how shall we tell
the bright petals
from the sun in the
sky concentrically

crowding the branch
save that it yields
in its modesty
to that splendor? (*CP2*, 396)

Indeed, it rehearses "Complete Destruction" (1921), an early attempt at the appearance of a double stop-short on the page:

It was an icy day.
We buried the cat,
then took her box
and set match to it

in the back yard.
Those fleas that escaped
earth and fire
died by the cold. (*CP1*, 159)

English quatrains are typically made up of four lines, six to ten syllables each, carrying three, four, or five stresses.[5] By contrast, the quatrains in

"Complete Destruction" and "The Chrysanthemum" consist of two-stress lines, three to six syllables each. In 1932 Williams named a poem in four short-line tercets "Poem" ("As the cat") (*CP1,* 352). As Henry Sayre surmises, his purpose was to urge readers to see it not as mere "*utterance*" but as "*utterance given the form of poetry.*"[6] For the same intent, in my opinion, Williams has named one *Brueghel* poem "Short Poem" and three other *Brueghel* poems "Poem." Two of the *Brueghel* pieces named "Poem" are, in fact, in quatrains, and one of them—"Poem" ("The plastic surgeon") is in tercets. "Poem" ("The rose fades") appears to be another quasi-double stop-short poem. Unlike "The Chrysanthemum" with two square-looking stanzas, however, each of this poem's stanzas contains two shortened lines:

> The rose fades
> and is renewed again
> by its seed, naturally
> but where
>
> save in the poem
> shall it go
> to suffer no diminution
> of its splendor (*CP2,* 413)

Beginning with "The rose" and ending with "splendor," "Poem" ("The rose fades") seems at once allusive to Williams's 1923 cubist masterpiece "The rose is obsolete" and to *Brueghel* poems such as "The Chrysanthemum."

The quasi-double stop-short form is rehearsed in "The World Contracted to a Recognizable Image" (*CP2,* 415–16) and "Histology" (419). According to Christopher MacGowan, Williams composed "The World Contracted to a Recognizable Image" after a brief hospital stay in the fall of 1959. On October 2, 1959, he wrote to his Italian translator Cristina Campo, suggesting that she slip into her forthcoming volume a version of that freshly composed piece, which he believed "sums up all of my work in a way which I haven't succeeded in achieving until now."[7] The poem pays tribute to an East Asian picture on a hospital wall, "probably Japanese / which filled my eye," setting aside "the small end of an illness" (*CP2,* 415–16).

Many more *Brueghel* poems consist of short-line quatrains. Among these are "Song" ("beauty is a shell") (*CP2,* 394–95), "The Polar Bear" (395), "The Stone Crock" (404–405), "Poem" ("on getting a card")

(417), "To Flossie" (417–18), "Portrait of a Woman at Her Bath" (418), "A Salad for the Soul" (421), and "Sappho, Be Comforted" (433–34). All eight of them have three or more quatrains and three of them—"The Stone Crock," "To Flossie," and "Sappho, Be Comforted"—include alternate indented lines or indented penultimate lines, respectively.

In a note to "Poem" ("on getting a card"), MacGowan informs us that Williams twice changed his mind about its inclusion in a sequence accompanying Mary Ellen Solt's essay "William Carlos Williams: Poems in the American Idiom." In a letter dated July 16, 1959, to Solt, the doctor-poet expressed uncertainty about its quality: "Maybe this isn't a poem at [all]: not an image in the G. damn thing—EXCEP the musical measure of its lines." He wrote again on that same day to instruct "Hold everything! .... I [had] liked that poem until I LOOKED at it carefully and discovered its total lack of an image."[8] Five days later, he wrote to Solt a third time to reverse his earlier judgment, saying that the poem "brings out just the image I wanted to emphasize."[9] Williams's uncertainty about that poem reaffirms his typical aesthetic inconsistency. When he wrote Solt on July 16, he was apparently thinking of "image" in terms of an object or a person verbally represented, whereas when he wrote her the third time he was thinking of it, as he had counseled David Wang, in terms of "the structural interest of a mathematical theorem" (Dartmouth), what Sayre calls "a visual sense of poetic form."[10] True, "Poem" ("on getting a card") does not contain a visual image, what T. S. Eliot calls an "objective correlative"[11] but with a single word ("but" or "technique") ending its first two quatrains, two or three monosyllabic words ("to hear," "nor is he,") popping up in the second lines of the third and the fourth quatrains, and a single word ("virtues") surfacing in the third line of its final quatrain, it displays "the structural interest of a mathematical theorem." Its five short-line quatrains are arranged not in one way, as in a Chinese double stop-short, but rather alternately in the following three ways:

Unlike "The Chrysanthemum" and "Complete Destruction" (1921), "Poem" ("on getting a card") and "Poem" ("The rose fades") are Williams's endeavors to make new his 1920s imitative adaptations of the Chinese stop-short form. Without his 1958–61 collaboration with David Wang on the Chinese poems, Williams's late-life reinvention would have been out of the question. Think of "The Newlywed's Cuisine," a re-creation of a late eighth-century stop-short which David Wang sent Williams in August 1958. Wang's bold manipulation of the Chinese minimalist form, his splitting of each of its four lines into two and rearrangement of them in four stanzas, may well have spurred Williams to try his hand at playing with the stop-short form in more innovative ways. To keep the rose from fading and from suffering "diminution / of its splendor," Williams knew, he must not only renew its modernist minimalist design but renew it with fresh innovations.

"The Dance" ("When the snow falls"), yet another *Brueghel* poem, is made up of nine quatrains with varied line length. Five of them— the first, the third, the sixth, the eighth, and the last quatrains—each include a nine- or ten-syllable line, and three of them—the fifth, the seventh, and the last—each contain a two- or three-syllable line. From the outset the poem seems an attempt to catch the rhythm of the dance of the snow:

> When the snow falls the flakes
> spin upon the long axis
> that concerns them most intimately
> two and two to make a dance
>
> the mind dances with itself,
> taking you by the hand,
> your lover follows
> there are always two (*CP2,* 407)

Its first two stanzas recall Williams's January 1958 attempts at Wang Wei's stop-short poems. The images chosen—"snow," "falls," "spin," and "dance"—moreover are reminiscent of the second half of "To the Shade of Po Chü-i"—"A girl passes, in a red tam, / the coat above her quick ankles / snow smeared from running and falling" (*CP1,* 133).

Just as the girl "in a red tam" leads the speaker of "To the Shade of Po Chü-i" to think of "death the bright dancer," so the spinning of the snowflakes causes the speaker of "The Dance" to imagine "the mind danc[ing] with itself":

> this flurry of the storm
> that holds us,
> plays with us and discards us
> dancing, dancing as may be credible. (*CP2*, 408)

Like *Spring and All* (1923), *Pictures from Brueghel and Other Poems* (1962) is a cubist collage of verbal representations. Only the first dozen lyrics in the 1962 volume are attempts to represent the Netherlandish Renaissance painter's masterpieces in words. None of the rest has anything to do with Brueghel or with each other. "Iris," "The Chrysanthemum," "The Woodthrush," and "Bird" are about iris, chrysanthemums, a woodthrush, and a bird; "Elaine," "Erica," "Emily," and "Suzy" concern the speaker's granddaughters Elaine, Erica, Emily, and Suzy. They are not meant to symbolize anything. Each poem creates a distinct perception whose meaning varies depending on who is reading in what mood. One of the "de-familiarizing" strategies used, as Perloff points out, is "repetition, both verbal and syntactic."[12] The influence has been attributed to Arthur Rimbaud and Gertrude Stein. It would be misleading, however, to claim that Rimbaud's *The Illuminations* and Stein's *Tender Buttons* were Williams's only models in his early avant-garde phase. He apparently drew on multiple sources of inspiration of which the mid-Tang poet Bai Juyi (Po Chü-i) was as important as Rimbaud and Stein. Consider Bai Juyi's "On His Boldness" in Waley's translation:

> At dawn I sighed to see my hairs fall;
> At dusk I sighed to see my hairs fall.
> They are all gone and I do not mind at all!
> I have done with that cumbrous washing and getting dry;
> My tiresome comb for ever is laid aside.[13]

Williams owned a copy of Waley's *More Translations from the Chinese*, which includes "On His Boldness." He could not fail to notice in the poem's second "I sighed to see my hairs fall" a shift in mood from regret to acceptance and amusement. This kind of repetition in Waley's versions of Bai Juyi points to Williams's repetition of the word *snow* in "To the Shade of Po Chü-i" for an altered effect. Whereas "snow" in the first two lines—"The work is heavy. I see / bare branches laden with snow"—evinces a note of desolation, "snow" in lines 6–7—"the coat above her quick ankles / snow smeared from running and falling"—suggests a sense of humor or liveliness.

Bai Juyi is dwarfed by his predecessor Du Fu in his mastery of the art of repetition. Williams had no idea how great Du Fu was until after reading Kenneth Rexroth's *One Hundred Poems from the Chinese* (1956). In the 1957 review mentioned in chapter 1, he cited two of Rexroth's versions of Du Fu to give Chinese poetry the highest praise: "Nothing comparable and as relaxed is to be found I think in the whole of English or American verse, and in French or Spanish verse, so far as I know."[14] The versions of Du Fu cited, "Dawn over the Mountains" and "Visitors," present similar scenes, in which, in Williams's description, "the person of the poet, the poetess, no, the woman herself (when it is a woman), speaks to us ... in an unknown language, to our very ears, so that we actually weep with her and what she says (while we are not aware of her secret) is that she breathes ... that she is alive as we are."[15]

No more than eight months after the publication of this review appeared in *Poetry,* Williams was challenged to re-create a version of Wang Wei's dramatic monologue, "The Lady of Lo-Yang" ("The Peerless Lady"). Was he sparked by Rexroth's Du Fu to make the version more dramatic and more conversational? At any rate, under his care the first two lines in David Wang's draft—"The lady of Lo-Yang lives across the street. / By her looks she's about fifteen years of age" (*CP2,* 501)—became "Look, there goes the young lady across the street / She looks about fifteen, doesn't she?" (*CP2,* 364). And the seventh line offered by David Wang—"Through gauze curtain she glides into her perfumed sedan chair" (501)—is rewritten as "Look, she's coming thru the gauze curtains to get into her chaise" (364). By inserting the interjection "Look" twice and by converting statements to rhetorical questions and the present tense to the present continuous tense, Williams succeeds in letting the reader directly hear the speaker chatter about his affluent neighbor's gorgeous young wife and her common background.

The repetition of "Look" is of course not in Wang Wei's original. Wang Wei is good at employing repetition for special effects, though. In the first Wang Wei stop-short Williams dealt with in January and February 1958, the word *man,* for example, is repeated in the first two lines to strike a Zen overtone. This repetition, reproduced in David Wang's "Empty hill not see man / But hear man's voice sound," is suppressed in both of Williams's versions, however. Similarly, in a Du Fu poem that

David Wang and Williams call "Profile of a Lady," the characters *shan* (meaning "mountain") and *quan* (meaning "spring") are repeated in the original to intensify a contrast. Williams was not even aware of these repetitions since they were not present in Wang's draft version: "Spring in the mountains is clear, / Mud underfoot" (*CP2*, 371). The couplet, if literally rendered, would be: "Spring in the mountains is clear, / Spring out of the mountains is mud."

As I have remarked elsewhere, the images of mountains and streams recur in "On Being Sixty," "Going to the Mountains with a Little Dancing Girl, Aged Fifteen," and other versions of Bai Juyi's late poems.[16] Recurrences of these images suggest a serene state of mind. As to why the Chinese poet is able to enjoy such tranquility in old age, an answer is given in the opening couplet of a version of his poem entitled "At the End of Spring (To Yuan Chen)": "The flower of the pear-tree gathers and turns to fruit; / The swallows' eggs have hatched into young birds."[17] Here the Tang poet typically equates the cycles of vegetable life and animal life with the cycles of the seasons, hence the serenity. The influence of Bai Juyi's occasional poems displaying his Taoist outlook seems to have returned to Williams in the final years of his life. While Bai Juyi's recurring images of mountains and streams appear to anticipate the numerous flower and bird poems in *Pictures from Brueghel,* the Chinese poet's characteristic equation of the cycles of all things in the world looks ahead to Williams's alertness to seasonal changes in his final lyrics.

The *Brueghel* poems seem as reflective of the cycles of the seasons as those Williams and David Wang appropriated from the Chinese. Li Bai calls his poem about a pretty girl by the mulberry road "Spring Song"; Wang Wei sets his "Lady of Lo-Yang" in summertime; and Du Fu tells a winter tale in "Profile of a Lady." Likewise, seasonal changes play a critical role in a large number of Williams's *Brueghel* poems. "Landscape with the Fall of Icarus" opens with the lines, "According to Brueghel /when Icarus fell / it was spring" (*CP2*, 385). The very first word of "The Corn Harvest" is "Summer!" (389). "Peasant Wedding" is held in autumn, as "a head / of ripe wheat is on / the wall beside" the bride at the banquet (388). As to "The Hunters in the Snow," "The over-all picture is winter" (386).

The endless cycles of the seasons go hand in hand with the endless cycles of human life, animal life, and vegetable life. "The Adoration of the Kings" in *Pictures from Brueghel* presents the birth of Jesus Christ.

"Children's Games" portrays children at school. "Peasant Wedding" and "The Wedding Dance in the Open Air" both depict specific wedding celebrations. "The Corn Harvest" and "Haymaking" delineate harvest scenes in different ways. In "The Parable of the Blind," six blind men are led to catastrophe one by one. In "Landscape with the Fall of Icarus" Icarus drowns in an ocean while villagers on shore go on with their normal lives.

The first dozen *Brueghel* poems are ekphrasis or verbal representation of visual representation. They re-create in words a portrait of questionable authorship and nine masterpieces of the Netherlandish Renaissance painter Pieter Brueghel (ca. 1525–69). During a 1924 trip to Vienna Williams and his wife, Flossie, made a point of going to the Kunsthistorisches Museum for its splendid Brueghel collection. In 1959, however, Williams had to rely on coffee-table editions of the Netherlandish master, especially Gustav Glück's *Pieter Brueghel the Elder* (1952), to paint in words Brueghel's portrayals of spirited peasant life.

The dozen picture poems (counting parts II and III of "Children's Games") each consist of seven to eight tercets with one to five words or one to seven syllables to a line. Williams's 1942 *Brueghel* poem "The Dance" ("In Brueghel's great picture") cannot be included in the sequence primarily because it is composed not in short-line tercets but in twelve continuous nine- to ten-syllable lines. The late *Brueghel* poems' shared minimalist, spatial design and balanced outlook can be traced to the influence of Tang dynasty poets, particularly that of Bai Juyi. The opening poem, "Self-Portrait," originally entitled "Self-Portrait: The Old Shepherd," portrays a genial old man:

> In a red winter hat blue
> eyes smiling
> just the head and shoulders
>
> crowded on the canvas

The Kunsthistorisches portrait that Williams painted in words was ascribed to Brueghel in 1924, but since the late 1920s that painting's attribution has been questioned. According to Christopher MacGowan, the painting, titled *Self-Portrait,* was ascribed to Jan van Eyck (ca. 1390–1441) in the 1950s, then to a follower of Jan van Eyck in the 1960s, and to Jean Fouquet (1420–81) more recently.[18] Williams would not have been uninformed of this problem with the portrait's attribution. The edition he depended on, Glück's *Pieter Brueghel the Elder*, does not reproduce the Kunsthistorisches portrait of a Ferrara court jester, which was for a long time taken as Brueghel's or some other artist's self-Portrait. "Self-Portrait" as the opening piece of *Pictures from Brueghel*, like the jester portrait frontispiece of *The Elder Peter Brueghel* published by New York's Willey Book (1938), is nothing but a joke. At any rate, Williams seems fond of the old man in "Self-Portrait." Smiling in a red winter hat, he is reminiscent of the vivacious girl in a red tam in Williams's "To the Shade of Po Chü-i." What's more, both Williams in old age and the poet of "Going to the Mountains with a Little Dancing Girl, Aged Fifteen" appear as dedicated to their craft and as uncaring about their appearances as the old man of "Self-Portrait":

> the eyes red-rimmed
>
> from overuse he must have
> driven them hard
> but the delicate wrists
>
> show him to have been a
> man unused to
> manual labor unshaved his
>
> blond beard half trimmed
> no time for any-
> thing but his painting (*CP2*, 385)

The second poem in the volume, "Landscape with the Fall of Icarus," opens with the phrase, "According to Brueghel," claiming rejection of Ovid's version of the myth. Unlike Ovid's plowman, who "stands stupefied, and believes [flying Icarus and Daedalus, son and father] to be / gods," Williams's plowman, following Brueghel's suit, goes on "ploughing / his field."[19] In fact,

> the whole pageantry
>
> of the year was
> awake tingling
> near
>
> the edge of the sea
> concerned
> with itself (*CP2*, 386)

People die natural or unnatural deaths every hour and every minute. Williams, like Brueghel the Renaissance painter, has reason to believe that when Icarus of ancient Crete drowned, the plowman in the field would go on plowing and the angler on the shore would go on angling.

In October 1958, it is worth noting, Williams suffered another stroke, the fourth since his first in 1951. During the recuperating period he had nothing better to do than pore over Brueghel's pictures in one coffee-table edition or another. His favorite Brueghel paintings unexpectedly kindled some energy and excitement. Soon he was not only re-creating Brueghel's masterpieces in words, but also suggesting revisions for David Wang's draft versions of Du Fu and other Tang poets. Taoist insight into the cyclical nature of life and death, its belief in less is more, and other notions inevitably entered Williams's representations of Brueghel. Brueghel's pictures are bright-colored and joyful. With the Chinese influence, Williams's representations of the Netherlandish Renaissance painter appear even more radiant and cheerful. In Brueghel's *The Fall of Icarus,* Icarus, one of the central subjects in Ovid's *Metamorphosis,* is represented insignificantly by a tiny leg disappearing into the green ocean. In the foreground are the unconcerned plowman, shepherd, and angler. This treatment is emulated by Williams in his ekphrastic poem. Whereas Icarus still claims the center in *The Fall of Icarus,* he takes a back seat in Williams's "Landscape with the Fall of Icarus." Life is rendered brighter in Williams's ekphrasis, where "the whole pageantry //of the year was / awake" on a spring morning. If the intended theme of the poem is humanity's indifference to death, then the poet approaching death himself is treating it not downheartedly, but matter-of-factly with a Du Fu/Bai Juyi-like serene state of mind.

The cold night world of Williams's "The Hunters in the Snow" is reproduced from Brueghel's painting of the same title. Less than a year before the composition of the *Brueghel* poems, we may recall, Williams had learned from David Wang an ancient Chinese philosophical notion. In his letter of May 20, 1958, he thanked Wang for enlightening his mind on the yin/yang balance, "making [him] realize what the poets are talking about" (Dartmouth). In painting *The Hunters in the Snow* in words, it must have occurred to the doctor-poet, the picture's accentuated icy cold and dark night, both yin elements, like Wang Wei's "deep woods," need to be counteracted by adding yang elements, like Wang Wei's "light." Against the chilly, pitch-dark background, therefore, he built up the warmth and brightness of "a huge bonfire //that flares wind-driven tended by / women who cluster / about it" (*CP2,*

386–387), which detail is but marginally featured in Brueghel's visual representation. The somberness of the painting is, in fact, further compensated for by Williams's vigilance, in his version, to jovial winter activities such as "a pattern of skaters."

"The Corn Harvest" consists of eight tercets, half of which are shaped like haiku—a six- or seven-syllable line set between two lines with two to four syllables each. As verbal representation of Brueghel's *The Harvesters* (figure 4), it has been faulted for its indifference to 92 percent of the painting's vivid details.[20] Contrary to Gustav Glück's edition of Brueghel, which offers two additional plates of details— one of the reapers at work and the other of a midday meal beneath a tree[21]—Williams's poem devotes more than half of its space to the description of

> a young

> reaper enjoying his
> noonday rest
> completely

> relaxed
> from his morning labors
> sprawled

> in fact sleeping
> unbuttoned
> on his back (*CP2,* 389)

James Heffernan perceptively argues that the poet's concentration "allows him to see certain things the critic overlooks."[22] The young reaper's midday sleep signals how strenuously he has worked in the morning. His relaxation is energy recharging for more field labor in the afternoon. Williams's equation of rest beneath a tree (yin) and hard work under the sun (yang), nonaction (yin) and action (yang) in a poem about corn harvest calls to mind "Spring," a haiku-like *Sour Grapes* poem probably inspired by Bai Juyi's "On His Baldness": "O my grey hairs! / You are truly white as plum blossoms" (*CP1,* 158). In it, aging is superimposed with spring rather than with autumn, and "grey hairs" are superimposed with "plum blossoms" rather than with yellow leaves or fallen leaves.

Everything has two sides, a dark side (yin) and a bright side (yang).

Figure 4. *The Harvesters,* Pieter Brueghel, 1565. (Metropolitan Museum of Art, New York, Rogers Fund, 1919)

From the Tang poets Williams seems to have learned to cheer him-self up in rocky times by focusing on the bright side of everything. Amazingly, after a fourth stroke and in the face of approaching death, Williams is able to imagine so much joy and hope even in Brueghel's gloomy pictures. It is not surprising to note a hilarious tone in Wil-liams's version of *The Dance Village,* depicting 125 wedding guests danc-ing in the wood. The elderly poet's title is "The Wedding Dance in the Open Air." It is only natural for the Netherland village revelers to spin, like Bai Juyi and his fifteen-year-old dancing companion, "round and around in / rough shoes and / farm breeches // mouths agape" (*CP2,* 390–91). What is surprising is the way Williams ends his version of *The Parable of the Blind.* The concluding lines—"one / follows the others stick in / hand triumphant to disaster" (*CP2,* 391)—are of course oxy-moronic. But Williams is probably trying to see things from the Taoist perspective, that is, to view misfortune as a blessing in disguise. Chinese in a disastrous situation would sometimes think of the parable of an old man who lost a horse. When his neighbors came to comfort him, he said that his loss could be a good thing. Indeed, a few months later, his horse returned with another horse. When his neighbors came to congratulate him, he said that this good luck might turn out to be misfortune. Strangely, a few days later, his son fell from the new horse and broke his leg. Due to his lameness, however, the young man was not chosen to fight in a war in which thousands of soldiers were killed. Williams is not likely to have heard of this Chinese parable. But from the Tang poets he has taken in the Taoist notion of nondiscrimination, that is, to view all things in the universe—life and death, vitality and old age, disaster and blessing—as the same. In "To the Shade of Po Chü-i," one recollects, the speaker catching sight of a girl running and falling over snow can think of nothing but "death the bright dancer." "Death the Barber," the fourteenth poem in *Spring and All,* is another example of capturing the yin/yang idea, perhaps with no knowledge of the terms *yin* and *yang.* In that poem the barber casually observes that "we die / every night—," to which the speaker responds by telling him "of old men / with third / sets of teeth" and "of an old man / who said / at the door—/ Sunshine today!" (*CP1,* 213).

Since not a few of the Brueghel pictures represented are set in wintertime with a seemingly somber tone, Williams finds it necessary to conclude the series with "The Rewaking," a poem in haiku-like tercets that will help clarify the volume's overall theme:

Sooner or later
we must come to the end
of striving

to re-establish
the image the image of
the rose

but not yet
you say extending the
time indefinitely

by
your love until a whole
spring

rekindle
the violet to the very
lady's-slipper

and so by
your love the very sun
itself is revived (*CP2*, 437)

Williams's choices of words such as "re-establish," "rekindle," and "revived" all point to the poem's motif given by its title. The image of the rose calls to mind Williams's most cubist poem, "The rose is obsolete" (*CP1*, 195), betraying his regret for the falling-off from that great little poem. Accordingly, "The Rewaking" hints simultaneously at his loving wife and his brand of modernist poetry. Like Bai Juyi's "At the End of Spring," Williams's final lyric brings to light the cyclical nature of all things in the universe—human and nonhuman, concrete and abstract. The poem can certainly be read as a dramatic monologue in which the dying poet engages his wife in a positive dialogue about life and death. But it can also be interpreted as an interior monologue in which the American modernist poet speaks to his muse about experimental modernism, its setbacks and renewal.

Williams made *Pictures from Brueghel and Other Poems* precisely during the heyday of postmodernist poetry. In the final phase of his life, he witnessed the Black Mountain poets, the Beat generation, and the confessional poets emerge to challenge the values championed by him and his fellow modernists. As a friend and mentor of Allen Ginsberg, Robert Lowell, and other younger American poets, Williams never seems to have questioned the worth and meaningfulness of their very personal and literal poetries. Nonetheless, by abandoning his own autobiographical tendency in *Journey to Love* and *Paterson,* Book V, and by returning to the modernist ideal of impersonality in his last book of verse, he took a stance not really sympathetic with his postmodernist friends' propositions and goals.

Impersonality as a poetic ideal opposed to romanticism was advocated by the modernists in the early decades of the twentieth century through essays such as T. S. Eliot's "The Tradition and the Individual Talent" (1919). Williams had always resented the way Eliot overshadowed his brand of modernist poetry, and he had always opposed Eliot's elitist style with endless allusions to European literature and culture. Despite all his resentment, it must be pointed out, Williams had not been critical of Eliot's advocacy of impersonality. Nor had he underestimated the merit of Eliot's modernist poetry. In fact, in March 1948, Williams told James Laughlin of New Directions that Eliot's *Four Quar-*

tets were "about the only poems . . . that are truly inventive (Pound not writing much) today."[23]

The literary models for Williams, from Rimbaud to Bai Juyi, are all upholders of the poetics of impersonality. In *On the Observation of Things* Song dynasty philosopher Shao Yong (1011–77) famously asserts, "to attain a state in which, to quote Laozi, 'he does nothing, yet there is nothing that is not done,' one must 'forget self.' "[24] The Chinese poets who adhere to forgetting self are like the American modernists who strive for "a continual self-sacrifice, a continual extinction of personality."[25] The poems of Wang Wei, Du Fu, and Bai Juyi are apparently impersonal but transparently personal. Similarly, Eliot's *The Waste Land* and Williams's "The Red Wheelbarrow," "Spring and All," and "Landscape with the Fall of Icarus," despite their shared impersonal appearance, each have a concealed authorial voice.[26] Bai Juyi's "On His Baldness" and Williams's "Spring" may seem personal, but since the speakers in these poems are conspicuously trying to clear themselves of egotism—or, in Shao Yong's words, to forget self—they are no less effective examples of "a continual self-sacrifice, a continual extinction of personality."

When faulting the modernist ideal of impersonality, postmodern poets and critics tend to target Eliot and evade Williams. Olson and Ginsberg called themselves students of Williams in all sincerity. At Ginsberg's request, the doctor-poet actually wrote introductions to two of Ginsberg's books of verse—*Howl and Other Poems* (1956) and *Empty Mirror* (1961). Lowell won Williams's approval for his *Life Studies* (1959). After reading *Life Studies* in manuscript, Williams wrote to Lowell on December 4, 1957, congratulating him for having advanced himself "as an artist and a man in the world."[27] All this must not mislead us into thinking that Williams had a very high opinion of the postmodernist poets, for he did not. In a posthumously published review of Olson's *Maximus,* Book II, he expressed his ambivalent feeling about the Black Mountain leader: "Sometimes he seems terrific and at others incredibly bad and self-deluded."[28] To Williams, "Ginsberg's long lines" meant "nothing."[29] At a 1959 symposium on the Beats he surprised everyone in the audience by drawing attention to some un-beatnik poetry, which he declared, "the 'beatniks' have much to learn from."[30] In a letter to Cid Corman on September 15, 1959, cited in the introduction, he gave away his true sentiment about the younger American poets in general: "When I see how unenlightened, technically unenlightened, many of our prizewinning poets are, I do not feel discouraged though my time is running out. Once in a while I can still do it." To Williams, fellow objectivist Louis Zukofsky was still "miles ahead" of them all when it came to reinventing the American poem.[31]

No one will raise doubts about Williams's impact on Olson, Ginsberg, Lowell, and other younger American poets. Nor will one deny the fact that Williams was generally friendly and sympathetic in his exchanges with postmodernist poets. But in the final analysis Williams and the majority of these younger American poets represent two different kinds of poetry. First, Ginsberg and Lowell after *Life Studies* signify a poetic direction opposite to the modernist ideal of impersonality. Admittedly, Williams's *Journey to Love* is an attempt to be personal, but Williams never really broke away from the poetics of impersonality. The Chinese poems he worked on with David Wang from 1958 to 1961 rekindled his passion for this ideal. As a result, he renewed the modernist principle of impersonality in his last book of verse. Second, Williams did not share with Ginsberg and late Lowell an antisocial standpoint. He too had dissatisfactions with the American society, but unlike Ginsberg and late Lowell, who, according to Williams, were "mentally much disturbed by the life which [they] had encountered about [them]," the doctor-poet, thanks to the influence of Tang dynasty poets, tried to keep an optimistic outlook, a serene state of mind.[32] If his dialogue with Bai Juyi around 1920 was partially responsible for his early minimalist, spatial design and tranquil state of mind, then his collaboration with Wang in 1958–61 helped in an important way to renew that design with fresh innovations and reinitiate that state of mind with genuine appreciation.

In the early 1960s, with Stein and Stevens gone and Eliot and Pound "not writing much," American modernist poetry seemed brought to the brink of extinction. It was at such a critical moment that Williams published *Pictures from Brueghel and Other Poems*. The centrality of this volume to Williams's late modernism is as acute as that of *Spring and All* to his early phase of avant-gardism. Williams's last book of verse should be viewed as the dying poet's public response to the postmodernist challenge. It should be regarded as a new milestone in his long career, signaling his return under cross-cultural textual and interpersonal influence to Pound's and his own anti-symbolist poetics of the early twentieth century, a poetics of depersonalization, anti-mimesis, and interculturalism.

THREE

Moore, Sze, and the Tao

MARIANNE MOORE SHARED with Pound and Williams a lifelong interest in Chinese culture.[1] Surprisingly, in her old age she acquired a more astute understanding of Chinese aesthetic than Pound and Williams. Indeed, in the foreword to *A Marianne Moore Reader* (1961), she refers to a lecture on Taoist aesthetic entitled "Tedium and Integrity in Poetry," which she gave at Mills College in Oakland, California, on October 16, 1957: "What became of 'Tedium and Integrity,' the unfinished manuscript of which there was no duplicate? A housekeeper is needed to assort the untidiness" (*CPr*, 550).

Not the entire manuscript of "Tedium and Integrity" was found, however, as she clarifies two paragraphs later: "Of 'Tedium and Integrity' the first few pages are missing—summarized sufficiently by: manner for matter; shadow for substance; ego for rapture" (*CPr*, 551). Of Moore's seven-page October 1957 lecture notes only part of the main body and the conclusion remained.

The surviving pages of Moore's typescript are kept at the Rosenbach Museum and Library in Philadelphia (and published as an appendix to my 2003 study *The Modernist Response to Chinese Art: Pound, Moore, Stevens*). Moore biographer Linda Leavell speculates: "This may have been one of Moore's most important essays along with 'Feeling and Precision' and 'Humility, Concentration, and Gusto' had she not lost the first four pages."[2] But is nearly half of "Tedium and Integrity in Poetry" really lost? Could it not be reconstructed if a recording of the lecture were found? With this possibility in mind I traveled to Mills College in May 2010. Thanks to the assistance of Janice Braun, Curator of the Mills College F.W. Olin Library Special Collections, a recording of the October 1957 lecture was indeed discovered. In her final de-

Figure 5. Marianne Moore, October 14, 1957. (Photograph by Imogen Cunningham, © 2017 Imogen Cunningham Trust)

cade, Marianne Moore (figure 5) might well have turned this lecture into an essay as important as "Feeling and Precision" and "Humility, Concentration, and Gusto." Leavell's speculation proves correct. This lecture provides essential clues about the later development of Moore's modernist poetics as manifest in her last two books of verse, *O to Be a Dragon* (1959) and *Tell Me, Tell Me* (1966). The discovery also brings to light what inspired her October 1957 lecture—a 1956 book about the Tao by a Chinese painter-writer, which she had read earlier that year. The Chinese aesthetic concepts and forms she learned from that book and then elucidated in the lecture would lead to her sudden renewal of experimental modernism in old age. Without access to the entire lecture, precisely how Moore introduced her theme of "Tedium and Integrity in Poetry," what impromptu remarks she made about modernist poetics and the Tao, and what new and old poems she read that night would remain lost to the reader.

As the sound recording attests, Moore began her forty-minute lecture at Mills College with a brief explanation of what she meant by "tedium":

> Tonight our topic is "Tedium and Integrity." How are we going to express it, a creative principle? It should in any case be the opposite of the uninstructed teaching the lesson, the unnecessary. It should be the initiate making explicit the intangible. Now, what kind of poetry is not tedious? What is tedium? One of my compositions is entitled "Poetry," and I said, "I, too, dislike it." What do I mean by that? I mean that we dislike manner for matter, shadow for substance, and ego for rapture.[3]

For Moore, modern poetry should be like modern painting that "centers much less on seeing the real world than on making of it another world." Or as she further explains in her Mills College lecture, poetry should make "exciting what did not exist until sensibility and imagination created it." Accordingly, she would find it tiresome to read any poetry with no vision of "another world" or no "sensibility and imagination" that created "another world." With this elucidation, Moore shifted to "integrity," referring first to Dr. Samuel Johnson, whom she considered "a man of integrity," and then to the English writer and illustrator Beatrix Potter (1866–1943) who, she said, had also testified to the wholeness of an artist's personal life and work. Having praised these Western men and women of integrity, she credited the idea of integrity, surprisingly, not to any of them but rather to Mai-mai Sze and her 1956 book in the Bollingen series, *The Tao of Painting,* published with a translation of *The Mustard Seed Garden Manual 1679–1701*:

> Now, this whole theme of integrity, for I would like to dispatch tedium for good, was suggested to me by *The Tao of Painting,* edited and with a translation by Mai-mai Sze. It was published by the Bollingen Foundation in 1956, and anything I say that is worth the hearing should be attributed to Ms. Mai-mai Sze. Well, Hsieh Ho, whose six canons of painting were formulated about AD 500, said, "The terms ancient and modern have no meaning in art."

And I indeed felt that art is timeless when I saw in the book review section of the *New York Times* last winter, a reproduction of a plum branch, a blossoming branch entitled "A Breath of Spring." ("Tedium and Integrity")

As I have noted in *The Modernist Response to Chinese Art,* Moore received her copy of *The Tao of Painting* along with two other books (Kenneth Clark's *The Nude: A Study in Ideal Form* and C. G. Jung's *The Collected Works,* vol. 1) from the Bollingen Foundation in January 1957. Just how thrilled she became by possessing these books is evident in a letter she wrote John Barrett on January 22, 1957: "you cannot imagine my excitement in possessing these books. The exposition of subjects and the terminology in discussing 'The Elements of a Picture' in the Chinese text is pleasure enough for a lifetime" (Rosenbach). Her admiration for *The Tao of Painting* is further revealed in her letter on September 5, 1957, to Barrett, in which she ordered five more copies of Sze's book for her friends: "Now!—I need some copies of the TAO and for two, enclose a check for fifty dollars and a memorandum of what I owe for conveyance will have to be made. I seem to make a salesman of you. . . . I have been talking to my friend Bryher [Annie Winifred Ellerman] about my so-called lecture in California TEDIUM AND INTEGRITY about how the Tao makes study charming and I cannot rest till she has this treatise—of all my friends the one perhaps, who deserves it most" (Rosenbach).

What first caught Moore's eye were no doubt the book's expertly chosen plates of Chinese ink paintings and calligraphy. She alluded to one of them, *A Breath of Spring* by Zou Fulei (figure 7), in her Mills College lecture, and she extravagantly praised another, *Early Autumn* by Qian Xuan (1235–1305), in her January 22 letter to Barrett:

If I were in a decline mentally, the insect and frog color-print in Volume I of the Tao would, I think, help me to regain tone. The accuracy without rigidity of the characterizations is hard to credit; the emerald of the leopard-frog and its watchful eye, the dragonflies, sanguine, brown and greenish gray against the fragile beetle of some kind, the climbing katydid and grasshopper on the move, the plausibility of all this life above the pumpkin-leaves and lace of lesser leaves, the bumble-bee so solid despite frail violet wings and trailing legs with thorny rasps, are something, I suppose, that one could learn by heart but never become used to. (Rosenbach)

For decades Chinese art had held a well-known fascination for Moore. Among proofs for this abiding fascination are her admiration for "mandarins and insects painted upon silk" by a Chinese hand in a 1925 *Dial* "Comment" piece (*CPr,* 151); her tribute to the plates of Chinese figures and landscapes illustrating Louise Wallace Hackney's *Guide-Posts to Chinese Painting* in a 1928 *Dial* review (*CPr,* 255), and her eulogy of Ming and Qing porcelain designs—"a Chinese / who imagined this masterpiece"—in "Nine Nectarines," a 1934 poem (*CPo,* 30). Yet until she read *The Tao of Painting* she had no objective understanding of what made Chinese art eternally fascinating. More importantly, she discovered to her amazement that much of the Tao or the aesthetic behind Chinese poetry and painting appeared akin to her own modernist poetics. Both favor an art that "centers much less on seeing the real world than on making of it another world" ("Tedium and Integrity"). She could invigorate her poetry by deliberately applying the Tao. She wished fervently to share her new insights with others, and precisely at that moment she received a lecture invitation from Mills College. It provided her with that opportunity.

"Tedium and Integrity" is thus Moore's homage to *The Tao of Painting.* Whereas *tedium* is Moore's term for Sze's locution "egotism," or *siyu* in Chinese, "integrity" is her expression for the Tao.[4] In chapter 1, "On Tao and the Tao," Sze stresses the indefinable nature of the Tao by quoting Laozi as saying in the *Dao De Jing* (*Tao Te Ching*), "the *Tao* that can be called the *Tao* is not the eternal *Tao*" (*The Tao of Painting,* 15).[5] "In Chinese writing, which is pictographic, of course," Moore observes in her October 1957 lecture, "a tao is a pair of legs, whereas the Tao has legs, arms, and a head—it's a total harmony, from head to foot" ("Tedium and Integrity"). Moore derives this symbolic meaning from Sze's analysis of the Chinese character 道 (*dao* in pinyin) in primitive form as a depiction of a head (on the right) beside a depiction of a foot (on the left), representing wholeness of head and foot, beginning and end, heaven and earth (*The Tao of Painting,* 16). We can see, then, why Moore has chosen *integrity* as her term for the Tao. The English word, too, emphasizes both aspects of the Taoist concept symbolized in the character 道 in primitive form—wholeness of all things (heaven and earth) and wholeness of character (individual from head to foot). Scrutiny of the character 道, moreover, reveals the foot on the left as both unmoving and moving. The dual character of the Tao—unmoving/moving, non-action/action—is summed up by Laozi's catch phrase *wu wei,* which means nonaction/action, or as Sze puts it, "outer passivity, inner activity" (17). The Tao is aptly compared to the forever-running water and forever-circulating air in space. "Space of any sort," writes Sze, "was regarded as filled with meaning since it was filled with *Tao*, in fact was *Tao*, an idea that inevitably had a profound influence on painting" (17). "To be able to reflect clearly the *Tao*," she further expounds, it is "helpful in emptying the heart of distractions, selfishness, and ignorance," what the Chinese call *siyu* (31).[6] This leads to Moore's theme of tedium or "egotism" in her October 1957 lecture. Since her college days, as Cristanne Miller has observed, Moore has been known for her avowed objection to egotism, which underlies her attraction to the Taoist insistence on clearing away all *siyu*.[7]

Sze, in chapter 2 of *The Tao of Painting*, turns her attention to the six canons of painting (*liu fa*) formulated by Xie He (Hsieh Ho) in AD 550, and Moore does the same in the second part of her Mills College lecture. For fifteen centuries Chinese art critics have used Xie He's six canons as criteria when judging works of art. Ironically, few of them have interpreted Xie He in his own terms.[8] In Xie He's original text (preface to *Gu Hua Pin* [*Ranking of Ancient Painters*]), each canon consists of six characters, the last two, a copulative phrase (*shi ye*), serving to break the first four into two phrases, one glossing the other. As Qian Zhongshu has pointed out, the copulative phrase at the end of each canon is accidentally dropped in *Lidai Minghua Ji* (Famous paintings through history) by Zhang Yanyuan (ca. 815–877), from which most art critics have cited the six canons.[9] Relying not on Xie He's text but on Zhang Yanyuan's, Western scholars have unavoidably misread the six canons. The first canon in Xie He's original words, for instance, is *qi yun, sheng dong shi ye*, or "breath resonance, which refers to liveliness and animation."[10] Taking the canon as an integral four-character phrase, Herbert Giles renders it as "rhythmic vitality," omitting the *qi* or breath element for readability.[11] In *The Flight of the Dragon* (1911) Laurence Binyon expresses dissatisfaction with Giles's translation, saying, "though terse and convenient, it does not seem quite to cover the full meaning of the original phrase."[12] He then offers his own interpretation: "We are probably nearer to its essence when we speak of the rhythmical movements of the body, as in games or in the dance. We all know, by experience, that in order to apply the energy of the body to the utmost effect, we must discover a certain related order of movements."[13]

His interpretation starts from "the rhythmical movements of the body." Although *qi* (breath) is still not translated, its meaning is suggested by this phrase. Ezra Pound reviewed *The Flight of the Dragon* in

Blast 2 (1915). Instead of quoting the above passage he draws attention to the first canon by capitalizing every word of another statement by Binyon, which ends with Giles's term: "FOR INDEED IT IS NOT ESSENTIAL THAT THE SUBJECT-MATTER SHOULD REPRESENT OR BE LIKE ANYTHING IN NATURE; ONLY IT MUST BE ALIVE WITH A RHYTHMIC VITALITY OF ITS OWN."[14]

Moore, too, had read Binyon's *The Flight of the Dragon* (her copy is kept at the Rosenbach Museum and Library in Philadelphia). However, it was Sze's summary of the first canon—"the idea that *Ch'i*[1] (the Breath of Heaven, the Spirit) stirs all of nature to life" (*The Tao of Painting,* 33)—rather than Binyon's statement about it that opened Moore's eyes to its aesthetic value. In her lecture, Moore, drawing on Sze, observes: "The first of these [canons] is basic to all and controls all the others, the world of the spirit, *ch'i*. This translation says, in the Cantonese version, it's pronounced 'hey.' They outdo the English, I think, in mystifying the reader regarding the actual pronunciation of words. And that word *ch'i* suggests exhaling a breath, cognate in meaning to *pneuma* and the Latin *spiritus*" ("Tedium and Integrity").

The Tao was evidently present in Moore's thought throughout her October 1957 lecture. Drawing to a close, she swiftly turns to the beginning, that is, to the symbol of the Tao as described by Sze, a circle whose "beginning (the head) and end (the foot) are the same" (*The Tao of Painting,* 16). Echoing Sze, Moore observes: "Everything must be in relation to the Tao, the center.... A circle's beginning, its head, and its end, or foot, are the same, unmoving and continually moving" ("Tedium and Integrity"). She adds: "As a symbol of the power of Heaven, the dragon, slumbering or winging its way across the heavens, has movement as a main characteristic" ("Tedium and Integrity"). Unsurprisingly, the dragon was to be the central symbol of Moore's next book of verse, *O to Be a Dragon* (1959).

In September 1957, when Moore was musing on *The Tao of Painting,* Mai-mai Sze, a fellow New Yorker (figure 6), was attracted to Moore's *Like a Bulwark* (1956). On September 28, 1957, coming across a review of this book of verse in the *Listener,* Sze could not resist clipping it out and sending it to Moore with a note: "You may perhaps not see this enclosed review in the London B.B.C. weekly *The Listener.* I thought that you might wish to have it" (Rosenbach). This note was followed by letters and conversations between the two writers that lasted for twelve years.

Figure 6. Mai-mai Sze, 1940. (Photograph by Carl Van Vechten, © 2017 Van Vechten Trust)

Mai-mai Sze (Shi Yunzhen 施蘊珍) was born in Tianjin, China, on December 2, 1909. Her father Alfred Sao-ke Sze (Shi Zhaoji 施肇基, 1877–1958) was the Republic of China's ambassador to Washington from 1935 to 1937. Her brother Szeming Sze (Shi Siming, 1908–98) was an initiator of the United Nations World Health Organization. Educated in England and the United States and holding a degree in the humanities from Wellesley College (1931), Sze made her acting debut in a 1936 Broadway show of S. I. Hsiung's *Lady Precious Stream* (adapted from Beijing opera's *Lady Wang Baochuang*). Her greater successes were, however, as a painter and as a writer. As a painter, she was better known for her portrait of Eugene O'Neill, printed on the cover of the program for *Iceman Cometh* (1946) and on the cover of the July 17, 1957, *Newsweek,* than for her landscapes in oil exhibited in London, Paris, and New York City. As a writer, she published her first book, a pamphlet about China, in 1944.[15] She was at the time a founder of the Chinese War

Relief Committee in New York City, and the pamphlet was an effort to support the war relief in China. Her second book, an illustrated autobiographical novel titled *Echo of a Cry: A Story Which Began in China,* came out in 1945.[16] The year 1948 saw the publication of her third book, *Silent Children,* a novel about refugee children in post-Second World War Europe.[17] During this period she also wrote an "East-West" column in the *New York Post* and contributed book reviews to the *New York Times.* It was her fourth book, *The Tao of Painting: A Study of the Ritual Disposition of Chinese Painting with a Translation of the Chieh Tzŭ Yüan Hua Chuan or Mustard Seed Garden Manual of Painting 1679–1701* (1956) that won her a lasting friendship with Moore.

The Tao of Painting not only gave an impetus to Moore's October 1957 lecture on "Tedium and Integrity in Poetry," it also inspired her book of verse, *O to Be a Dragon.* Upon the publication of *O to Be a Dragon* in April 1959, Moore sent Sze an inscribed copy. In the enclosed letter (April 18, 1959), she acknowledged her debt by calling Sze "angel to me and friend of the dragon-symbol": "Just please realize my gratitude, the fond thoughts you evoke—the celestial reveries for which you are responsible; my universe [is] enlarged and ever expanding by receiving from Mr. Barrett the TAO OF PAINTING—the mustard-seed garden and above all Volume II" (Rosenbach).

How *The Tao of Painting* impacted *O to Be a Dragon* is the topic of my earlier work *The Modernist Response to Chinese Art* (2003). I am not returning to any of the poems examined there except the title piece, which I shall reconsider in the light of the recently discovered sound recording of "Tedium and Integrity in Poetry." Moore, before her trip to Mills College, had been asked to read a few of her poems after her lecture. What she chose for the occasion were "O to Be a Dragon," "A Face," "The Wood-Weasel," "Bird-Witted," and "Silence," and translations of two fables of La Fontaine—"The Scythian Philosopher" and "The Cat and the Mouse." The first poem she read that night was an early version of "O to Be a Dragon." Introducing the poem, she referred to *Sequoia,* the student literary journal of Stanford University, and to Lynn White, Mills College president from 1943 to 1958:[18]

> Before I read this, I want to say what I forgot to say last night at Stanford. Pardon me, the editors of the *Sequoia* were really very unusually persevering about my contributing to *Sequoia.* They said they'd be very glad to publish this. They'd heard I was to give a lecture. And I said, well it belonged, it was the property of Presi-

dent White. "Well, we'd be glad to publish it too." "No," I said. And then I thought, and I will say this obligingly, that I thought of this: I was at a party the other night, and a gentleman who seemed to be an expert in every field, we were talking about the Chinese and these symbols, and he said, "O, to be a dragon!" Symbol of the power of Heaven! So I thought there's something.

> If I had, like Solomon . . .
> my wish . . . O to be a dragon,
> of silkworm
> size or immense; at times invisible.
> Felicitous phenomenon! ("Tedium and Integrity")

The poem indeed appears in the fall 1957 issue of *Sequoia* with a headnote stating that "MARIANNE MOORE . . . was kind enough to write this poem especially for SEQUOIA" and with a drawing of a dragon contributed by Bill Davis, a graduate student in the Stanford Art Department:

> If I could have my wish—if I, like Solomon,
>   could have my wish—
>
> my wish . . . Oh to be a dragon,
> a symbol of the power of Heaven—sometimes
> of silkworm size; immense; at times invisible!
>   Felicitous phenomenon.[19]

In this version published in *Sequoia,* the opening line is changed from "If I had, like Solomon . . ." to "If I could have my wish—if I, like Solomon"; "could have my wish—" is inserted between the first two lines to become line 2, and "a symbol of the power of Heaven—sometimes" is inserted between the second and third lines to become line 4.

The 1959 book version of "O to Be a Dragon," like the *Sequoia* version, has six lines. However, in addition to changes in mechanics, the first line is shortened to "If I, like Solomon," "sometimes" in line 4 is deleted, "of silkworm" in line 5 is moved to line 4, and the first semicolon in line 5 is changed to "or."[20]

Among the distinguishing characteristics of Moore's poetry are the juxtaposition of observations and quotations, the omission of quotation marks around quotations, and the use of endnotes to acknowledge sources of quotations. While the first two of these characteristics are evident in "O to Be a Dragon," the last is not. There *are* two notes for this poem when it makes its appearance in *The Complete Poems*, neither of which, however, elucidates its quotations—"a symbol of the power of Heaven" and "of silkworm . . . invisible"—from volume I of *The Tao of Painting*. The first note concerns "dragon" in its title, directing attention to volume II of *The Tao*, "Modern Library edition, page 57," source of "secondary symbols" other than the "dragon"; and the second note is about Solomon's wish (*CPo*, 290). In other words, here Moore has experimented with unacknowledged quotations in the true sense. The poem is a collage of observations and quotations. Sandwiched between an opening statement and an exclamation are three quotations in the 1959 "O to Be a Dragon" (two quotations in its 1957 version), of which I have identified two in *The Modernist Response to Chinese Art*: "a symbol of the power of Heaven" is a quotation from Sze's *The Tao of Painting*, (81) and "of silkworm / size or immense; at times invisible" derives from the sixth-century BC philosopher Guanzi, translated by Sze (82–83). What a reader would not know is that "O to be a dragon" is also a quotation, as Moore revealed first in her October 1957 lecture and then in the 1961 foreword to *A Marianne Moore Reader*. In the latter, Moore describes how "a friend at a party—an authority on gems, finance, painting, and music. . . exclaimed obligingly, as I concluded a digression on cranes, peaches, bats, and butterflies as symbols of long life and happiness, 'O to be a dragon!'" (*CPr*, 551). That exclamation inspired Moore to improvise her 1957 dragon poem.

Indeed, "O to Be a Dragon" calls to mind T. S. Eliot's *The Waste Land*, a modernist masterpiece largely made up of borrowed words, written or spoken. Like *The Waste Land*, Moore's pithy dragon poem looks ahead to twenty-first-century modernists' citational texts such as Susan Howe's *The Midnight* (2003) and Charles Bernstein's *Shadowtime* (2005).[21] In *Unoriginal Genius* (2010), Marjorie Perloff describes framing, citing, and recycling as poetic strategies characteristic of a global world of hyper-information.[22] While Perloff's illustrations—*The Waste Land*, *The Midnight*, and *Shadowtime*—are book-length works, Moore's "O to Be a Dragon" is a minimalist poem.

Moore's admiration for the Chinese dragon may be traced to 1923, when in separate letters to her brother John Warner Moore and friend Bryher she paid tribute to "a dragon in the clouds" in the Metropolitan Museum's exhibition of Chinese paintings.[23] The Chinese dragon resurfaces in her 1932 poem "The Plumet Basilisk": "As by a Chinese brush, eight green / bands are painted on / the tail—" (*CPo*, 22). One thing that distinguishes her 1957 dragon poem from "The Plumet Basilisk" and other lyrics before her encounter with Sze's *The Tao of Painting* is its compact form. Moore's poems are typically medium-sized. Her occasional short pieces consist of eight to ten lines. By contrast, the dragon poem Moore read at Mills College is even shorter than the six lines it has in 1959.

In *The Modernist Response to Chinese Art,* I assert that "O to Be a Dragon" is as good an attestation as "The Plumet Basilisk" to Cristanne Miller's claim about "authority" in Moore: "Authority lies somewhere between the sources of Moore's information, her suggestive use of that material, and the reader's construction of an intellectual or moral argument from the poem's suggestions."[24] But because in "O to Be a Dragon" Moore has concealed the sources of her information and restrained from detailing, it is harder to identify "references to myth and divinity within the poem."[25] On the other hand, with less detail, the reader has greater freedom to make imaginative claims.[26]

Moore's compact late style can be attributed to the influence of *The Tao of Painting,* especially its elucidation of the fifth canon of painting. Moore in her October 1957 lecture attaches greater importance to this canon that accounts for the use of space than to most other canons, calling it applicable "very closely ... to writing" ("Tedium and Integrity"). She extensively cites Sze's statements and quotations about the fifth canon, emphasizing on the one hand the expressiveness of empty space aptly used, and on the other hand the bad taste of overproduction. Citations from volume I of Sze's *The Tao* justifying the relevance of empty space include: "Space of any kind is regarded not as empty but as filled with meaning. In fact, it is synonymous with the Tao"; "Hollow trees were not just hollow trees; they are filled with meaning"; "The space in a wheel, the spaces between the spokes make the wheel, not the spokes or the bars"; "And it's not a set of walls but the space in a room that is its usefulness."[27] Citations from volume II, which presents the *Mustard Seed Garden Manual of Painting,* criticizing abundance and excessiveness include: "if a man had eyes all over his body, he would be a monstrosity.... A landscape with people and dwellings in it has life, but too many figures and houses give the effect of a market place" ("Tedium and Integrity"; *The Tao of Painting,* 264).

As I have designated elsewhere, "I May, I Might, I Must," "To a Chameleon," and "A Jelly-Fish" in *O to Be a Dragon* are poems resurrected from Moore's uncollected early oeuvre. Citations from *The Tao of Painting* favoring the use of empty space over crowdedness must have contributed to Moore's shortening of these poems before collecting them into *O to Be a Dragon*. The 1959 version of "A Jelly-Fish," for instance, has but half the size of its 1909 version. Eight lines were removed from the original version to make it look good in the Taoist sense.

Moore's late compact style manifests itself first in "O to Be a Dragon." The title poem of her 1959 book echoes what she observes in her Mills College lecture: "Symbolism, as I said, is a characteristic of Chinese thinking, and as a symbol of the power of Heaven, the dragon, slumbering or winging its way across the heavens, has movement as a main characteristic. At will, it can change, be the size of a silkworm, or swell so large as to fill the heaven and earth, thus representing totality" ("Tedium and Integrity").

The Tao of Painting, responsible for "O to Be a Dragon," was partially responsible for many other celestial reveries in the 1959 volume: "The Arctic Ox (or Goat)," "Saint Nicholas," "Combat Cultural," and "Leonardo da Vinci's," to name but a few considered in *The Modernist Response to Chinese Art.*[28]

The contexts I have been developing seem appropriate for reassessing Moore's final version of "Poetry" (1967), which from a chronological point of view will be reassessed in chapter 4. Twice in four years Moore referred to Zou Fulei's *A Breath of Spring* (figure 7), reproduced in *The Tao of Painting* as suggestive of the Tao or integrity. By giving it the title *A Breath of Spring,* the artist clearly intended to draw the viewer's eye to the vast empty space surrounding the plum branch; or in Moore's words, from "the real world" to "what did not exist until sensibility and imagination created it" ("Tedium and Integrity"). This fourteenth-century masterpiece may well have emboldened Moore to shorten "Poetry" from five six-line stanzas to a skeleton of three lines. According to her protégé Grace Schulman, Moore's editor at Viking, Edwin Kennebeck, was shocked by her idea of abbreviating "Poetry" to three lines. Editor-in-chief Marshall Best, warned Kennebeck, "would fall dead when he saw it." But Moore retorted, "the rest of it seemed to be padding."[29] Moore's aesthetic outlook changed after *The Tao of Painting.* When printed in her *Complete Poems* (1967), the new "Poetry" indeed appears somewhat like Moore's beloved ink plum against a blank space:

I, too, dislike it.
    Reading it, however, with a perfect contempt for it, one
        discovers in
    it, after all, a place for the genuine. (*CPo,* 36)

Figure 7. *A Breath of Spring,* Zou Fulei, mid-fourteenth century. (Freer Gallery of Art, Smithsonian Institution, Washington, D.C.; purchase, Charles Lang Freer Endowment, F 1931.1)

This was not Moore's first attempt to shorten the original "Poetry" (1919), however. In 1924 when she had a chance to revise this poem for a second edition of *Observations* (1925), she pared it down from five eight-line stanzas to thirteen lines without a stanza division. In 1931 Harriet Monroe wanted to add Moore's "Poetry" (1919 or 1925) to a new edition of *The New Poetry: An Anthology* (originally published in 1917). Instead of submitting either of the earlier versions, she rewrote it in three five-line stanzas.[30] In her 1957 Mills College lecture Moore told us that she trapped herself by giving this poem the title "Poetry": "It gave the impression that I was going to define poetry" ("Tedium and Integrity"). What she actually wanted to say in "Poetry" was simply that she disliked anything in poetry that was not genuine. Her final version was an effort to expel all the details meant to make her position vividly intelligible.

The final version of "Poetry" calls to mind not only Zou Fulei's *A Breath of Spring* reproduced in *The Tao of Painting,* but Williams's "Spring" and Pound's "In a Station of the Metro." Coincidentally, Pound's metro poem has an early version virtually the size of Moore's 1935 further revised "Poetry," in five six-line stanzas.[31] An obvious difference between the male poets' modernist abbreviations and Moore's 1967 "Poetry" is that whereas Williams's and Pound's haiku-like poems retain some colorful and tangible details ("my grey hairs! / . . . white as plum blossoms" in Williams's "Spring" and "Petals on a wet, black bough" in Pound's metro poem), Moore's does not. But isn't abstraction also a characteristic of high modernism? In fact, in Charles Altieri's view, "poetry must be abstract . . . . The genuine . . . resides less in anything we say about the poem than in what we do, as we try to cut through the images to the mobile inventiveness that underlies them and gives them a 'place.'"[32] To the Moore after *The Tao of Painting,* details such as "a wild horse taking a roll" (*CPo,* 267), quotations such as "we / do not admire what / we

cannot understand," and even her own witty statement "imaginary gardens with real toads in them" (*CPo,* 267) appear as padding or extra eyes
over a human body, what Laozi calls "surplus food and unwanted fat."[33]
"A textual void," as Andrew Kappel points out, is "a silence more eloquent than the finest phrases."[34] "A wild horse taking a roll," "a tireless
wolf / under a tree," and so on all stand for "the genuine" after all. The
space left blank beneath the three-line "Poetry" in *The Complete Poems,*
on the other hand, is "charged with meaning to the utmost possible degree."[35] As Altieri observes, echoing Laozi, the final version of "Poetry"
is "a remarkably active form of passivity."[36] In the sixth poem of *Spring
and All,* "To Have Done Nothing," Williams similarly tries to express in
English what Laozi has taught: "for everything / and nothing / are synonymous"; "only to / have done nothing / can make / perfect" (*CP1,*
192).[37] By refusing to give any detail that facilitates the comprehension
of "Poetry," Moore proves herself to be an astute student of the ancient
Chinese philosopher. To the final version of "Poetry," she has subtly
and satisfactorily applied the very teaching of Laozi that Williams has
articulated in English.

FOUR

Sze's "Permanent
Gifts" and Moore's
Last Achievement

MAI-MAI SZE BEGAN corresponding with Moore at a time when Moore was already a widely anthologized and commonly admired poet. Compared with Moore's famous protégés Elizabeth Bishop, Randall Jarrell, and Robert Andrew Parker, Sze was but a stranger in the US literary and art worlds.[1] Yet ironically, this stranger with a single substantial book found her way into Moore's later work more profusely than most of her other friends. The two New York writers shared diverse interests. After *O to Be a Dragon* (1959) they continued to correspond and to meet for real conversations for many more years.

In 1961–62, Sze spent nearly a year in Europe and North Africa with her companion, the costume designer Irene Sharaff (1910–93), for the filming of *Cleopatra* (1963).[2] Upon return home she gleefully found among her piles of unopened mail a copy of *A Marianne Moore Reader* with Moore's "generous and friendly inscription." In her letter on July 14, 1962, Sze first apologized for her long silence and then asked if Moore had located her typescript of "Tedium and Integrity in Poetry": "you mentioned it in a letter—Mills College was it not? I would like very much to read it—could I?" (Rosenbach). In 1963, Moore traveled with Bryn Mawr classmate Frances Browne and her sister Norvelle Browne to Greece and Italy. While in Venice, Moore stopped by Ezra Pound's cottage in the Via Querini, virtually next door to Cici's Pensione Restaurant. Upon return, she had a Roman ceremonial bronze shipped to Sze. Coincidentally, Sze was rereading Moore's 1944 essay "Feeling and Precision," ending with the statement, "So art is but an expression of our needs; is feeling, modified by the writer's moral and technical insights" (*CPr*, 402). Thanking Moore for the bronze piece in a letter dated November 21, 1963, Sze could not help but exclaim, "What power!" (Rosenbach).

In January 1964, Sze visited Moore's Brooklyn home. Over tea and biscuits Sze and Moore and a couple of other guests exchanged their favorite fairy tales. Sze did not expect that Moore would, after her visit, write a letter to retell the shared fairy tales in vivid detail.[3] In a reply on January 26, 1964, Sze thanked Moore for "sending me your 'retelling'—unique telling of the three fairy tales," adding that "I've had a lovely time with them and you! I like very much the happy photograph of you with the branches of winter plum" (Rosenbach). Unfortunately, Moore's letter retelling the fairy tales has been lost.[4] Had that letter survived, it would not be difficult to figure out from Moore's retelling if one of the fairy tales might be Sze's and if one or another fairy tale had resurfaced in a mid-1960s Moore poem.

Sze used to address Moore as "Dear Miss Moore" or "Dear Marianne Moore." Early in 1965 she began to address her more familiarly as "Dear Marianne" (Sze to Moore, January 2, 1965; Rosenbach). On September 10, 1965, Sze brought up the topic of the Vietnam War. In her letter to Moore, she quoted what President Lyndon Johnson had said that morning—"I think I'm in good shape"—adding that the remark "made me remember how it feels coming up for air after anesthesia & an operation, like Mrs. Gradgrind in 'Hard Times'" (Rosenbach). In a postscript she paid a tribute to Moore's two-page, single-poem book *Silence* (in a limited edition), just published by L. H. Scott: "I wish LHS at his press in Harvard Yard would print a selection of your poems together in the size & format & paper & cover & type of "Silence"— done with such impeccable taste—this is, I'm sure, the Tao of printing" (Rosenbach). The effect of that accolade on Moore was to manifest itself in the way she and Viking prepared *The Complete Poems* in 1967.

After living in the yellow brick and limestone apartment house in Brooklyn for thirty-six years, Moore moved back to Manhattan in the winter of 1965–66. As her letter to Moore on February 17, 1966, indicates, Sze was among the first to be invited to visit her new apartment on West Ninth Street (Rosenbach). For more than a decade it had been Sze who would telephone Moore for casual conversations. On August 2, 1966, Sze invited Moore to dine with her and Irene Sharaff at their East 66th Street apartment. In that letter she gave her phone number so that Moore might call to say if she would or would not come (Rosenbach).

For Moore, Sze's most precious gifts were not souvenirs from her

European and North African trips, and nor her 1968 Christmas gift of a custom-designed violet shirt. "We are delighted to think of you in the violet shirt & hope we shall see you in it soon," wrote Sze (to Moore, December 18, 1968; Rosenbach). They were her 600-plus-page tome *The Tao of Painting* and a subscription to the *Times Literary Supplement*. Shortly after the two began exchanging letters, Sze found that Moore had no access to the *TLS*. The London weekly literary review soon found its way to Moore's Brooklyn apartment, and it was renewed year after year. In the decade 1958–68, the *TLS* provided the two writers with numerous interesting discussion topics. In a letter to Sze on November 20, 1963, for instance, Moore referred to an August 16, 1963, *TLS* review ("The Elephant and the Mouse") that compared Dr. Johnson to the elephant and Boswell to the mouse: "'Comparing all our acquaintance to some animal or other,' wrote Mrs. Thrale, 'we pitched upon the elephant for [Johnson's] resemblance, adding that the proboscis of that creature was like his mind most exactly, strong to buffet even the tyger, and pliable to pick up even the pin.'"[5] Moore was an avowed elephant fan. In a 1918 poem, "Black Earth," she assumes the persona of a dark elephant called "Melanchthon," characterizing him as witty, selfless, and generous.[6] Reading the above-mentioned *TLS* review, Moore naturally approved of its likening Dr. Johnson's wit and generosity to that of an elephant.

Sze never worked together with Moore on any poems, but by passing onto her the spirit of the dragon and the substance of the six canons of painting through *The Tao of Painting* and giving her a yearly subscription to the *TLS* since January 1958, she became one of Moore's secondary collaborators. Moore on several occasions owned her debt to *The Tao of Painting*. In her 1957 Mills College lecture, she emphasized that her theme of integrity "was suggested to me by *The Tao of Painting,* edited and with a translation by Mai-mai Sze" ("Tedium and Integrity"). When sending a copy of *O to Be a Dragon* (1959) to Sze, she called Sze "friend of the dragon-symbol" (Rosenbach). In the foreword to *A Marianne Moore Reader* she elaborated: "And the Tao led me to the dragon in the classification of primary symbols, 'symbol of the power of heaven'—changing at will to the size of a silkworm; or swelling to the totality of heaven and earth; at will invisible" (*CPr,* 551). Moore was similarly grateful for Sze's gift of the *TLS*. In her letter dated April 18, 1959, she virtually called it an educator, a source of inspiration: "What significances it has lent my life. . . . My books are peopled with clippings from the Times Supplement" (Rosenbach). On November 20, 1963, she thanked Sze again for giving her the *TLS* and sharing with her personal feelings about its reviews: "Affording me luxury week by week—*educating me*—and I do not afford myself even the luxury of thanking you!" (Rosenbach). To say that Moore in her last decade carried much of the spirit of the Tao in her mind is an understatement. Indeed, the Taoist aesthetic continued to work almost everywhere in Moore's final book of verse, *Tell Me, Tell Me* (1966).

The opening poem of *Tell Me, Tell Me,* "Granite and Steel," celebrates the Brooklyn Bridge, designed by the German immigrant John A. Roebling (1806–69) and completed in 1883. Spanning the East River, it connects the two New York City boroughs, Manhattan and Brooklyn, where Moore had homes in different time periods. To Moore, the bridge is not so much a hub of communications as it is an artwork. It looks like a Chinese dragon in an ink painting, blending the designer's personality with the blue sky and the brown river. In "the celestial reveries," she envisions the bridge as changing from image to image—from "Caged Circe of steel and stone" to a "seagull's wing" and "a double rainbow." In the third stanza, lines borrowed from Hart Crane echo the spirit of the Tao—modern architecture united with nature, and heaven united with earth:

"O path amid the stars
crossed by the seagull's wing!"
"O radiance that doth inherit me!"
—affirming inter-acting harmony! (*CPo,* 205)

Images such as "path amid the stars," "seagull's wing," and "inter-acting harmony" are reminiscent not only of the Tao as "Wholeness or Oneness" (*The Tao of Painting,* 16) but also of the dragon, the symbol of the Tao, "slumbering or winging its way across the heavens" ("Tedium and Integrity").

Sze devotes a chapter of *The Tao of Painting* to the six canons of painting formulated by Xie He in AD 550. The first canon of painting, "breath resonance," as "a direct manifestation of [possessing *ch'i,*] this creative power of Heaven" (*The Tao of Painting,* 33), is illustrated with sensual imagery in "Blue Bug," a poem more immediately inspired by a photograph of eight polo ponies printed in the November 13, 1961, *Sports Illustrated.* In Linda Leavell's opinion, this is "Moore's most ambitious self-portrait since 'The Paper Nautilus.'"[7] Indeed, in the speaker's imagination, one of the polo ponies, nicknamed "Blue Bug," is galloping with breath resonance:

> In this camera shot,
> from that fine print in which you hide
> (eight-pony portrait from the side),
>   you seem to recognize
>   a recognizing eye,
>   limber Bug. (*CPo,* 218)

All of a sudden, the spirited pony is metamorphosed into the African American ballet dancer and choreographer Arthur Mitchell (b. 1934):

> bug brother to an Arthur
> Mitchell dragonfly,
>   speeding to left,
>   speeding to right; reversible (*CPo,* 218)

While envisioning the dancer and choreographer in the polo pony, the speaker seems also to perceive the breath resonance of ancient Chinese music: "like 'turns in an ancient Chinese / melody, a thirteen / twisted silk-string three-finger solo.'" Is the speaker imagining *guzheng* music, the *guzheng* being an ancient Chinese plucked string instrument?[8] The breath resonance in the polo pony, the ballet dance, and the *guzheng* melody further calls up in the speaker's mind's eye the rippling clouds and waves in the Qing dynasty Yellow-River scroll:[9] "There they are, Yellow River- / scroll accuracies." This miraculously shifts to

> the acrobat Li Siau Than,
>   gibbon-like but limberer,
>   defying gravity,
>   nether side arched up,
>   cup on head not upset—
> China's very most ingenious man. (*CPo,* 219)

Binyon's reading of the first canon, his linkage of it to "the rhythmical movements of the body," seems familiar to Yeats as well as Williams perhaps due to Pound's boost of it in *Blast* 2 and in private conversations.[10] Writing on the artistry of Japanese Noh dance, Yeats credits its special worthiness not in "the human form but in the rhythm to which it moves."[11] The "black winds" in Williams's fifth *Spring and All* poem, as Barry Ahearn points out, is a metaphor for "emotional energies pulsing through humanity and the forms they adopt."[12] As such it alludes to the first canon of painting. Among the "humanity and the forms they adopt" are Pound's *Cathay* poem "Song of the Bowmen of

Shu," circus rider "May Worth's equestrian arts," and "the play of [our] body—the quiver / of its strength—" (*CP1*, 191). Like Moore's "Blue Bug," Williams's "Black Winds" is a modernist endeavor to elucidate the workings of Xie He's first canon, breath resonance. Whereas none of Williams's illustrations is Chinese (not even the rhythmic beauty of Pound's "Song of the Bowmen of Shu"), all of Moore's except the photograph from *Sports Illustrated* and the example of Arthur Mitchell come from the Orient: Chinese *guzheng* music, Chinese scroll painting, and Chinese acrobat. What about polo, popular in many European countries? From *Encyclopedia Britannica* (1911), Moore could have learned that polo was first played in Persia, fifth century BC. It became popular in Tang dynasty China in the seventh century AD, as is depicted in the murals unearthed from Tang Prince Zhanghuai's tomb in the Qianling Mausoleum in Shanxi, China.

The ballet star in "Blue Bug" reappears as a central figure in "Arthur Mitchell," which refers, as Moore reveals in her note to the poem, to his dancing in the role of Puck:

> Slim dragonfly
> too rapid for the eye
>   to cage—
> contagious gem of virtuosity—
> make visible, mentality.
> Your jewels of mobility
>
>   reveal
>   and veil
>   a peacock-tail. (*CPo*, 220)

Puck is the clever, mischievous elf in Shakespeare's *A Midsummer Night's Dream*. In the 1964 Lincoln Kirstein and George Balanchine ballet production of the play at New York City Center, Mitchell miraculously captured the breath resonance of Puck dancing the dragonfly dance. In her poem "Arthur Mitchell," Moore likewise catches the breath resonance of the ballet dancer in that role. Once more the modernist poet proves herself to be a transformable Chinese dragon, "a symbol of the power of Heaven—of silkworm / size or immense; at times invisible" (*CPo*, 177).

Sze's presence continues to be felt in *Tell Me, Tell Me*. Two poems in which elephants figure tie back to the painter-writer by way of her weekly gift, the *TLS*. The August 16, 1963, *TLS* account of Dr. Samuel Johnson and James Boswell provided Moore with a new way of admiring her favorite animal, the elephant. In "Charity Overcoming Envy," the elephant appears as a carriage for Charity in her battle against Envy. Instead of trampling the dog-riding Envy, it only "scarcely scratched" his cheek (*CPo*, 216), like Dr. Johnson, whom Moore considers her role model, "a man of integrity" ("Tedium and Integrity"), judiciously leveling a warning. In lines 23–25, "The elephant, at no time borne down by self-pity, / convinces the victim / that Destiny is not devising a plot." Moore's characterization of Charity on the elephant and Envy on the dog could be partially patterned on the *TLS* sketches of Samuel Johnson and James Boswell. The exchange between the self-assured Charity/elephant and the insecure Envy/dog resembles Johnson's confidence and compassion as distinct from Boswell's continual need for Johnson's affirmation and approval. As the *TLS* review notes, Boswell, when emulating the masterful Johnson, was always aware of his shortcomings.[13]

In "Old Amusement Park: *Before it became LaGuardia Airport*" Moore describes a pair of pachyderm statuary:

> The park's elephant
> slowly lies down aslant;
>
> a pygmy replica then rides
> the mound the back provides. (*CPo*, 210)

The description is, likewise, reminiscent of Boswell in the *TLS* review. When the elephant falls "aslant," the pygmy tumbles with it, as his fortunes are inseparable from the elephant's. According to the review, Boswell would often ask the impelling question: "What would Johnson say of this?"[14] He, like the pygmy in "Old Amusement Park," was unable to act without Johnson's elephantine intellect.

Dr. Johnson is not the only figure Moore pays tribute to in *Tell Me, Tell Me*. In "W. S. Landor," a fifteen-line poem, she extols the English writer Walter Savage Landor (1775–1864). With a heroic impulse to leave his home country, England, and join the Spanish national army against Napoleon, Mr. Landor, known for his prose *Imaginary Conversations* and poem *Rose Aylmer*, showed himself to have a heart as good as gold. He could

> throw
> a man through the window,

yet, "tender toward plants," say, "Good God,
the violets!" (below). (*CPo*, 214)

Integrity means for late Moore "uprightness, honesty . . . a thing of
which all the parts are there," a thing that "has not been touched or
diminished but is left whole" ("Tedium and Integrity"). Mr. Landor
displayed all these qualities. He was "Accomplished in every // style /
and tint," yet when asked about "infinity and eternity," he would hon-
estly and uprightly respond, "I'll / talk about them when I understand
them" (*CPo*, 214).

"An Expedient—Leonardo Da Vinci's—and a Query" is an homage to da Vinci (1452–1519), a more eminent man of integrity. The
Italian Renaissance master had patience "so that 'great wrongs / were
powerless to vex,'" memory "making past present—/ like 'the grasp of
the gourd, / sure and firm,'" and a passion with which "he drew flowers, acorns, rocks—intensively." "An Expedient—Leonardo da Vinci's"
in the title refers to *Leda and the Swan,* his biggest and most important
work, said to have been deliberately destroyed. Although da Vinci was
"Peerless, venerated / by all," after *Leda and the Swan,* "he succumbed //
to dejection" (*CPo*, 212). A question is raised in the closing stanza of
the poem:

> Could not Leonardo
> have said, "I agree; proof refutes me.
> If all is mobility,
>   mathematics won't do":
> instead of, "Tell me if anything
>   at all has been done?" (*CPo*, 213)

These lines, as Bernard Engel has noted, "indirectly assert that the proof
of an artist's greatness is in what he creates, not in his theories."[15]

Between 1957 and 1963, as I noted in my earlier book *The Modernist
Response to Chinese Art,* Moore returned again and again to the theme
of her Mills College lecture. Some of my previous examples include
her 1958 review of the American painter Robert Andrew Parker (*CPr,*
500–502), three *O to Be a Dragon* poems—"The Arctic Ox (or Goat),"
"Combat Cultural," and "Leonardo da Vinci's"; and a 1963 essay, "The
Knife" (*CPr,* 564–68). Moore's theme of tedium and integrity continues to manifest itself in a variety of ways in *Tell Me, Tell Me* (1966).

In "To a Giraffe" the giraffe is a metaphor for T. S. Eliot and the modernist ideal of impersonality he upholds. As Ruth Carrington has pointed out, in the mid-1940s Moore already began referring to her friend Eliot as a giraffe.[16] In a letter to Eliot on November 16, 1946, Moore wrote: "Dear San Tomas (as you appear in the Morley classification of American fauna, under giraffes), For a giraffe to cook a gosling does not seem very kind, but it is; and I shall not hamper you further with impractical considerations."[17] In his reply of November 21, 1946, Eliot refuted: "Dear Marianne: But it was very mischievous of him to classify me under Giraffes, unless anybody is a Giraffe who has dwelt in the Giraffe house; my proper classification is under Elephants."[18] My reading of "To a Giraffe" suggests that Moore continued to think of Eliot as this long-necked animal in the 1960s.

The poem can be interpreted as Moore's commentary on the changing poetic style in the late 1950s to early 1960s. In those years, Moore witnessed her aesthetic values—the values of modernist poetry—being challenged by those of postmodernist poetry. On November 1, 1956, Lawrence Ferlinghetti's City Lights Bookstore published Allen Ginsberg's *Howl,* the landmark book of the Beat generation. Ginsberg's antisocial stance did not impress Moore; nor did the rawness of his poetic language. At the request of fellow poet and father of Allen, Louis Ginsberg, Moore in the summer of 1952 read a manuscript of the Beat poet's early work, eventually published as *Empty Mirror: Early Poems* (1961). In a letter to Allen Ginsberg on July 4, 1952, her disapproval of his poetry is already visible: "Your disgust worries me and I can't make clear what I mean without being objectionable. . . . *Empty Mirror* is too literal, you don't get behind it. You don't see that it is? It is 'treatment.' It is your 'taste.' Note, however, you did not choose [the] title, 'His heart was a bag of shit'; or 'Existence is a load of shit.' Any line that occurs in the course of the work as your pronouncement should be able to serve as a title. . . . Here is the proof that something is wrong. What is it? the old hackneyed truism; affirm or die. If I feel negative, why can't I say I am?"[19]

A few days later, in a separate letter to Louis Ginsberg on July 11, 1952, Moore further explains the reason for her resistance to his son's poetry manuscript: "Self-centeredness and negative writing in the name of realism are self-destruction, I feel. Yet, as older fighters against disillusion and 'injustice,' we must have compassion on the malaise of younger persons."[20]

It was four years after these exchanges and one year after Ginsberg's reading of *Howl* at Six Gallery in San Francisco that Moore pointedly criticized "self-centeredness and negative writing" again in her two-part UCLA lecture "Idiosyncrasy and Technique": "We are suffering from too much sarcasm, I feel . . . . what I was so urgent to emphasize is reduced in the First Psalm to a sentence: Blessed is the man who does not sit in the seat of the scoffer" (*CPr*, 511–12). Months later, she received a letter from the University of California Press, commissioning her to edit that lecture for publication.[21] She most probably sent Sze an extra copy of her edited manuscript for suggestions, for in a letter to Moore on October 10, 1957, Sze wrote: "How very nice of you to write me the note & to tell me you have been thinking of me (in connection with the article)! I fear that parts of the Tao opus could well illustrate the other half of your title" (Rosenbach). Whereas Moore began the second part of her lecture ("Idiosyncrasy") by chiding sarcasm, she disclosed in the first part of it ("Technique") what frequently motivated her revisions and omissions: "My own revisions are usually the result of impatience with unkempt diction and lapses in logic; together with an awareness that for most defects, to delete is the instantaneous cure" (*CPr*, 507). Sze's reply of October 10, 1957, virtually encouraged Moore also to link the Tao to both parts of her lecture "Tedium and Integrity in Poetry" to be given in October 1957. While integrity is her tribute to the Tao, tedium implies her critique of the Beat generation and its very personal and literal poetry. Moore makes this clear in her lecture:

> Chinese philosophy, Ms. Mai-mai Sze observed, might be said to be psychology—a development of the whole personality; and egotism—or what the Buddhists call ignorance—obscures a clear view of the Tao. It is unusual, in my experience at least, to come on a book of verse which has not a tincture of animosity, sarcasm, grievance, or some sense of injury, personal or impersonal—general. And I feel very strongly what Señor Jiménez, the Spanish poet, says in referring to something else to what is not poetry: "There is a profounder profundity than wistful egocentricity." ("Tedium and Integrity")

Moore's comments in "Tedium and Integrity" are reaffirmed in "To a Giraffe." The opening of the poem, according to Bernard Engel, might be interpreted as saying: "if the artist is not to be personal or literal, and should be innocent, he or she is required to work always at the highest reach."[22] Like the giraffe, such an artist is "an animal that pleasures [us] because it is 'unconversational.'"[23] Certainly the speaker had in mind Eliot (a giraffe) and herself (an elephant) when stating this in "To a Giraffe." Both became aware of the threat of extinction to their kind of poetry in the early 1960s. The poem thus continues in variant heroic couplets:

> When plagued by the psychological,
> a creature can be unbearable
>
> that could have been irresistible;
> or to be exact, exceptional
>
> since less conversational
> than some emotionally-tied-in-knots animal. (*CPo*, 215).

Carrington convincingly argues that these couplets allude to Moore's friend, Robert Lowell, who was "certainly 'plagued by the psychological' when he was writing his 'not cooked, but raw' poems of this period about his recurring bouts with mental illness, his periodic hospitalizations, and his conflicts with family members."[24]

Would the giraffe, or modernist poetry, become extinct in the face of the rise of very personal and literal postmodern poetry? The speaker offers an answer in the next stanza: "After all / consolations of the metaphysical / can be profound" (*CPo*, 215). Her choice of the word *metaphysical* further reveals that she had in mind Eliot, the author of "The Metaphysical Poets," and Eliot's brand of modernism. To her, no poetry, neither modern or postmodern, impersonal or personal, could be perfect: "In Homer, existence // is flawed." Despite their respective shortcomings, she predicts, modernist poetry and postmodernist poetry will journey side by side "from sin to redemption, perpetual" (*CPo*, 215).

The theme of "Tedium and Integrity" is also evident in the title poem of Moore's 1966 collection. It begins with a question, reasserting that notion:

> where might there be a refuge for me
> from egocentricity
> and its propensity to bisect,
> mis-state, misunderstand
> and obliterate continuity?" (*CPo*, 231)

"Egocentricity" is precisely what Moore in her Mills College lecture speaks of as "tedium," or "what the Buddhists call ignorance." For Moore after *The Tao of Painting*, as for classic Chinese poets and artists, egocentricity obscures a clear vision of the Tao and makes profound art impossible. In *The Tao of Painting*, Sze attributes this notion to the fifteenth- to sixteenth-century neo-Confucian thinker Wang Shouren (also known as Wang Yangming, 1472–1529), who views the mind of an artist or a poet as one with Heaven when cleared of egocentricity. He is cited as saying, "Every time we extend our intuitive knowledge, we clear away the obscurings, and when all of them are cleared away, our original nature is restored, and we again become part of this Heaven" (*The Tao of Painting*, 30). The concept is further traced to the ancient Chinese philosopher Liezi (Lieh Tzŭ), whose saying "To a mind that is still, the whole universe surrenders" is cited by Sze (*The Tao of Painting*, 18) and by Moore in her Mills College lecture. What Liezi and Wang Shouren have stated, it might occur to Moore, anticipate Eliot's notion of art making as "a continual self-sacrifice, a continual extinction of personality," and Gertrude Stein's recommendation for emptying-out of selfhood.[25] "Creatively speaking the little dog knowing that you are you and your recognizing that he knows," writes Stein, "that is what destroys creation."[26] According to Marjorie Perloff, what Stein is trying to say is that "a strong awareness of oneself, of *identity*, is the enemy of artistic creation, which depends precisely upon an emptying-out of such selfhood."[27] So the modernists' experiment with extinction of personality or emptying-out of selfhood is from the Chinese point of view following the Tao.

What helped such artists as Henry James and Beatrix Potter remain exempt from egocentricity? To the speaker of "Tell Me, Tell Me" it is their "Chinese / 'passion for the particular'" (*CPo*, 231). Potter's tailor of Gloucester, despite sickness and fatigue, "cut a masterpiece of cerise—" commissioned by the newly elected mayor for his wedding the next morning (*CPo*, 231). Having run out of cherry-colored silk, the tailor could not go on and finish his commission, so he sent his cat to buy a twist of fine thread in that color. While the cat was gone, the tailor released the cat's mice, detained under teacups. Finding his mice gone, the cat retaliated by hiding the twist of silk he had bought, frustrating the tailor. All this is in Potter's marvelous illustrated book *The Tailor of Gloucester* (1902). Moore has, however, picked up the story from Margaret Lane's *The Tale of Beatrix Potter*, as she tells us in her Mill College lecture. Thus in "Tell Me, Tell Me" the speaker continues:

> In this told-backward biography
> of how the cat's mice when set free
> by the tailor of Gloucester, finished
> the Lord Mayor's cerise coat— (*CPo*, 232)

The story serves as a lesson on how to fight self-centeredness. The integrity of the tailor of Gloucester motivated his cat's mice to finish the commission on his behalf, thus saving him from despair. Potter's tailor sets a fine example for all artists and poets. What else besides "Chinese / 'passion for the particular'" can fight egocentricity? The speaker tells us that her own "defense" is "deference" "Passion for the particular" is a professional tip; "deference" is moral advice. How can the two go together? Moore in her Mills College lecture calls our attention to what Mai-mai Sze has emphasized, the Chinese view "that painting is not a profession but an extension of the art of living" (*The Tao of Painting*, 5). "Authorship in China," Moore clarifies, "is integral to education; it's not a separate proficiency to be acquired." To relate this to the American literary scene, she comments, "It's rather humbling to those of us who spend, devote, a great deal of time to incidental aspects of writing" ("Tedium and Integrity"). "Tell Me, Tell Me" thus verifies what Moore said to Sze in the November 16, 1963, letter, acknowledging *The Tao of Painting* as one of Sze's "permanent gifts," which she tried to put into use "along with some incurable ignorances" (Rosenbach).

Modernism arose not out of the effort of a single genius but the collective efforts of numerous avant-garde artists and poets working closely together. Just as the collaboration of Pablo Picasso and Georges Braque ushered in cubism, which broke ground for revolutionary artistic concepts, the gathering together of Ezra Pound, Hilda Doolittle (H.D.), and Richard Aldington brought about imagism, which changed the nature of poetry written in English. Among Pound's collaborators were also Mary Fenollosa and Baosun Zeng (Pao Swen Tseng). Had not Mrs. Fenollosa provided her late husband's Chinese poetry and Japanese Noh drama notes, Pound could not have made *Cathay* (1915) or *"Noh," Or, Accomplishment* (1916). Similarly, had not Miss Zeng interpreted the Chinese manuscript poems of a screen-book from Japan and furnished these poems' background information, Pound's memorable "Seven Lakes" canto (Canto XLIX) would have been out of the question.[28] T. S. Eliot's most notable collaborator was Pound, whose radical revisionary efforts helped make Eliot's *The Waste Land* the modernist masterpiece it is. Marianne Moore's collaborators included H.D., Bryher, Eliot, and her mother, Mary Warner Moore. Whereas H.D. and Bryher were responsible for the publication of Moore's first book of verse, *Poems,* in 1921, Eliot personally selected the poems for the 1935 *Selected Poems of Marianne Moore,* arranged them, and wrote the introduction. As to Moore's mother, she was for decades the first reader and critic of Marianne Moore's draft poems, contributing in her way to her daughter's poetic style. Arguably, Moore's friendship with Mai-mai Sze not only satisfied her lifelong thirst for Chinese culture but helped in a small way to fill the void in her career left by the death of her mother. Sze's *The Tao of Painting* came to Moore at an opportune moment. It served to boost Moore's confidence about her modernist aesthetic— her rejection of the romantic ego, fusion of moral standards with art, and use of blank space to suggest meaning.

Linda Leavell points out that late Moore poems show "her ambivalence about her own fame": she desired "silkworm-size obscurity" at the same time she enjoyed "dragon-size visibility."[29] Hilton Kramer, in a review of the 1981 *Complete Poems,* blames Moore for permitting the media to publish her long list of names offered to the Ford Motor Company for one of their new automobiles, making her visible as "the very archetype of the quaint literary spinster."[30] The overwhelming majority of Moore's critics since that assessment "ignore her late work."[31] The media image of Moore as an indiscreet correspondent with the Ford Motor Company should in no way obscure her late triumphs. Leavell reminds us of John Ashbery's October 1966 review of *Tell Me, Tell Me,* in which he considers Moore "with the possible exception of Pound and Auden, the greatest living poet in English."[32] To him late Moore is as admirable as early or middle Moore. Indeed, the best poems of *Tell Me, Tell Me,* in his view, display "a new style whose late, queer clarity resolves the fragmented brilliance of the early work."[33] *The Complete Poems,* which came out the following year, only increased Ashbery's respect for late Moore. In a November 1967 review for the *New York Times Book Review,* he declares that "after rereading her in this magnificent volume," he is "tempted simply to call her our greatest modern poet." This, he stresses, is despite his affection for "her chief competitors, including Wallace Stevens and William Carlos Williams." To him our critics "underestimate Miss Moore" when they simply concur with Eliot that her work belongs to "that small body of durable poetry written in our time."[34] Some of her most commendable qualities, those that her peers do not have and those that are newly developed—"her new, tough simplicity" and her "quick effect of wholeness"—remain barely recognized.[35]

It is true that in the 1950s and '60s Moore improvised a few poems that have negatively affected her literary reputation, but during this period she also wrote some of her most brilliant and most innovative modernist lyrics. The majority of Moore's poems after *The Tao of Painting* retain her early avant-gardism with a new minimalist tendency, a queer lucid style, and an increased respect for harmony between nature and humanity, what the Chinese call "wholeness of Heaven and Earth." Otherwise Ashbery, a great poet and literary critic himself, after rereading *The Complete Poems,* which omits "Melanchthon" ("Black Earth"), "Old Tiger," and twenty-six lines from the 1935 version of "Poetry," would not have been tempted to single her out in 1967 as "our greatest modern poet."

FIVE

Fang as Pound's
Teacher of Naxi
Pictographs

HOW DID THE SURVIVING old guards of American modernism respond to the changing literary climate in the early 1960s? As I have shown in chapters 2 and 4 respectively, in 1960 Williams brought out twelve *Brueghel* poems that re-initiated his early modernist minimalism; and from 1962 to 1964 Moore published "To a Giraffe" and other lyrics that saluted the disparaged modernist ideal of impersonality. Whereas Williams and Moore stoutly took up the postmodern challenge, their generally more contentious colleague Ezra Pound grew increasingly silent. In 1961 the former champion of modernism did not publish a single poem or prose piece, nor did he speak to any visitors, which vexed his old friends, especially Marianne Moore, who wrote to him on August 18, 1961: "I am worried. I hear from Lester Littlefield that you aren't thriving. Neither am I but am going to. And so are you" (Beinecke).

But had Pound really stopped speaking? On July 9, 1962, as I have noted in my introduction, after a urological operation at a private medical facility in Rapallo, he wrote to fellow modernist E. E. Cummings in the United States, asking "do you evuh read contemporaries? I mean are there any fit for me to read[.] I strongly suspect there *has* been some good stuff since 1930."[1] So he had not stopped purposeful exchanges with cherished friends after all. The question raised gives away his sustained reading interest, and the comment made after it—"I strongly suspect there *has* been some good stuff since 1930"—reassures us of his confidence about the renewal of literary modernism.

In 1966, less than a year after the passing of T. S. Eliot, Pound broke his silence to write in honor of his lifelong friend: "His was the true Dantescan voice—not honoured enough, and deserving more than I ever gave him." With this said, he lamented, "Who is there now for me to share a joke with?" Then, to the reading public overwhelmed by the postmodernists, he admonished, "I can only repeat, but with the urgency of 50 years ago: READ HIM."[2]

Pound had not ceased revising and rearranging his final cantos either. In the summer of 1962, the *Paris Review* issued Donald Hall's 1960 interview with him and two of his new cantos—"From Canto CXV" and one of the "Canto CXVI" variants.[3] In the winter of 1963–64, *Agenda* printed "Sections from New Cantos," one of them from Canto CXII, imagining the idyllic landscape of Lijiang (Li Chiang):

> By the pomegranate water,
> > in the clear air
> > > over Li Chiang
> The firm voice amid pine wood,
> > > many spirits are at the foot of
> > > > Hsiang Shan[4]

Writing on *Drafts and Fragments of Cantos CX–CXVII* (1969), Peter Stoicheff asserts that Pound "attempts to render a paradise of natural, private, and poetic harmony there, and some of the passages are among the most limpid and lyrical of *The Cantos*."[5] When making this claim Stoicheff may well have in mind the above passage along with the passage in Canto CXVI, which Stephen Sicari views as signaling "the clearest and most powerful moment of retrospection":[6]

> but about that terzo
> > third heaven,
> > > that Venere,
> again is all "paradiso"
> > a nice quiet paradise
> > > over the shambles,
> and some climbing
> > before the take-off,
> to "see again,"
> the verb is "see," not "walk on." (*C*, 816)

Lijiang, in southwest China, was first made known to the English-speaking world by the Austrian-American anthropologist and botanist Joseph F. Rock (1884–1962) through his monographs about its people the Naxi (Na-khi) and their literature. It was to recur again and again in Pound's *Drafts and Fragments*. As Ronald Bush contends, these final cantos mark, on the one hand, a turning away from "the idiom of the *Pisan Cantos*," and on the other hand, a departure from the "condensed political discourse" of *Thrones*.[7] Indeed, *Drafts and Fragments* is stylistically closer to Pound's *A Draft of XVI Cantos* (1925) than to *The Pisan Cantos* (1948), *Section: Rock-Drill* (1955), or *Thrones* (1959), which is to say that it exhibits the renewal and development of his modernist poetics of the 1910s and 1920s, a poetics of transforming transparency into opacity, history into fiction, and personality into impersonality.

For one thing, *Drafts and Fragments* is concise, graphic, and poignant, stylistically reminiscent of Pound's imagist and vorticist *Lustra* (1916). In Peter Makin's words, "everything is slimmed down, made lean in words and full in implication."[8] Wyndham Lewis, for instance, emerges in "From CXV" as Courage incarnate: "Wyndham Lewis chose blindness / rather than have his mind stop" (*C*, 814). So does Olga Rudge in "Fragment" (1966): "Her name was Courage / & is written Olga" (*C*, 824). For Makin, "the process and the result of abbreviation are like those in Beckett."[9] For me they bring to mind late Moore, who in 1967 cut "Poetry" down from twenty-nine lines to three lines. For another thing, the final sequence of *The Cantos* includes no allusion to Confucius or Confucian maxims, and the paradise being written is not the Confucian Apricot Temple, nor the Confucius-admired Zhou (Chou) dynasty, nor the thrones of the Confucian emperors Kangxi and Yongzheng ("Kang Hi" and "Young Tching"), but rather the "quiet house" of Torcello (*C*, 797) with a mosaic Madonna "over the portal" (*C*, 815) and Rock's enigmatic world of Lijiang inhabited by the nature-loving, non-Confucian Naxi.[10]

The intricate Naxi religious rite ^{2}Muan ^{1}bpo—the sacrifice to heaven—makes its debut in Canto XCVIII of *Thrones:* "Without ^{2}muan ^{1}bpo ... but I anticipate" (*C*, 711). Lijiang first appears in Canto CI of *Thrones:* "at Li Chiang, the snow range, / a wide meadow" (*C*, 746).

Carroll F. Terrell is not wrong in identifying Rock's 1939 bilingual narrative, "The Romance of ^{2}K'a-^{2}mä-^{1}gyu-^{3}mi-^{2}gkyi," his 1948 treatise, "The ^{2}Muan ^{1}Bpö Ceremony or the Sacrifice to Heaven as Practiced by the ^{1}Na-^{2}hki," and his 1947 study, *The Ancient Na-khi Kingdom of Southwest China*, as sources of the Naxi passages in *Thrones* and *Drafts and Fragments*.[11] But was Rock the person who first introduced Pound to Lijiang and its ethnic culture? Did Pound ever come into contact with a Naxi native? Fredric Jameson urges us to historicize. He opens *The Political Unconsciousness* with his catchphrase: "Always historicize!"[12] To reassess Pound's cantos with the Naxi motifs, we must historicize, that is, situate these cantos in their largely overlooked cross-cultural textual and extratextual contexts. Newly excavated materials reveal that Pound relied on multiple sources to compose his Naxi passages, of which there were, besides Rock, a Lijiang native and a Russian writer who had lived among the Naxi people for many years.

Pound and Rock exchanged letters between 1956 and 1958. Only one letter from Rock to Pound, dated January 3, 1956, has survived in the Beinecke Library at Yale University.[13] In it Rock refers to a "Na-khi boy" and two of his papers on the Naxi given to Pound by Professor Giovanni Giovannini of the Catholic University of America in Washington, DC: "My friend Pao-hsien Fang, a Na-khi boy whose parents I used to know for many years in Likiang, Yunnan, sent me a letter written to him by Prof. G. Giovannini of the Catholic University of America. In the letter Mr. Giovannini told Fang that he had given you two of my papers on the Na-khi, a very romantic people among whom I lived for 27 years" (Beinecke).

Was Pound acquainted with Rock's Naxi friend Pao-hsien Fang? He certainly was. The Beinecke Library at Yale University keeps two Christmas cards Paul Pao-hsien Fang and his wife sent the Pounds in 1957 and 1963, respectively. The Lilly Library at Indiana University preserves an additional card from the Fangs to the Pounds, dated 1959. On the back of the 1959 card Paul Pao-hsien Fang acknowledges Pound's return of his books. His autograph note also reveals his familiarity with Pound's interest in the *Yi jing* hexagrams and with Pound's ongoing project about the Naxi for his final cantos: "Thank you for these books you sent back and the beautiful binding with your precious signature. Is the design of 八 卦 [hexagrams] in this greeting card appropriate? I wish more cantos from you will resurrect 麗 江 [Lijiang], after the Revolution, Republic, People's Republic, Commune etc. Please let us hear from you!" (Lilly).[14]

Pound's daughter, Mary de Rachewiltz, keeps in the Pound Library at Brunnenburg, Italy, yet another greeting card from the Fangs to the Pounds dated Christmas 1959 (figure 8). On the front is a family photograph and on the back a note in Paul Fang's hand: "We follow your work with gratitude: my beloved country and my beloved village will be immortalized through your pen and your words."

Paul Fang surely had received a copy of Pound's *Thrones de los Cantares XCVI–CIX* (published in December 1959). Especially appealing to him would have been the two lines in Canto CI depicting an auratic code of Naxi culture ("auratic" in Walter Benjamin's sense), their

Figure 8. Greeting card from the Fangs to the Pounds, Christmas 1959. (© 2017 Josephine Fang; courtesy of Mary de Rachewiltz)

women's costume which displays the Naxi worship for nature: "With the sun and moon on her shoulders, / the star-discs sewn on her coat" (*C, 746*).

How well did Pound know Paul Pao-hsien Fang? To get answers to questions such as this, one must find Paul Fang, and through him, Pound's side of their correspondence. In the summer of 2003, I located Pao-hsien Fang, a retired Boston College professor of physics, living in Belmont, a suburb of Boston, and continuing his research in the development of solid state electronics for his own company, F. S. Lab. The role Paul Fang played in Pound's composition of the Naxi passages in *The Cantos* has long gone unnoticed. The neglect of him as a Cantos source is partly due to our slow recognition of the importance of cross-cultural interpersonal influence and partly due to confusing him with Achilles Fang (1910–95), the Harvard scholar who contributed a lengthy note to Pound's *Confucius: The Great Digest and Unwobbling Pivot* (1951) and an introduction to Pound's *The Classic Anthology Defined by Confucius*

(1954). Indeed, for a fairly long time the greeting cards Paul and Josephine Fang sent the Pounds were mixed up with the Pound-Achilles Fang materials at the Beinecke Library.[15]

What do we know about Paul Pao-hsien Fang? How did he get to know Pound? Pao-hsien Fang (Fang Baoxian 方寶賢) was born to a Naxi family in Lijiang on August 18, 1922. His father Fang Guoshen (方國琛) owned a grocery store in Lijiang's Old Town, and his uncle Fang Guoyu (方國瑜, 1903–83) was China's foremost Naxiology scholar, the compiler of *A Dictionary of Naxi Pictographs* (1979, 2005), a more reliable source of the Naxi pictographic language than Rock's *Nakhi-English Encyclopedic Dictionary* (1963). Paul Fang left home at age fourteen to attend a middle school in the provincial capital Kunming, where his professor uncle Fang Guoyu lived and where he first learned Mandarin Chinese, a language quite different from his mother tongue, Naxi. It took fifteen days to walk from Lijiang to Kunming, Paul Fang told me in an August 2003 interview. At that time the Kunming–Burma Road that was the route from Lijiang to Kunming had not yet been completed, and while most Naxi villagers rode horses up and down mountain paths to Kunming, he preferred traveling on foot.

In 1944, before graduating from the National Southwestern Associated University in Kunming, Paul Fang was awarded a scholarship to study in the United States.[16] That year awarded the same competitive scholarship and put in the same NSAU prep class for graduate study in the United States was Chen Ning Yang, cowinner of the 1957 Nobel Prize in Physics (with Tsung Dao Lee). Fang first studied at Ohio State University, where he earned a BS degree and an MS degree in physics. In 1950 he began working on a PhD in physics at the Catholic University of America in Washington, DC. There he met and married Josefine (Josephine) Maria Riss from Austria, who held a PhD from the University of Graz (1948) in Austria and was working toward a master's degree in library science at CUA. Among their friends was English professor Giovanni Giovannini, who in 1952 became their firstborn child's godfather.

In the summer of 1953, Professor Giovannini took Paul Fang, then a fresh postdoc and CUA research associate in physics, to visit Ezra Pound, who was incarcerated in St. Elizabeths Hospital on charges of treason for having made antigovernment broadcasts in fascist Rome. The American poet, Giovannini told Paul Fang, had translated into English *Ta Hio* (1928) and *Confucian Analects* (1951). His English versions of Li Po (Li Bai) and other Chinese poets were collected in a volume called *Cathay* (1915). As a regular visitor and a family friend, Giovannini knew of Pound's passion for Chinese culture. By introducing Paul Pao-hsien Fang to the poet, he opened a new window for him, a window to a little-known ethnic Chinese culture.

Starting that summer, Paul and Josephine Fang visited Pound count-less times. More than once or twice they took their oldest daughter, Paula, and son, David, with them to the government hospital, whose green lawns, like a public park's, delighted their young children. On Ezra Pound's birthdays Josephine would make a special kind of cake she knew the poet loved, and it was Paula who would carry it to Pound. In a letter to the Fangs on January 6, 1959, Dorothy Pound recalled one of their visits: "Paula may remember bringing EP his birthday cake at St. E's."[17] Such friendly visits continued for five years until May 1958 when Pound was released from St. Elizabeths Hospital.

Pound held a well-known fascination for China. Before meeting Paul Fang, however, his enthusiasm for China was strictly reserved for main-stream Chinese culture, the Han culture, especially the Confucian cul-ture. Until the summer of 1954 Pound never expected that he would in his senior years begin studying with a Naxi man the working picto-graphic language of his people and learning about their religious rites.

In June of that year Harvard University Press published a trade edi-tion of *Shih-ching: The Classic Anthology Defined by Confucius.* Pound, as the translator of *Shih-ching,* experienced little excitement. What he really wanted was a scholarly edition of the Confucian odes with a Chi-nese seal text and a sound key, a project that was to be forever shelved.[18] With a visitor originally from China, he could not help venting his frustration by referring again and again to the Harvard-trained orien-talist Ernest Fenollosa (1853–1908) and his essay "The Chinese Writ-ten Character as a Medium for Poetry" (edited and published by Pound in 1919 and 1936). One day, when Pound began quoting Fenollosa and marveling at the Chinese character in primitive form again, Paul Fang, a man of few words, surprised the eloquent American poet by remark-ing that his people, the Naxi, still relied on a pictographic language to communicate. This was the first time he confided to Pound that he was not a Han Chinese but a Naxi man from Lijiang, a thriving town on China's ancient southern Tea Road to India, Burma, Malaysia, and other south or southeast Asian countries.

Lijiang was the center of the ancient Naxi kingdom, which flour-ished from the eighth to the eighteenth centuries.[19] Its green world, along with its unique ethnic culture, had lured Joseph Rock to live there for twenty-seven years (from 1922 through 1949), collecting rare flora from its virgin forests and rescuing the Naxi pictographic language and religious literature, which were on the brink of extinction. And it would soon be turned into what Terrell terms an "image of the archetypal holy city" in Pound's *Thrones* (1959):[20]

> at Li Chiang, the snow range,
>   a wide meadow
> and the [2]dto-[1]mba's face (exorcist's)
>   muy simpático
> by the waters of Stone Drum,
>   the two aces
> Mint grows at the foot of the Snow Range (C, 746)

"The earthly paradise over Lijiang is real," Paul Fang confirmed in a follow-up interview in September 2007. Starting from 1972, with the normalization of the United States-China relations, he traveled to Lijiang (meaning "Beautiful River") every year as a United Nations TOKTEN (Transfer of Knowledge through Expatriate Nationals) expert, helping Kunming and Lijiang scientists develop solar cell production and use. In 2003, on the one-hundredth anniversary of his linguist-historian uncle Fang Guoyu's birth, Paul Fang, accompanied by wife, Josephine, six of their children, and four of their grandchildren, returned to his beloved hometown for the thirty-third time. And in the summer of 2007, at age eighty-five, he made his last trip to Lijiang with two of his grandchildren. "The 'Snow Range' remains as majestic and unpolluted as it has ever been," he told me upon return.

> So do "the waters of Stone Drum" at the first bend of the Yangtze outside of Lijiang Old Town. A stone drum unearthed in the sixteenth century and erected there ever since serves as a reminder of god's concern over the feud between two proud Naxi tribes. The disturbed god is said to have interfered with the tribal strife by sending a white-hair angel to beat a wooden drum day and night till the two tribes ceased fire. Upon the dispersion of the tribal troops, the white-haired angel changed into a stone statue and her wooden drum into a stone drum.

I asked him if he had related to Pound this charming legend? The answer was "quite possible."[21]

Pound, nevertheless, was less interested in the Lijiang landscape than appreciating the Naxi heritage—its pictographic writing and religious rites. Paul Fang was too modest to consider his role as important, but his visits to St. Elizabeths Hospital actually served to open Pound's eyes to a China beyond the Chinas of Ernest Fenollosa, M. G. Pauthier, Joseph-Anne-Marie de Mailla, James Legge, and Achilles Fang, resulting in a change of course in his late cantos.[22]

Pound was of course eager to see with his own eyes Paul Fang's people's working pictographs. These eleven-hundred-year-old symbols are preserved in the fifteenth-century murals in Baisha Village six miles northwest of the Old Town of Lijiang (figure 9) and in Naxi dongba ([2]dto-[1]mba) scriptures as aid to the performances of various religious rites.[23] From that point onward, whenever Paul Fang showed up at St. Elizabeths Hospital, Pound would ask him to draw a few Naxi pictographs and teach him how to pronounce them. Paul Fang could not tell me how many Naxi pictographs he had taught Pound, but he remembered showing him how to draw and pronounce the Naxi pictographs for the sun (a radiating circle within a larger circle pronounced "bi") and for the moon (a simple depiction of the crescent moon pronounced "le"). Having learned the Naxi pictograph for the moon, Pound would reproduce it along with the Naxi pictograph for "fate's tray," a depiction of a sieve, in Canto CXII to make peculiar music and sense:[24]

Artemisia
Arundinaria
Winnowed in fate's tray

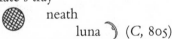

neath

luna) (C, 805)

The sieve sign ● (pronounced "mu") appears in "The [2]Muan [1]Bpö Ceremony," where Rock defines it as "a large winnowing tray made of the small bamboo (Arundinaria)," embodying "a fate, a life."[25] Whether Pound learned the sieve pictograph first from Fang or from Rock, the above lines from CXII exhibit the poet's attachment to his own recommendations made in 1918 and 1929, respectively: a poet should "fill his mind with the finest cadences he can discover, preferably in a foreign language," and poetic language should be "charged with meaning to the utmost possible degree."[26] Amazingly, the passage involves Naxi, a little-known foreign language, both pictographically and phonetically. There is near rhyme across English and Naxi ("le" for the moon with "tray" above it) as well as alliteration across Latin and Naxi ("luna and le").

In 1955, with a job offer from Philco Corporation, Paul Fang and

Figure 9. Baisha mural with Naxi pictographs meaning "pregnant," "passing a chain bridge," "chieftain," "love," "beat grain," "hunt," "go fishing," "birth," "mount," and "set a trap." (Photograph by Zhaoming Qian; © 2017 Zhaoming Qian)

his family moved to Dresher, a suburb of Philadelphia. That fall, Joseph Rock returned to the East Coast from Hawaii (where he served as research professor of oriental studies at the University of Hawaii) and paid Paul Fang a visit. Rock had been a friend of Paul Fang's parents since Paul's childhood. When in Lijiang in the 1930s and '40s, the anthropologist-botanist borrowed sums of local silver dollars from the elder Fang, which he repaid in the early 1950s by wiring American dollars to Paul Fang in Washington, DC. Before departing, Rock took out of his briefcase two of his publications—"The Romance of ²K'a-²mä-¹gyu-³mi-²gkyi" and "The ²Muan ¹Bpö Ceremony"—and autographed them before giving them to Paul Fang. As these rare papers would answer most, if not all, of Pound's trying queries about Naxi rites, Paul Fang sent them to St. Elizabeths Hospital through Professor Giovannini.

As Rock's letter on January 3, 1956, to Pound reveals, in November or December 1955 Paul Fang forwarded to Rock a letter from Giovannini, informing him how Pound had gotten these papers and how profoundly he had been impressed by Rock's commitment to studying and saving the Naxi pictographic language and literature.[27] Having learned of Pound's interest in his work, Rock wrote his first letter to the poet at St. Elizabeths Hospital. It was Paul Fang, along with Giovannini, who had put Rock in touch with Pound, initiating a correspondence between the two learned men.

In the summer of 1956, Paul Fang resigned from Philco to join the National Bureau of Standards in Washington, DC. When he resumed

Figure 10. Ezra Pound on the St. Elizabeths Hospital lawn, 1956. (© 2017 Mary de Rachewiltz; courtesy of the Beinecke Rare Book and Manuscript Library, Yale University)

visits to St. Elizabeths Hospital, Pound (shown in figure 10) would keep him longer for his Naxi lessons. At age seventy to seventy-one the incarcerated poet intensified his study of Naxi people's working pictographic language. One of his regular visitors, David Gordon, reminisced seeing on the walls of Pound's St. Elizabeths cell Naxi pictographs copied from Rock's works.[28] What Gordon probably did not know was that Pound had a private tutor for his Naxi lessons. During these sessions Pound would pick a word here and a word there from "The Romance of ^{2}K'a-^{2}mä-^{1}gyu-^{3}mi-^{2}gkyi" or "The ^{2}Muan ^{1}Bpö Ceremony" and ask Paul Fang to pronounce them and explain their meanings.

Paul Fang's copy of "The Romance of ^{2}K'a-^{2}mä," kept at his Belmont home, bears some of his glosses and corrections for Pound. On page 9, for instance, above the phonetic symbol "^{1}Yu-" is the English word *sheep* in Paul Fang's hand.[29] From the Naxi pictograph for "shepherd," a figure with a sheep's head, Pound could have guessed what "^{1}Yu-," in Rock's "^{1}Yu-boy," meant. Paul Fang's gloss here points to Pound's insistence on making certain what each part of a Naxi compound pictograph signified. In "The Romance of ²K'a-²mä" Rock provides the original pictographic text of the romantic tragedy of ²K'a-²mä-¹gyu³mi-²gkyi and her shepherd lover ²Ndzi-²bö-¹yü-²lä-¹p'ĕr with translation and explanatory notes. So the word Pound paid special attention to concerns one of the protagonists' means of livelihood.

Rock's phonetic system with hyphens and superscripts is meant to help readers pronounce unpronounceable Naxi pictographs. Still, Pound wanted to hear the words spoken by a Naxi native speaker. Since his purchase of a copy of *Mathews' Chinese-English Dictionary* in 1948, Pound had been studying Chinese phonetics.[30] Relying on this dictionary with a sound key to each character, he was able to transcribe the "singing syllables" of the Confucian odes. Whenever Paul Fang's compatriot and friend at CUA, Veronica Huilan Sun, visited, he would ask her to read aloud a few Confucian odes.[31] Similarly, he took advantage of Paul Fang's native fluency of Naxi. His alertness to Naxi phonetics is made evident by Paul Fang's gloss to the Naxi pictograph for "cuckoo" on page 53 of his copy of "The Romance of ²K'a-²mä."[32] In describing the pronunciation of this Naxi word, Rock notes that "the word '³gkye-²bpu' is the most difficult to pronounce; it is really ³tgkye or ³tkhye." In the margin next to this comment is written in Paul Fang's hand "eng geek." No doubt, it was at Pound's request that Paul Fang facilitated the "unpronounceable" Naxi pictograph.

On that same page, one will notice, Paul Fang corrects a mistake in Rock's description of the Naxi pictograph for "three spring months." His copy, loaned to Pound in 1955–58, shows that the number 4 in "4 horizontal lines" for "≡" beneath the Naxi sign for the moon (meaning "months" here) is crossed out and changed to 3.[33] Going through passages in Rock's works with Pound, it is certain that Paul Fang facilitated far more unpronounceable words and corrected far more inaccuracies than those that have been recorded. It is a pity that Paul Fang's copy of "The ²Muan ¹Bpö Ceremony" with more of his glosses has not been located. According to Pound's daughter, Mary de Rachewiltz, the copy of "The ²Muan ¹Bpö Ceremony" at Brunnenburg is not Paul Fang's.[34] The few recorded examples, nonetheless, are sufficient proof that Paul Fang was to Pound more than an interpreter of Rock's works about the Naxi; he was to the poet a passionate private tutor of the Naxi language and culture.

Pound was equally curious about Naxi religious rites. Did Naxi people believe Buddhism? Or did they believe Taoism? Were they anti-

Confucian? Having left home at a young age, Paul Fang was not able to answer Pound's questions such as these. Nonetheless, on his early visits to St. Elizabeths Hospital (1953–55), he did tell Pound that the most important religious rites observed by the Naxi people were the ²Muan ¹bpo and ²Ndaw ¹bpo or the sacrifice to Heaven and the sacrifice to Earth.

> On the ninth day of the first moon, my folks, that is, the entire Fang clan, would go to the foot of Jade Dragon Snow Range for the ²Muan ¹bpo, and on the ninth day of the seventh moon, we would go to the same spot for the ²Ndaw ¹bpo.[35] On the altar for the ²Muan ¹bpo and ²Ndaw ¹bpo are three trees, a juniper in the center embodying our ancestors and two chestnut trees on its sides embodying Heaven and Earth. "²muan" means Heaven, "²ndaw" means Earth, and "bpo" means white. In the Naxi language adjectives follow nouns.[36]

Fang's account, simple and lucid, would invite more questions from Pound. Precisely because he could not match Pound's queries about the ²Muan ¹bpo and ²Ndaw ¹bpo, he counted himself lucky to be able to obtain in the fall of 1955 a copy of Rock's essay about the ²Muan ¹bpo, which he wasted no time sending to Pound.

²Muan ¹bpo, or the sacrifice to Heaven, recurs four times in *Thrones*. In Canto XCVIII, the first "Sacred Edict" canto, between a rendition of Emperor Yongzheng's ("Yong Tching's") commentary on "grip[ping] the earth in good manners" (*C,* 709) and a rendition of his commentary on "敬 reverence" and "order 孝" or showing respect to and filial love for the elders (*C,* 711) is Pound's first reference to the ²Muan ¹bpo for worshipping nature and ancestors. The contextual arrangement here alludes to the ritual's present-day usage as described by Paul Fang rather than its past usage as defined by Rock. As I have stated above, Paul Fang refers to the juniper on the altar as symbol of "our ancestors," whereas Rock in "The ²Muan ¹Bpö Ceremony" interprets it as "Emperor" or "god."[37]

"Without ²muan ¹bpo ... but I anticipate" (*C,* 711). The line in Canto XCVIII is supposed to enrich its neo-Confucian context, that is, Emperor Yongzheng's emphases simultaneously on "the colour of nature" (*C,* 709) and "filial piety" (*C,* 711), as rendered by Salt Commissioner Wang Youpu ("Ouang-iu-p'uh") in colloquial Chinese and by missionary sinologist F. W. Baller in English, but what about the ²Muan ¹bpo itself?[38] The Naxi occultist ritual is defined first in Canto CI, where a dongba priest (²dto-¹mba) "muy simpático" chants a ²Muan ¹bpo prayer "by the waters of Stone Drum":

> "May their pond be full;
> The son have his father's arm
> and good hearing;
> (noun graph upright; adjective sideways)
> "His horse's mane flowing
> His body and soul are at peace." (*C*, 746–47)

And then in Canto CIV, where the importance of the ritual is underscored: "Without ²muan ¹bpo / No reality / Wind over snow-slope agitante" (*C*, 759). And further in Canto CVI with a description of the ritual's altar: "the juniper is her holy bush / between the two pine trees" (*C*, 773–74).

In *Drafts and Fragments* the ²Muan ¹bpo ceremony recurs twice, first in Canto CX:

> heaven   earth
> in the center
> is
> juniper
> The purifications
> are snow, rain, artemisia,
> also dew, oak and the juniper (*C*, 798)

and then in Canto CXII:

> If we did not perform ²Ndaw ¹bpö
> nothing is solid
> without ²Mùan ¹bpö
> no reality
> Agility, that is from the juniper,
> rice grows and the land is invisible (*C*, 804)

Carroll Terrell is correct in identifying Rock's "The ²Muan ¹Bpö Ceremony" as the source of most ²Muan ¹bpo references in *Thrones* and *Drafts and Fragments*. In this treatise prepared with the assistance of a Naxi dongba priest, Rock concedes that "²dto-¹mbas are seldom invited to assist in the performance of the ceremony."[39] "Their participation in such a ceremony," he clarifies, "must have been at the height of their influence, which is now very much on the wane, or almost nil."[40] Yet he has translated from a Naxi manuscript in his possession

not only a prayer customarily chanted by the oldest male of each worshipping family but also three dongba prayers, one to Heaven, one to
Earth, and one to the juniper.[41] None of the prayers given offers a clue
to where Pound's prayer in Canto CI originates—"May their pond be
full; / The son have his father's arm / and good hearing." Terrell traced
it to Rock's 1955 essay, "The ^{1}D'a ^{3}Nv Funeral Ceremony."[42] But there
is no proof for Pound's access to that paper prior to the publication of
Thrones in 1959. Besides, it is doubtful that Pound would want to bor-
row a prayer from a Naxi funeral ceremony for the ^{2}Muan ^{1}bpo rite.
Who else before 1959 could have given Pound the idea of such a prayer?
Who else before then could have recounted to Pound the Naxi legend
about "two aces" fighting over "the waters of Stone Drum"?

Furthermore, in Canto CI the dongba (^{2}dto-^{1}mba) performing the
^{2}Muan ^{1}bpo is portrayed as having a facial gesture "muy simpático"
(*C,* 746). Rock's "The ^{2}Muan ^{1}Bpö Ceremony" offers nothing very
sympathetic about his dongba. They are presented instead as mixing
various kinds of herbs to chase demons and spirits and as preparing
other kinds of herbs for people to "attain an age of a hundred years
and ... not die."[43] In the Chinese history cantos Pound denounced
taozers (Taoist priests) "babbling of the elixir / that wd/ make men live
without end" (*C,* 288) and taozers who caused "HIEN of TANG" to
die "seeking elixir" (*C,* 313). What could have persuaded Pound, who
had condemned "taozers, hochang [Buddhist monks] and debauchery"
(*C,* 302), to put aside his prejudice against non-Confucian Chinese religions? There were many factors contributing to his change of attitude,
among which was Paul Fang's personal influence. In a 1954 or 1955
conversation with Pound, Paul Fang described how in one summer he
and two other Naxi boys broke into a chamber in the Puji Lamasery
and alarmed Lijiang's most revered lama, Shenlou Hutuktu. Instead of
scolding them, the Grand Lama, said to be a saintly incarnation, greeted
the boys amicably. Shenlou Hutuktu, born of Lijiang Naxi parents, was
a close friend of Paul Fang's grandparents and parents. After his grandfather's death, the Grand Lama stayed in his parents' house for two
months, personally preparing his grandfather's funeral and other religious rites. Paul Fang shared this family story also with Peter Goullart.[44]
In 1941 Shenlou Hutuktu and Goullart met in Chongqing, the wartime
capital of China. Surprisingly, on that occasion the Grand Lama pre-
dicted that the Russian journalist would soon visit Lijiang.

Like ordinary men and women, authors are influenced not only by
their reading and viewing but also by interactions with people sur-

rounding them. Among those who extratextually influence writers, artists, and common people alike are parents (such as Maxine Hong Kingston's mother, whose "talk stories" play a key role in *The Woman Warrior*), teachers (such as D.T. Suzuki, who contributed some Zen idea to John Cage's composition 4′33″), friends (such as Hayashi, the art dealer whose trade in work by Eishi, *Women Beside a Stream Chasing Fireflies,* sparked Monet's *Springtime*), and even strangers (such as a nameless Japanese Noh enthusiast, who through chanting the Noh vocal part lent Yeats the rhythm for his Noh-like play *At the Hawk's Well*).[45] Evidence of cross-cultural interpersonal influence tends to be wasted if no one strives to retrieve it from clues left by an author, a collaborator, or a third-party witness.[46]

Yeats and Pound were among the few creative artists who almost instantly acknowledged their debt to guides from East Asia. Around 1914 Yeats had virtually given up theater. A dance with Noh gestures performed by a Mr. Itō from Japan made Yeats change his mind. The Noh-like dance inspired him to create *At the Hawk's Well* (1916), a play for dancers. The Japanese dancer Michio Itō (1893–1961) was invited to portray the hawk guard in the play. Through rehearsal after rehearsal Yeats became increasingly aware of the expressive power of Itō's dance. According to Curtis Bradford, the Irish playwright cut a thrice-repeated song and several speeches, which taken together "indicate a fuller dependence on the dance as an expressive means."[47] *At the Hawk's Well* marked Yeats's transition to modernism. In "Certain Noble Plays of Japan" (1916), he acknowledged what he owed to Itō: "My play is made possible by a Japanese dancer whom I have seen dance in a studio and in a drawing-room and on a very small stage lit by an excellent stage-light. In the studio and in the drawing-room alone where the lighting was the light we are most accustomed to, did I see him as the tragic image that has stirred my imagination."[48] Similarly, in *Gaudier-Brzeska* (1916) Pound recorded the precise manner in which the nameless Japanese officer's turning of an emotion into a haiku, through Victor Plarr's recounting, inspired him to abbreviate his thirty-line metro poem to its final version.[49] The anonymous Japanese officer's cross-cultural interpersonal influence resulted in a breakthrough in Pound's poetry. His narrative in *Gaudier-Brzeska* seems analogous to Wordsworth's half real, half fictional "Michael," which Geoffrey Hartman describes as a case of "cultural rhetoric" whose aim "is often to give voice to the voiceless, representation to those who are anonymous and marginalized."[50] Without Wordsworth's poem no one would know

Michael's misery. Without Pound's testimony no one would be aware of Plarr's and the nameless Japanese navy officer's roles in the making of Pound's metro poem.

Lesser-known individuals exert an extratextual influence on canonical creative artists no less than vice versa. The problem is where to locate evidence of the lesser knowns' cross-cultural interpersonal influence? Not all authors acknowledge such influences. Even if some of them sometimes do, they may not specify what material effects are produced in which work. Williams, for example, in a letter of May 1958 gives credit to David Wang for his knowledge of the yin/yang principle. Moore in a letter of September 1963 expresses gratitude to Sze for "affording me luxury week by week—*educating me*." Neither poet indicates relevant material effects in his or her exact work. The daunting task of bringing to light hidden or forgotten effects of acknowledged cross-cultural interpersonal exchange and, moreover, absorbing new insights into textual criticism, has been left to the critic.

Clues of cross-cultural interpersonal influence provided by a collaborator have the same problem. Paul Fang's confirmation that he taught Pound how to draw and pronounce the Naxi pictograph for the moon means very little with regard to its effect on Pound until we find that Rock uses that pictograph in "The ²Muan ¹Bpö Ceremony" and "The Romance of ²K'a-²mä" to signify "night" or "month" rather than "moon" and that he pronounces it "²hä" or "²haw" rather than "le" as Fang taught Pound.[51] Fang's personal story illustrating Grand Lama Shenlou Hutuktu's compassion and benevolence by itself is even less significant. Nevertheless, when this exchange, interpersonal in nature, is set against textual proofs, proofs such as Pound's sympathetic response to the Naxi rite stories in Peter Goullart's *Forgotten Kingdom,* as I shall explore in the next chapter, it becomes serviceable as circumstantial evidence for any role in Pound's changed attitude toward non-Confucian Chinese religions—say, his portrayal of a dongba priest's visage as "muy simpático" in Canto CI. As to clues of cross-cultural interpersonal influence provided by a third-party witness, specific instances in a second-generation modernist will be considered in the coda.

SIX

Naxi Rites and
Vortex in Pound's
Final Cantos

NAXI RITES in *Drafts and Fragments* are the best index of Pound's turn-ing away from Confucianism. They are also the best index of his sudden renewal of early avant-gardism in old age. Whereas the ²Muan ¹bpo rite recurring in *Thrones* at least retains to a degree the Confucian respect for the elders, the ²Hăr-²la-¹llü or wind sway ceremony at the center of Pound's final cantos is straightforwardly anti-Confucian. Han lovers in modern China would elope to dodge arranged marriages. Naxi lov-ers would instead seek double suicide to forestall the Confucian mari-tal practice introduced to their culture in the sixteenth to seventeenth centuries. By doing so, they believed that their spirits would roam "with the wind and clouds, in the perpetual embrace of love, never to be re-born, never to be sent to an infernal region, but to live inseparably to the full in a state of eternal youth."[1] According to the Naxi code of customs, without the wind sway ceremony performed, the unattended spirits of the deceased lovers would roam with the wind in the wilder-ness, bringing illness and calamity to their families and villages.

Going over "The Romance of ²K'a-²mä-¹gyu-³mi-²gkyi" with Pound at St. Elizabeths Hospital, Paul Fang drew attention to the pop-ularity and the effect of this Naxi version of *Romeo and Juliet*. It was known to every single Naxi boy and girl, and under its influence, two young lovers in his Old Town neighborhood carried out their death pact in a forest, which compelled their parents to hire dongbas to per-form the ²Hăr-²la-¹llü rite for their unattended spirits (see figure 11).

Such casual conversations prepared Pound for his reading of Rock's "Romance of ²K'a-²mä," which in turn led to his brilliant rendition of the ²Hăr-²la-¹llü rite in Canto CX, the opening canto of *Drafts and Fragments*:

Figure 11. Naxi dongbas performing the ²Hăr-²la-¹llü rite, 1939. (Photograph by Joseph F. Rock)

²Hăr-²la-¹llü ³k'ö

of the wind sway,

The nine fates and the seven,

and the black tree was born dumb,

The water is blue and not turquoise

When the stag drinks at the salt spring

and sheep come down with the gentian sprout,

can you see with eyes of coral or turquoise

or walk with the oak's root? (*C,* 797)

In her analysis of a 1923 version of Canto VIII, the first Malatesta canto, Marjorie Perloff highlights Pound's experimentation with several strategies that are characteristic of high modernism.[2] These include juxtaposition of "verbal elements, fragmented images, and truncated bits of narrative," "condensation and modernization" of mid-fifteenth-century archival documents, and sudden switch from "updating of history" to a voice in the past, the voice of a fifteenth-century Italian historian.[3] Fragmentation, condensation, modernization, and updating all point to the ingenious uses of borrowed words. The ²Hăr-²la-¹llü ³k'ö passage in Canto CX, therefore, like Moore's "O to Be a Dragon," at once recalls Pound's first Malatesta canto and anticipates contemporary citational texts such as Susan Howe's *The Midnight* and Charles Bernstein's *Shadowtime.*

The images and bits of narrative in this nine-line passage (from "²Hăr-²la-¹llü ³k'ö" to "or walk with the oak's root"), like those in Canto VIII, are lopped off from diverse sources, namely various sections of "The Romance of ²K'a-²mä." The line "The nine fates and the seven," for instance, is the fragmentation of a footnote in "The Romance of ²K'a-²mä": "a man has nine fates ²ngv = nine, hence a boy is often addressed ²Ngv-¹tzĕr, and, as a girl has seven fates, she is addressed ²Shĕr-¹tzĕr, ²shĕr = seven; both are endearing names."[4] The line "and the black tree was born dumb" is the condensation of five lines of prose in a different section of the same source: "She twisted a rope, a new rope (she) took, to the tree she went to commit suicide (to die), the black crown of the tree waved, ²K'a-²mä-¹gyu-³mi-²gkyi's heart was faint, the black tree was born dumb (was born without a mouth), here to commit suicide, here to decompose (the tree) did not invite her (did not say), hence she did not commit suicide and again returned."[5]

Going over this allusive and disruptive passage, the reader is forced to guess meaning from the context, or in Perloff's words, "participate in the poem's action."[6] Just as in Canto VIII where Pound's rendition of a formal Sigismundo letter is suddenly switched to "the voice of the Renaissance chronicler," so toward the end of this passage in Canto CX, the fragmented images hinting at the Naxi girl's failed suicidal attempts and her somberness are abruptly shifted to her boyfriend's despairing cry let out upon his catching her hung body on a Mt. Sumeru oak branch: "can you see with eyes of coral or turquoise / or walk with the oak's root?"[7] This cry will echo with deeper frustration and anguish seven lines below: "can'st'ou see with the eyes of turquoise?" (*C,* 798).

For John Peck Canto CX with the "²Hăr-²la-¹llü ³k'ö" passage presents a "suicide night world."[8] For Emily Mitchell Wallace, Canto CX is an elegy "paying tribute [to deceased friends] so that their spirits will not be troubled in this world or go into the next world *unattended* or unaccompanied by his love."[9] "These friends include, but are not limited to," clarifies Wallace, "Wyndham Lewis, 1957; Ernest Hemingway, 1961, H.D., 1961; e. e. cummings, 1962; Joseph Rock, 1962; William Carlos Williams, 1963; T. S. Eliot, 1965."[10] Canto CX *is* an elegy, but since the "²Hăr-²la-¹llü ³k'ö" passage has a draft version composed as early as

December 1958, its elegiac mood was initially aroused not by Hemingway, Cummings, Rock, Williams, or Eliot.[11] Rather, it was stirred up by Lewis, who passed away on March 7, 1957, and, in a way, also by H.D. (Hilda Doolittle), who, as Ronald Bush has pointed out, "from a sanatorium in Switzerland in 1958 had sent [Pound] a memoir of their time together (*End to Torment*, later published in 1979)," and who then passed away on September 21, 1961.[12]

Wallace is absolutely right in asserting that Canto CX with the ²Hăr-²la-¹llü rite at the center "focuses not on the manner of death or ways of dying, but on ways of responding to the death of a loved one and to the possibilities of life after death."[13] No matter how it is interpreted, Canto CX signals a shift in Pound's outlook, a parting from Confucianism, especially that of Canto XIII, where Kung is quoted as saying "nothing of the 'life after death'" (*C*, 59). The passage offers blessings to the spirit of the deceased Naxi girl, who, in the elderly poet's mind, deserved to enjoy free love in the next world, a world with no Confucian marital practice or parental interference with their children's love or marriage. It offers blessings also to H.D., whose youthful love life, like the Naxi girl's, was nipped in the bud, as is recollected in her memoir *End to Torment*:

> We had climbed up into the big maple tree in our garden, outside Philadelphia. . . . .
>
> "No, Dryad," he says. He snatches me back. We sway with the wind. There is no wind. We sway with the stars. They are not far.
>
> We slide, slip, fly down through the branches, leap together to the ground. "No," I say, breaking from his arms, "No," drawing back from his kisses. . . . .
>
> . . . My father said, "Mr. Pound, I don't say there was anything wrong *this time*. I will not forbid you the house, but I will ask you not to come so often." . . . .
>
> "You must come away with me, Dryad." "How can I? How can I?" His father would scrape up enough for him to live on. I had nothing. . . . The engagement, such as it was, was shattered like a Venetian glass goblet, flung on the floor.[14]

Rock informs us that ²Hăr-²la-¹llü or the ceremony for the spirits of Naxi lovers' suicides literally means "Wind sway perform."[15] H.D. speaks of her unforgettable time together with Pound figuratively in terms of "sway[ing] with the wind."[16] It is only natural for Pound to think of both the Naxi girl and H.D. when rewriting and rearranging the "wind sway" passage for Canto CX.

In the mid to late 1950s, partly due to the textual and extratextual influences of Joseph Rock and Paul Fang, Pound slowly opened himself up to non-Confucian Chinese religions. By 1956, the poet of *The Cantos* owned up to Georgetown University student William McNaughton, a regular visitor to St. Elizabeths, his senseless prejudice against Taoism and Buddhism in the past: "There's no doubt I missed something in Daoism and Buddhism. Clearly, there is something valid, meaningful, in those religions."[17] Despite what he said, he continued to resist putting into *Thrones* (1959) the anti-Confucian "²Hǎr-²la-¹llü" passage he had drafted. In the spring of 1958, Pound got a copy of Peter Goullart's *Forgotten Kingdom* (1955). Before long he was captivated by its breathtaking stories illustrating the creditability and suggestiveness of non-Confucian Naxi religious rites.

Born to a well-educated Russian family, Peter Goullart (1901–75) lost his father at age two. During the Bolshevik Revolution, he and his widowed mother fled from Moscow to Paris, from where they traveled farther to China. In 1924 his mother died while exiled in Shanghai. Wandering alone and searching for sustenance, young Goullart developed an interest in Taoism and became a Taoist devotee in a monastery in Hangzhou. He made a living by guiding wealthy Western tourists from Shanghai to Hangzhou, Guangzhou, Hong Kong, Hanoi, Singapore, and Bangkok. Japan's invasion into China and its neighboring countries made tourism in the region impossible. Following China's war of resistance against Japan (1937–45), Goullart became a representative of "Gung Ho" or the International Committee for the Promotion of Chinese Industrial Cooperatives. In 1941, as a "Gung Ho" agent, he journeyed to Lijiang, Yunnan Province, where he met Rock and Paul Fang. The fascinating Naxi culture Goullart observed during his nine-year sojourn generated his debut travel book *Forgotten Kingdom* (1955). Paul Fang, after reading it, sent a letter to Goullart, congratulating his old friend on publishing a best seller with "obvious affection" for his beloved hometown: "I cannot say the same about Dr. Rock, not because he is restricted to archaic writings, but because I had one occasion to meet him in the U.S. when his only adjective about Likiang seems to be 'primitive'" (JFC).

At Paul Fang's recommendation, Pound began reading *Forgotten*

Kingdom. One of the things that must have enthralled the poet was Goullart's account of how the Naxi people preserved not only the genuine Confucian instruments but also the Confucian music scores "lost" during the First Emperor of China's burning of the Great Books. The Confucian music scores are said to have survived only in fragments in some remote Taoist monasteries.[18] This fascinating revelation should have increased Pound's respect for the nature-loving and tradition-honoring Naxi people, who, as Goullart claims, simultaneously and sincerely believed in "Lamaism (Tantric Buddhism), Mahayana Buddhism, Taoism and Confucianism in addition to their ancient religion of Animalism and Shamanism."[19]

What must have impressed Pound more profoundly, as Wallace has noted, would be the common Naxi belief in the existence of spirits "somewhere near, just on the other side of the veil":[20]

> The Nakhi ... lived in close and intimate contact with the world of spirits. They believed that the immensity of space was inhabited by big and small deities, spirits of the dead and a host of nature's spirits both good and bad. The relationship between mankind and these many spirits was not considered hypothetical or conjectural but factual and authentic.... If there was an apparition, materialization or direct voice, people did not shrink from it but investigated the matter with sympathy and interest. In a word, a visitor from the unseen was treated as a person, with proper courtesy.[21]

The excerpt is likely to have struck a chord in Pound's youthful interest in the spirit of romance or in Greek myth, arising "when someone having passed through delightful psychic experience tried to communicate it to others and found it necessary to screen himself from persecution."[22] That interest had inspired "The Tree," the opening poem of *Personae* (1926), a poem from the earlier "Hilda's Book": "I stood still and was a tree amid the wood, / Knowing the truth of things unseen before."[23]

Furthermore, in *Forgotten Kingdom* Goullart offers a vivid description of a ²Hăr-²la-¹llü rite for the spirits of a double suicide held by both the boy's and the girl's parents, which he had witnessed as an invited guest. Seven dongba priests wearing five-petal diadems on their heads slowly danced around the small flags bearing the boy's and the girl's names: "'Come! Come! Appear! Come!' they commanded in a metallic and hypnotic voice.... There was a deadly stillness and a gust of ice cold wind filled the courtyard. Just for an instant, one brief moment, we all felt that the lovers had returned and stood there by their likenesses. I thought at first the impression was entirely mine: but, with a burst of weeping, the two families prostrated themselves as one man before the little altar."[24] This vivid account, more than Rock's "The Romance of ^{2}K'a-^{2}mä" or Fang's personal story, brought Pound, vis-à-vis the elegiac mood of an authentic ^{2}Hăr-^{2}la-^{1}llü rite, the mood of his "^{2}Hăr-^{2}la-^{1}llü ^{3}k'ö" passage in Canto CX.

On June 30, 1958, Ezra and Dorothy Pound, accompanied by Marcella Spann, an English teacher from Texas, boarded the Italian ship line *Cristoforo Colombo* en route to Naples with the manuscript of *Thrones* and copies of *Forgotten Kingdom,* "The ^{2}Muan ^{1}Bpö Ceremony," and "The Romance of ^{2}K'a-^{2}mä" in their luggage. Upon arrival at Brunnenburg Castle, home of Boris and Mary de Rachewiltz, Pound got word from Giovannini that Paul Fang had asked about his copies of Rock's papers. On July 15, 1958, Pound wrote Paul Fang from Brunnenburg to say that his copies of "The ^{2}Muan ^{1}Bpö Ceremony" and "The Romance of ^{2}K'a-^{2}mä" were not lost or given away: "I have found your Mùen Bpo & K'A MA gyu in my luggage. Are you in a hurry or do you merely want to know they are safe. Sorry for confusion" (JFC).

Of course, Paul Fang was not in a hurry to get back his copies of the Rock monographs. Nonetheless, before he had a chance to tell Pound in writing that he could keep these papers for as long as he wished, Dorothy had already put them in the mail across the Atlantic. When the package reached the Fangs' Washington, DC, apartment, Paul Fang opened it to find his copy of "The Romance of ^{2}K'a-^{2}mä" rebound with a hard cover signed in red ink by Pound (figure 12): "Sorry the binder has omitted Rock's dedication to Fang" (JFC).

For three years from 1955 to 1958 Pound had used "The Romance of ^{2}K'a-^{2}mä" so frequently that its signed soft cover had been worn off. Pound thought that Rock's dedication would mean a lot to Fang. Unexpectedly, however, Paul Fang valued Pound's signature more dearly than Rock's. His appreciation is expressed in a note on the back of his 1959 card to the Pounds: "Thank you for these books you sent back and the beautiful binding with your precious signature" (Lilly).

Until his death in October 2011 Paul Fang held that Lijiang was brought alive to the English-speaking world less by Joseph Rock than by Peter Goullart and Ezra Pound. To him Goullart's and Pound's Lijiang was more palpable and joyful.

Even before finalizing the *Thrones* manuscript for his Milan and New York publishers, Pound had fallen under the spell of some powerful lyr-

Figure 12. Ezra Pound to Paul Fang, 1958. (© 2017 Mary de Rachewiltz and the Estate of Omar S. Pound; courtesy of Josephine Fang)

icism from the Naxi materials. In mid to late July 1958, Pound's daughter's and son-in-law's Brunnenburg Castle "set deep in the mountains," as Ronald Bush states, "began to resonate with the melancholy legends of the Na Khi."[25] Goullart, a Western journalist and sojourner of Lijiang for nine years, would be a help with higher proficiency than Paul Fang for imagining Naxi in Pound's final cantos. That summer at Brunnenburg, Pound learned from his Australian protégé Noel Stock that Goullart was planning a trip to Europe. On August 5, 1958, he wrote Goullart, offering him a night or two at his Egyptologist son-in-law's fifth-floor flat in Rome should Goullart want to meet him there. With this said, he continued: "AND (again if Stock is correct in your itinerary), we should be delighted to put you up here, probably for more nights than you will be able to spare. At any rate, hope to meet you somewhere in Italy" (Beinecke). To write a paradise over Lijiang in his final cantos, Pound would be obliged to delve into all of Rock's monographs about the Naxi. In his letter of August 5, 1958, he asked Goullart for assistance: "If, by the way, you have any idea how I can get copies of [Rock's] Na Khi stuff I wd/ be grateful for the information. Have had to send Fang's copies back to him, and have now only the Muan Bpo" (Beinecke).

The anticipated meeting between Pound and Goullart did not take place until 1960. The Russian writer went to London instead that summer, which fact is confirmed by Dorothy in her reply of January 6, 1959, to the Fangs' 1958 Christmas card with a family photograph (see fig. 8, p. <oo>). The letter opens with references to Mary's children and the Brunnenburg Castle near Merano and the Austrian border, followed by messages from Pound:

Dear Famille Fang,
We were most interested in the family Fang photograph. Thank you. Only 2 children here, 11 & 9 years. The boy goes to school in Merano—the girl is still going to the village.

Mrs. Fang may know Merano? We are close to the frontier— the mountains are huge—at present snow half way down. The Castello is very ancient, built on Roman foundations—we have, luckily, good wood stoves.

Ezra very often reads to us after tea time his own Cantos—and the *Odes;* but the cold weather rather slows him up.

He sends messages—that Goullart got to London, & has arranged for publication of another book with Murray, that B[oris] de R[achewiltz]'s (see enclos.) book is most important. His newest book is from a different papyrus than the old Badge & has excellent illustrations.

Have you any idea of Rock's whereabouts? He seems to have disappeared again!

You can always get news of us from G. Giovannini, as we are in touch with them.

Hoping you are all well, and with our very best wishes for 1959.
Paula may remember bringing EP his birthday cake at St. E.'s.

most sincerely
Dorothy Pound (JFC)

The book Goullart had arranged for publication in London was *The Monastery of Jade Mountain* (1961), an engaging autobiographical account of his sojourn in the monastery of Jade Emperor Mountain in Hangzhou, studying the *Dao De Jing* (*Tao Te Ching*) and other Taoist classics. On a 1962 visit to Brunnenburg, Goullart gave Pound and Boris de Rachewiltz a copy of that book. While there, he was urged by

Pound and de Rachewiltz to send Rock their greetings first on January 29, 1962, and then again on February 28, 1962.[26] A photograph of him and Pound on the Brunnenburg terrace (taken that spring) was printed inside the dust jacket of his next book, *River of the White Lily: Life in Sarawak* (1964).

Eight months after sending messages through Dorothy, on August 25, 1959, Pound wrote from Rapallo to inform Paul Fang of the arrival of the long-awaited Rock book, *The Ancient Na-khi Kingdom of Southwest China* in two volumes. He must have written Rock both before and after his departure from the United States. Having not heard from him for over a year, he again asked his whereabouts:[27]

> Dear Mr Fang
> I have at last got hold of Rock's "Ancient Kingdom" with its fine photographs.
>
> Have you his Vienna address?
>
> Can you urge him to contact the Forschungsinstitut in Frankfurt?
>
> The widow Frobenius is a friend, and my name useful there.
>
> also can he stop at my daughter's [?]
>
> Mary de Rachewiltz, Schloss Brunnenburg-Tirolo
> MERANO Italy,
>
> My son in law is doing nicely in Egyptology, and should be useful in contacts in Rome. Not that Rock needs them. BUT the more we correlate the better.
>
> Goullart's book is very lively. You could also ask Rock about Goullart who stayed with him in Li-Chiang
>
> > cordially yours
> > E. Pound (JFC)

Earlier that summer, Pound had made a version of Canto CX. Many factors were at work in Pound's mind in the summer of 1959 when he rewrote and rearranged that version. Among them were not only the much-discussed friction between his women and the apathy at Brunnenburg and Rapallo, but also his memory of a past relationship brought back by H.D.'s *End to Torment,* obsession with the Naxi girl's romantic tragedy kept alive through rereading of Rock, and disillusionment about Confucianism, as revealed in Donald Hall's 1960 interview with him: "I might have done better to put Agassiz on top instead of Confucius."[28]

This version is close to the final text of CX in *Drafts and Fragments,* opening with a beach scene:

Thy quiet house
The crozier's curve runs in the wall,
The harl, feather-white, as a dolphin on sea-brink
I am all for Verkehr without tyranny
      —wake exultant
          in caracole
Hast'ou seen boat's wake on sea-wall,
        how crests it?
What panache?
      paw-flap, wave-tap,
        that is gaiety,
Toba Sojo,
      toward limpidity,
         that is exultance,
    here the crest runs on wall
che paion' si al vent' (*C,* 797)

This scene with a feather-white flying over a beach seems to involve Dorothy Pound or Marcella Spann, both with Pound at the time of its composition.[29] Spann had been a regular visitor to Pound at St. Elizabeths Hospital for two years while teaching English at a junior college in Washington, DC. She was then serving as Pound's secretary. Whether it was Dorothy or Marcella Spann who triggered his poetic imagination, what was envisioned in the lines was the poet's former "Dryad" on the wind (Dante's "al vent"), whose 1907–8 private engagement with him had been "shattered like a Venetian glass goblet" due to parental interference, and who was at the moment intimately identified with the young Naxi girl ^{2}K'a-^{2}mä.[30]

What follows in Canto CX's final version is the above discussed "^{2}Hăr-^{2}la-^{1}llü" passage. Surrounding the "^{2}Hăr-^{2}la-^{1}llü" passage are the beach scene above and a Chinese poem in a single vertical line (not in characters but in sound symbols) and a rehearsed ^{2}Muan ^{1}bpo ceremony scene below:

Yellow iris in that river bed
      yüeh$^{4.5}$
      ming^2

$$mo^{4.5}$$
$$hsien^1$$
$$p'eng^2$$

Quercus on Mt Sumeru
   can'st 'ou see with the eyes of turquoise?
      heaven   earth
         in the center
            is
         juniper
The purifications
      are snow, rain, artemisia,
      also dew, oak and the juniper
And in thy mind beauty, O Artemis,
      as of maintain lakes in the dawn,
Foam and silk are thy fingers,
                  Kuanon, (C, 798)

The single-line Chinese poem, "yüeh$^{4.5}$ ming^2 mo$^{4.5}$ hsien^1 p'eng^2,"
meaning "the moon bright no former friend(s)" or "under the bright
moon, no former friends," makes clear that the poet's nostalgia is for
his past friends, deceased or alive. Written in a fragmentary and impersonal style, these lines bluntly challenge the dominant poetic trend of
the 1960s. Despite the contrary literary climate, in Canto CX indeterminacy supplants fixity, fiction replaces event, and impersonality over-
rides personality.

In February 1960 Pound was interviewed by American poet and
critic Donald Hall. Three months later he sent Hall a typescript of a
few more unfinished cantos including a version of Canto CX. As Ronald Bush has shown, in the middle of their exchanges about the texts,
Pound stopped responding to Hall, who was hoping to publish these
new cantos in the *Paris Review*. It was not until September 24, 1961,
when he all of a sudden resumed his revisionary efforts.[31] On September 21, 1961, Hilda Doolittle died of complications from a serious stroke
in the Red Cross Hospital in Zürich, Switzerland. Her passing unexpectedly made Canto CX a perfect elegy for her as well as for Wyndham Lewis. Had the sad news of H.D.'s passing pushed Pound back into
work? H.D. had been on his mind—the H.D. in her last years haunted
by his words of 1908, "You must come away with me, Dryad," and her
father's words of 1906 or '07, "Mr. Pound, I don't say there was anything
wrong *this time*."[32] In Canto CX, it seems, the Naxi girl's words, "and

the black tree was born dumb," and her lover's words, "can you see with eyes of coral or turquoise / or walk with the oak's root?" mingle with Pound's and Mr. Doolittle's words which haunted H.D. in her last days. In a letter to H.D., dated November 6, 1959, Pound made a touching comment on her memoir: "there is a great deal of beauty," followed by a postscript, dated November 13, 1959: "Torment title excellent, but optimistic" (Beinecke).

A week or so before Christmas 1959, Paul Fang read the Naxi passages in *Thrones* with great gusto: "With the sun and moon on her shoulders, / the star-discs sewn on her coat / at Li Chiang" (*C*, 746) and "Na Khi talk made out of wind noise, / And North Khi, not to be heard amid sounds of the forest / but to fit in with them unperceived by the game" (*C*, 758).

His memories of how Pound had longingly listened to his Naxi stories and pushed him for more came back. Had he explained to the aging poet that a Naxi woman wore a sheepskin cape with seven round discs representing seven stars? In 1924, in a village at the foot of Lijiang's Snow Range, Rock took photographs of several Naxi women in costumes. Some of these photographs are reproduced in "The Romance of ²K'a-²mä-¹gyu-³mi-²gkyi" (1939). A beautiful Naxi woman appears in two of these. While in one photograph she is by herself, in the other photograph (figure 13) she is with two other Naxi women. The woman on the left in this photograph is visibly "with the sun and moon on her shoulders, / the star-discs sewn on her coat" (*C*, 746). That photograph reappears in *The Ancient Na-Khi Kingdom of Southwest China,* volume I. Its caption offers no clue whatsoever about the large discs on her shoulders as the sun and the moon or the smaller discs on her back as stars.[33]

As I have noted in chapter 5, Paul Fang wrote on the back of a 1959 Christmas card to the Pounds: "my beloved country and my beloved village will be immortalized through your pen and your words" (Mary de Rachewiltz).

Although Paul Fang was a bashful scientist, he was never at a loss for words to admire Pound's cantos. In a letter to Peter Goullart of September 1962, he observes: "No doubt you have seen some of his cantos. I am not engaged in the field of literature, but I enjoyed so immensely these moments I visited Mr. Pound and listened to his extolling expressions about our beloved land and people" (JFC). Similarly, in a June 2005 letter to me, he again stressed the value of Pound's cantos about the Naxi: "I appreciate so much the work of Pound with his imagina-

Figure 13. Naxi women in costumes, 1924. (Photograph by Joseph F. Rock)

tion and his profound thoughts, even with very limited resources. Today the resources have been vastly expanded. Naturally, people in Lijiang would be very interested and very grateful to Pound's work and your up-to-date scholarship."[34]

In the early 1960s Paul and Josephine Fang continued to send the Pounds greeting cards. The last of those survived is signed simply, "From the Fangs / Christmas 1963" (Beinecke). Just as his Naxi lessons at St. Elizabeths Hospital, along with Rock's papers, kindled astonishing creative energy in Pound, resulting in a new direction in *The Cantos*, Fang's remarks about Lijiang being "immortalized" by his work inspired the elderly poet to continue his dialogue with the Naxi while renewing early avant-gardism in his final years. Paul Fang (figure 14) never worked with Pound on any of his cantos, but by loaning Pound his Rock monographs about the Naxi, teaching Pound how to write and pronounce Naxi pictographs such as the one for the moon, and explaining to Pound the Naxi religious rites, [2]Muan [1]bpo and [2]Hǎr-[2]la-[1]llü, he contributed no less than a primary collaborator to Pound's final modernist project.

Pound never acknowledged the Fangs' greetings of the early 1960s.

Figure 14. Paul Fang, 1959. (© 2017 Josephine Fang)

By then he had stopped communicating with the outside world. Nonetheless, his imaginings of the Lijiang green world and exchanges with the Naxi people through his cantos carried on. From CXII, whose early versions were drafted in mid 1958 to late 1959 and whose final text was fixed in 1961, is entirely devoted to Lijiang. It opens with a rendition of a part of the ²Muan ¹bpo ceremony called the "³Ch'ou ³Shu," or smoking out of evils clinging to people like "a chief's daughter," or creatures such as owl or wagtail or fire-fox, an anti-Confucian religious rite Pound would have denounced a decade or two before:[35]

> . . . owl, and wagtail
> and huo³-hu², the fire-fox
> Amrta, that is nectar
> > white wind, white dew
> Here from the beginning, we have been here
> > from the beginning
> From her breath were the goddesses
> > ²La ²muṇ ³mi

If we did not perform ²Ndaw ¹bpö
                    nothing is solid
without ²Mùan ¹bpö
                    no reality
Agility, that is from the juniper,
rice grows and the land is invisible (C, 804)

Following this is the poet's imagining of an earthly paradise arising
from the ²Muan ¹bpo ceremony, which turns out to represent an actual scenic spot in the now famous Black Dragon Pool Park half a mile
north of Lijiang's Old Town (figure 15). To the east of the Black Dragon
Pool is Lung Wang's, or the Dragon King Temple, built in 1737 during
the reign of the Qing emperor Qianlong. Behind Lung Wang's temple
is Hsiang Shan, or the Elephant Hill. As a plaque at the park entrance
indicates, the pool, also excavated in 1737, is "the water-head of the
water system in Lijiang Old Town, a World Cultural Heritage Site":

By the pomegranate water,
                    in the clear air
                         over Li Chiang
The firm voice amid pine wood,
                    many springs are at the foot of
                                   Hsiang Shan
By the temple pool, Lung Wang's
                    the clear discourse
                              as Jade stream

玉 Yü⁴

河 ho² (C, 804)

This passage with its last seven lines re-created from a footnote in
"The ²Muan ¹Bpö Ceremony" exemplifies late Pound's visualized eco-
criticism.[36] Here the aging poet is at once celebrating the natural and
environmental beauty of an earthly paradise and commenting on what
makes it possible for the ultimate realization of harmony between humanity and nature. Lijiang, 2,400 meters (7,874 feet) above the sea level,
is claimed to be nearer to the sky than most other historic cities around
the world. The Naxi people with their women still wearing star discs
on their backs are claimed to be closer to nature.

Figure 15. The Black Dragon Pool in Lijiang, 2010. "By the temple pool, Lung Wang's / the clear discourse / as Jade stream" (*C*, 804). (Photograph by Ellen Satrom)

The last five lines of "From CXII" return to the ²Muan ¹bpo ceremony:

> Artemisia
> Arundinaria
> Winnowed in fate's tray
> ⬤ neath
> luna ☽ (*C*, 805)

These lines recall Canto I, a modernist rendition of Homer's Odysseus performing an ancient Greek ritual of descent to the underworld—"Poured we libations unto each the dead, / First mead and then sweet wine, water mixed with white flour / . . . / A sheep to Tiresias only, black and a bell-sheep" (*C*, 3)—to bring the blind prophet of Apollo in Thebes to foretell his future. The language of Canto I is not solely Pound's, but ply over ply Homer's Greek, Andreas Divus's Renaissance Latin, and Pound's "Seafarer" English. Here the last five lines of "From CXII" imagine the Naxi people performing the ²Muan

[1]bpo , a ritual of ascent to Heaven—placing "[2]bbue" (Artemisia) and "[1]mun" (a winnowing tray made of the small bamboo or Arundinaria) over a slaughtered pig (or pig's head) and pouring spring water through them.[37] The language of "From CXII" is not solely Pound's either, but a mixture of the languages of the Naxi dongbas (the "winnowing tray" pictograph and the "moon" pictograph), Rock's Latin-English ("Arundinaria"), Mathews' Chinese ("玉河", "Yü[4] ho[2]"), and Pound's *Thrones* English ("Winnowed in fate's tray").

Whereas Canto I includes no Chinese, From CXII has not only Chinese (both characters and Wade–Giles romanization symbols) but also Naxi pictographs. The characters and pictographs set in larger sizes demand attention. They function to guide the reader's eye to look and peruse in several directions. Take 玉河, for example. As soon as the reader's eye hits the two Chinese characters, it will glance first from left to right to see their transliterations, "Yü[4] ho[2]," and then from right back to left to regard their shapes, 玉Yü[4] with one drop of water on the lower right corner and 河ho[2] with three drops of water on the left side. Having done so, the reader's eye will automatically glance up to catch the meaning of 玉 河 first in "Jade stream" and then in "the clear discourse." Of course, the reader can peruse the lines with Chinese characters and Naxi pictographs in other ways. But whichever direction is taken, his or her reading will be "more spacious than linear," because one or another foreign sign is there to compel him or her to pause, contemplate, and read.[38]

The two cantos composed half a century apart are both intended as a linguistic journey through opacity to intensity and multiple meaning. While one is a daring attempt to initiate experimental modernism, the other is a no less courageous effort to renew it in an era of opposition to high modernist values. Compare its intensity in terms of length— no more than thirty lines—to that of, say Canto LXXXV, made up of 320 lines, or Canto XCIX, made up of 524 lines. Note Pound's imagism/vorticism or "avant-garde phase of modernism" re-initiated and sharpened. For "direct treatment of the 'thing' whether subjective or objective," heed "pomegranate water," "clear air," and so on highlighting the untainted green landscape of Lijiang's Black Dragon Pool, or "owl," "wagtail," and "fate's tray" side by side with its corresponding Naxi pictograph portraying the [2]Muan [1]bpo ceremony being performed.[39] For "to use absolutely no word that does not contribute to the presentation," note the thirty-line cubist collage of Latin, Chinese, Naxi, and English on a flat surface, "VORTEX, from which, and through which, and into which, ideas are constantly rushing."[40] For "to compose in the sequence of the musical phrase, not in sequence of a metronome," consider the couplings of English and foreign cadences, such as assonance and near rhyme across English and Naxi ("fate's tray / mu neath / luna le") and alliteration across Latin and Naxi ("luna / le").[41] For Eliot as for Pound, any form makes meaning. Here what we contemplate is not so much English and Latin rhyming with Naxi as Western civilization rhyming with Eastern civilization.

The Cantos is not a "rag-bag" of random subject matter after all. The poet laments in Canto CXVI: "And I am not a demigod, / I cannot make it cohere" (*C*, 816).[42] But hardly has he uttered these apologetic words when he has taken them back and declared in a louder voice: "it coheres all right / even if my notes do not cohere" (*C*, 817).

East-West Exchange
in the Eighties and
at the Millennium

WERE WILLIAMS, MOORE, AND POUND the only creative artists who
renewed themselves thanks to a degree of East Asian influence? Louis
Zukofsky also benefited from Japan and China in his renewal of modernism in the 1960s. Richard Parker has considered the objectivist
champion's innovative treatment of "Ryokan's Scroll" in *I's (pronounced
eyes)* (1963).[1] After decades of Buddhist study in Japan and the United
States, Gary Snyder reemerged in the 1990s as a late modernist. His long
poem *Mountains and Rivers without End* (1996; reprinted 2008) opens
with two epigraphs, one adapted from a poem by the Tibetan Buddhist
sage Jetsun Milarepa (ca. 1052–1135) and the other adapted from an essay ("Painting of a Rice-Cake") by the founder of the Japanese Sōtō
school of Zen Dogen Zenji (1200–53).[2] Anthony Hunt has explored
the former Beat poet's eclectic use of Buddhist ideas.[3] If we extend
our horizon beyond the borders of the United States, we shall have the
comparable examples of the British poet Lee Harwood and the Canadian poet Steve McCaffery. Whereas Tony Lopez has discussed the role
a Chinese character from the *Yi jing* plays in Harwood's "Chên.震"
(1974), Marjorie Perloff has examined a visual rendition of Pound's
metro poem—fourteen Chinese characters surrounding a photo-
graphed Western eye—in McCaffery's *Seven Pages Missing: Selected Texts
1969–1999* (2001).[4] I shall have little to add to the previous discussions.
What interest me are a playwright's and an architect's East-West exchange in the 1980s and at the millennium, their promise to confirm
and expand the notions discussed. Arthur Miller's *Death of a Salesman* in Beijing (1983) and I. M. Pei's new Suzhou Museum (2002–6),
like my key illustrations, involve late-life East-West interaction. Williams, Moore, and Pound stayed in the West to interact with the East.

By contrast Miller and Pei traveled from the United States to China to embrace the East. Unlike the three modernist poets who worked with individual Eastern partners on a one-on-one basis, the playwright and the architect collaborated with whole teams of Chinese professionals on their respective projects.

Admittedly, Arthur Miller's *Death of a Salesman* has very ordinary colloquial dialogue, but it is not a purely realist play. Miller has blended into his realism some expressionist and surrealist qualities. Like Eugene O'Neill's *The Emperor Jones* (1920), *Death of a Salesman* involves the audience emotionally in the audiovisual aspects of its protagonist's dream world. In addition the play presents the protagonist, a character in reality, as constantly vis-à-vis characters in illusion. For his expressionist use of sound and lighting and for his creation of "surreal" characters, Christopher Innes in "Modernism in Drama" refers to Miller as a successor to O'Neill's modernism "disguised beneath a naturalistic surface."[5] *Death of a Salesman,* in Matthew Roudané's view, is "even more inventive" than O'Neill's *The Emperor Jones* or Elmer Rice's *The Adding Machine* (1923). The action of *Salesman,* argues Roudané, "ignores the linear, chronocentric unfolding of time."[6] The 1949 play was revived on Broadway in 1984. Directed by Michael Rudman, it made a hit followed by a 1985 television version directed by Volker Schlöndorff. The gravity of the 1984 *Salesman* and its 1985 TV version is hardly in dispute. But what has been less well understood is the importance of the 1983 production of *Salesman* in Beijing directed by Miller himself and starring Chinese actor Ying Ruocheng, best known in the West for his role as Kublai Khan in the 1982 NBC miniseries *Marco Polo.*

The 1984 and 1985 productions of *Salesman,* with Dustin Hoffman in the title role, may be awe-inspiring, but as far as the playwright's own development of theatrical expressionism and surrealism is concerned, neither version of the classic American drama can be compared with the 1983 *Salesman* in Beijing. In 1978 Arthur Miller made his first visit to China where he came to know Ying Ruocheng (英若誠, 1929–2003) from the Beijing People's Art Theatre (BPAT). The two artists met again in New York City in 1982. It was decided then that Ying was to translate *Salesman* into Chinese and that Miller was to direct a BPAT production of it based on Ying's translation. Intense collaboration between the American playwright and a Chinese cast led by Ying began in March 1983. Modernist strategies such as concurrent display of present and past actions and expressionist use of sound and lighting were at the time still new to most Chinese theater artists. Miller had never worked harder than he did that spring. For over six weeks, as his log, published as *Salesman in Beijing* in 1984, reveals, the sixty-eight-year-old American playwright and director spent all mornings and evenings in the daily routine of rehearsals, "cajoling, educating and finally electrifying" the BPAT cast and crew into an understanding of his modern American drama.[7]

On the very first day of rehearsal Miller told the cast through an interpreter that their stepping over the line that stood for the wall of the kitchen on the set would signal their entry into the confounded mind of Willy Loman, an unsuccessful traveling salesman and a self-deluded victim of false American values.[8] This remark baffled the cast and the crew present, for although they had read Ying's Chinese version of his script, none had paid sufficient attention to his opening stage directions, whose fourth paragraph indicates: "Whenever the action is in the present the actors observe the imaginary wall-lines, entering the house only through its door at the left. But in the scenes of the past these boundaries are broken, and characters enter or leave a room by stepping 'through' a wall onto the forestage."[9]

One key to the success of any *Salesman* production concerns a set onstage that filters through Willy's brain confusing past and present. The technical issues of such a set were resolved by Elia Kazan and Jo Mielziner, the director and set designer of the original *Salesman*. In 1983 Miller worked as closely with Han Xiyu and Fang Kunlin, the BPAT set designer and lighting engineer, as he did with Kazan and Mielziner in 1949. A mock-up of the 1949 set that Han Xiyu and his assistants had created looked the same. But the same, in Wittgenstein's view, is never quite the same.[10] Each duplicate of the original is bound to have what Marcel Duchamp calls the *infrathin,* or difference barely noticeable to the layman.[11] Miller instantly discerned that the stairway supposed to be on the left was placed on the right. Han insisted that by moving the stairway to the right the Lomans' master bedroom and kitchen would appear closer to the audience. But Miller suspected that his change was simply intended to put his own stamp on the set.[12]

If the reversal of the Loman house layout in Han's set did not impress anyone, his solution to the mechanism that allowed the actors portraying Willy Loman's sons, Biff and Happy, to exit from their upstairs beds unseen and reappear from the wing sixteen years younger in a memory sequence really pleased Miller. In the original production, as Miller recalls, a winch that was supposed to lower the two beds on platforms (concealed by bedcovers) often got stuck, resulting in embarrassing situations. At Miller's suggestion, Han created two hinged slabs that could be inclined to let the actors secretly slide down into the space beneath the stage. The mechanism, really a product of Miller's collaboration with Han, made a difference to the first memory scene in act 1. On the opening night, when Biff and Happy emerged as teenagers from the wing to the cue of Willy speaking through the wall of the kitchen, "Just swingin' there under those branches, Boy, that would be . . . ," the audience was enthralled, wondering if four actors might be playing Biff and Happy, two as the thirtysomething Loman brothers and two as Willy Loman's subjective, imaginary projections of them in their teenage days.[13]

In 1949 Mielziner contrived a lighting program that magically displayed the salesman's house onstage sometimes in "an angry glow of orange" and sometimes "covered with leaves," as required by Miller's stage directions.[14] To repeat the 1949 Broadway success, Miller invited Fang Kunlin, his BPAT lighting collaborator, to try "flooding the stage with the shadows of leaves to indicate that Willy has made the mental leap into the past."[15] The playwright-director was doubtful that Fang would meet his challenge. What he did not know was that the use of lighting to project a character's inner thoughts was not really new to Fang. In the previous year he had collaborated with director Lin Zhaohua on Nobel laureate Gao Xingjian's first experimental play, *Signal Alarm*. Gao Xingjian, then also a BPAT member, had similarly invited Fang to use lighting and sound effects to designate his central character's entry into memories and imaginings.[16] The 1982 BPAT production of *Signal Alarm* "with its bold slicing of space and shuttling in time," according to Henry Zhao, captivated its audiences.[17] Despite what Miller called "the damned primitiveness of their lighting equipment," Fang, "through means invented by himself," solved all the difficult problems and triumphed in bringing out "the effect of light filtering through the leaves of two elms." Miller, overjoyed with the brilliant result, admitted that Mielziner, along with Kazan and himself, "never really succeeded with this in the original New York production, which was in every other respect a scenic triumph." Fang's contribution "really gave a sense of sunlight through the branches and dense leaf structures of a great tree."[18]

Miller worked more tirelessly with the cast in an effort to re-create his 1949 masterwork. Elsewhere I have discussed how he guided Zhu Lin as Linda to perform in the funeral scene "with real feeling and poignancy."[19] Here I want to focus on his endeavor with BPAT support-ing actors to reimagine three surreal characters—Ben, Biff, and Willy's Woman in Boston. The actor Zhong Jiyao, who played Ben, took it for granted that he was to play a ghost. He was confused when told to play Ben as in Willy's daydreams. He remained clueless until Ying explained in plain Chinese that Ben "simply voices Willy's thoughts," sometimes expressing Willy's regret not to have gone to Alaska with him and sometimes articulating Willy's false pride in bringing a fortune to Biff by self-destruction.[20] This was not the only time Ying helped Miller out of a dilemma in directing *Salesman* in Beijing, which led him to call Ying "my rock, a man of double consciousness, Eastern and Western, literary and show business."[21]

Miller found the actors Li Shilong and Zhong Jiyao, who played Biff and Ben, being too stiff in their rehearsal of a daydream combat scene. When in China in 1978 he and his wife, Inge Morath, watched a Beijing opera performance of *The Women Generals of the Yang Family* and a Kun opera performance of *The White Snake*.[22] For Miller Kun opera was "more lyrical than Peking opera and more of a chamber piece."[23] Re-calling the acrobatics of *The White Snake*'s second act, where "the her-oine [was] attacked by spears thrown from *four directions simultaneously*" and neither she nor the spear throwers were hit, Miller felt that the BPAT actors might pick up something from the way traditional Chi-nese operas depicted violence onstage.[24] So he made a point of clarify-ing his intention to portray Willy's imagining of a supernatural power Ben had over young Biff and reminded them of "the marvelous cho-reography of the Beijing opera battles, where nobody loses his aplomb, nobody is actually hit, and yet the effect of battle is amply produced."[25] Hearing this, Li Shilong and Zhong Jiyao both winked knowingly at him. Li as Biff instantly did some fist smacks in the air, and Zhong as Ben returned with a few gestural blows in a Beijing opera style, which brought the boy down on his back only to turn around and face Ben's umbrella pointing at his eyes. These acrobatic movements curiously succeeded in producing an impression of flash and otherworldliness, a physical realization of Willy's floating daydream onstage.

An even more telling example of how East-West exchange ener-gized the renewal of innovation in *Salesman* in Beijing involved the actress Liu Jun, who played the Woman in Boston. Willy's reverie of the woman is triggered first in act 1 by Linda calling him "the hand-somest man in the world," and then in act 2 by the giggling of a cheap, common girl with whom Happy is flirting in a New York chophouse scene. According to Miller's log, instead of following his direction, Liu Jun "invented all her business."[26] She "enters Willy's memory of the fateful night when Biff discovered him with her, in a baroque fashion that would be on the very verge of the intolerable by conventional New York standards. On her line 'Whyn't you have another drink, honey, and stop being so damn self-centered?' she slowly circles him as in a dream, offering a drink with a long white silk shawl flowing over her back and outstretched arms."[27]

All this appeared so "un-American" to Miller at first that he almost decided to reject it. But that night he took another look at her lines in his script and realized that he "indeed had originally intended a hallucinatory surrealism which had somehow gotten lost in the various productions, including the original."[28] An actor as a primary collaborator could refine, enrich, or mess about with a playwright's or a director's character. In Liu Jun's case, her seemingly contorted re-creation of the Woman in Boston, that is, her deliberate slow circling united with the ritual unfolding of a self-introduced white silk shawl to produce a single surrealist impression, happens to have rescued Miller's originally intended effect lost in all his play's previous productions.

Was Liu Jun's Woman in Boston mimicking Mei Lanfang dancing the dance of Yang Guifei (Yang Kue Fei) in *The Drunken Beauty,* spinning while singing "tonight as in a dream, seeing the jade rabbit ascending in the east"? Or was she with the long white chiffon draped across her back and down her arms copying Mei Lanfang dancing the dizzying sword dance of Lady Yu in *Farewell My Concubine?* Like other veteran BPAT actors, Liu Jun had done Beijing opera—it was part of their training. In her performance she no doubt brought in certain Beijing opera elements. Beijing opera was first introduced to the West in the 1930s. The great Chinese opera singer-actor Mei Lanfang toured New York and Los Angeles in 1930 and Berlin and Moscow in 1935. As Xiaomei Chen has pointed out, his anti-mimetic but convincing portrayals of female characters had an impact on Constantin Stanislavsky, Gordon Craig, Bertolt Brecht, and Sergei Eisenstein.[29] Speaking of Mei Lanfang and these Western theater artists, Georges Banu asserts, "Mei Lanfang was living proof that the actor they envisioned could exist. What is the theatre if not the incarnation of the invisible in a corporate body? The Chinese actor was the crystallization of their visionary spirit."[30]

For Yeats, as Christopher Innes notes, "the least representational mode of performance" is the dance.[31] In 1915–16 the Irish poet and playwright discovered his model in Michio Itō's Noh-like dance with a style of theater "close to pure music . . . that would free [the stage] from imitation."[32] Beijing opera and Noh drama share a tendency both to resist realism and to unite theatrical elements (costumes, props, dance, and so on) into a single perception, which coincides with the modernist passion for nonrepresentation and internal unity. In Beijing opera Brecht identifies an ideal illustration of his concept of "alienation effects." Brecht first introduces the concept "alienation effects" in an essay, "Alienation Effects in Chinese Acting" (1936), in which he describes the notion as "playing in such a way that the audience was hindered from simply identifying itself with the characters in the play."[33] John Willet who translated and edited the essay explains, "a penciled note on the typescript (Brecht-Archive 332/81) says: 'This essay arose out of a performance by Mei Lan-fang's company in Moscow in spring 1935.'"[34] In Brecht's view Mei Lanfang's "A-effect is a transportable piece of technique; a conception that can be prised loose from the Chinese theatre."[35] Miller and his BPAT collaborators implemented that insight. By incorporating elements of Beijing opera, they succeeded in creating "A-effects" in *Salesman*'s reverie sequences, thus remaking *Salesman,* or in Stein's words, rendering it "something else."[36]

The success of *Salesman* in Beijing excited Miller into new creativity in the mid-1980s. In 1984, before the Rudman-Hoffman revival of *Salesman* on Broadway was over, he published *Salesman in Beijing,* with photographs by Inge Morath, documenting the East-West collaborative enterprise with specifics that would otherwise have fallen into oblivion. In 1985 the Dustin Hoffman stage version of *Salesman* was produced for television. Then 1987 witnessed the publication of Miller's autobiography *Timebends: A Life.* Both the 1984 and 1985 productions of *Salesman* benefited from his presence at their rehearsals. Volker Schlöndorff in 1985, if not Michael Rudman in 1984, could also have read Miller's *Salesman in Beijing* with a remarkable account of Liu Jun's lyrical portrayal of the Woman in Boston. Its effect is reproduced in Volker Schlöndorff's second hotel scene, in which Biff (John Malkovich) crumbles in agony as his adolescent esteem for Willy vanishes. In Christian Blockwood's documentary of the stage-to-screen process, Miller appears a foot away from Schlöndorff when the second Boston hotel scene is shot. Two words he whispers into Schlöndorff's ear are "slow motion."[37] The woman, played by Kathryn Rossetter, shows up not in a black slip as required by Miller's 1949 stage directions but in a white chemise. Hearing repeated knocks at the door, Willy, played by Dustin Hoffman, thrusts into her hands a matching long-sleeve kimono-style robe while pushing her into the bathroom. The white satin robe she flings over her back when exiting the bathroom makes us think of Liu Jun's self-introduced white scarf. Just as Liu Jun's woman spins eerily with her white shawl down her arms, Kathryn Rossetter's woman circles around surrealistically with her white robe over her back to fall into Willy's bed. All is captured by Schlöndorff's cameraman, in Marilyn Ferdinand's words, in "slow motion in a POV shot of Biff watching [it] . . . suggesting an image in Biff's mind rather than what probably happened."[38]

Subsequent revivals of *Salesman* have paid no less attention to "alienation effects" in their memory sequences. It has become customary for the Woman in Boston to dance a bit as in a dream in the second hotel room scene. Molly Price playing that part in Mike Nichols's 2012 *Salesman,* for instance, did "a poignantly hapless shimmy" while giggling shrilly, which was at once reminiscent of the seductive ragtime sway, Mei Lanfang's dance in *The Drunken Beauty,* and Liu Jun's slow turns in *Salesman* in Beijing.[39]

Ieoh Ming Pei (b. 1917) is widely accepted as the last modernist in the art of architecture. His modernism blends the accomplishments of several pioneering masters of modernist design—Frank Lloyd Wright (1867–1959), Le Corbusier (1887–1965), and Walter Gropius (1883–1969). His first success, the National Center for Atmospheric Research (NCAR) in Boulder, Colorado (1961–67), echoes Wright's Taliesin III, which James O'Gorman calls "not a mere building but an entire environment in which man, architecture and nature form a harmonious whole."[40] Pei's Camille Edouard Dreyfus Chemistry Building at Massachusetts Institute of Technology (1964–70), simple and smooth in white concrete and glass, is reminiscent of the Swiss-French architect Le Corbusier, whose lectures on modernism at MIT are remembered by Pei as "the most important days in my architectural education."[41] His tendency to unite sculpture, painting, and foliage with architecture by and of itself is characteristic of the Bauhaus, the German laboratory of twentieth-century modernism, whose founder Walter Gropius and faculty member Marcel Breuer were his professors at Harvard Graduate School of Design.[42]

Because of Pei's openness to new ideas, Jacqueline Kennedy in 1964 chose him over such masters as Ludwig Mies van der Rohe and Louis Kahn to be the designer of the John F. Kennedy Library in Massachusetts. "He didn't seem to have just one way to solve a problem," Kennedy said. "He seemed to approach each commission thinking only of it and then develop a way to make something beautiful."[43] Nearly two decades later, for the same reason, French president François Mitterrand stood firm against objection to his selection of Pei as the renovator of the Grand Louvre, resulting in Pei's famous glass-and-steel pyramid, a new landmark in Paris.

Throughout his long career, Pei never shifted away from modernism, not even during the 1970s and 1980s when *modernism* became an unsung word. In the late 1970s, Philip Johnson, formerly a fellow modernist, abandoned modernism to embrace postmodernism. Ironically, Johnson's postmodernist AT&T Building (now the Sony Building) in New York City (1978–82) failed to please the American public as much as Pei's National Gallery of Art East Building in Washington, DC (1968–78), characterized by a humanized modernism.[44]

I. M. Pei's case of East-West exchange is far more complex than those of the other modernists. On the one hand, as a Chinese American he does not have to cross a tremendous cultural boundary to meet the East. It is not so surprising that he came to his ancestral home with a Chinese imagination. On the other hand, Pei left China in 1935 when he was eighteen. Having lived in the United States for over six decades, he no longer qualifies as a local Chinese. He has not completely lost touch with the cultural identity of his ancestors, but he more strongly identifies with the Western culture than with contemporary Chinese culture. To catch up with China today he too needs to interact with it via interlocutors from there, that is, with local Chinese people "defined by language, history, place, and tradition."[45] His interaction with China is somewhat different from his fellow modernists'. While other modernists' interaction with China involves concepts jarringly foreign, his is basically a process of refreshing memories of Chinese concepts or of updating old Chinese concepts. Whether it is to learn things vastly foreign or to relearn things forgotten, his fellow modernists' aspiration and his aspiration are the same: to re-initiate creativity and revitalize modernism.

Pei had an opportunity to interact with local Chinese in 2002–6 when he designed the new Suzhou Museum. Suzhou, one hundred miles northeast of Shanghai, is Pei's ancestral home. As a teenager he spent summers there learning about Chinese culture at his grandfather's knee and in his family garden, the Grove of Stone Lions, named for a lionlike sculpture there. It was twelve years after his retirement that Pei accepted the Suzhou municipal government's request to design the new Suzhou Museum. This was a job after Pei's own heart. Sixty years earlier at Harvard, Pei had designed for his master's thesis a Shanghai art museum with a stream running through a tea garden, which Gropius pronounced "the finest piece of student work I've ever seen."[46] The Suzhou Museum commission gave Pei an opportunity at once to expand his youthful imagination, "to pay a debt to the culture from which [he] came," and to make amends of an earlier, not completely satisfactory effort to blend Eastern and Western aesthetics.[47] Pei had worked very hard on that earlier project in China—the Fragrant Hill Hotel (1979–82). The four-story luxury hotel in Beijing was unmistakably modern. With moon gates, diamond-shaped windows, and trickling waters, it also evoked ancient Chinese history and culture. Nonetheless, it received less than enthusiastic response. In Pei's mind it was a disappointment.

The new Suzhou Museum was a second chance for Pei, but it also presented some of the toughest challenges. After surveying various spots on the outskirts of Suzhou, Pei and the city officials decided that the most suitable site for the new museum would be in the Old Town district across from a nineteenth-century palace, Prince Zhong's Mansion, and backed against two UNESCO World Heritage Sites, the Garden of the Humble Administrator and the Grove of Stone Lions. The city officials showed Pei great respect, but they set daunting limitations for the commission. While the new museum should be modern, they said, it also had to be designed in the traditional Suzhou style—with white stucco walls and curved tile roofs.[48] Although they wanted ample space to showcase Suzhou's magnificent collection of Chinese art, they also required it to be no more than 52.5 feet high.[49]

Unlike most other architects, Pei views demanding clients as potential collaborators who will challenge him to explore new concepts and forms. "It's a mutual challenge," he once said, "I challenge the client, of course. You have to. But they challenge me."[50] Speaking of his exchanges with atmospheric scientists for NCAR, Pei acknowledged, "I would not have been able to create a building of those articulated forms were it not for their special requirements."[51] Are the city officials the only people Pei thinks of as his collaborators? Pei's biographers have not emphasized enough his ability to listen to local experts' opinions and to pool their wisdom. A May 1, 2002, news report by Wang Jun entitled *Bei Yuming zhaokai dashihui* or "Pei Meeting Local Masters" reveals that right after the selection of the museum site Pei met with Chinese designing gurus to discuss optional solutions to the commission's thorny issues. Some suggestions made by the local experts coincided with Pei's thoughts while others inspired more ambitious ideas, turning a single master's project into a collaborative pursuit.[52]

According to the news report, on April 29, 2002, merely three days after his eighty-fifth birthday, Pei traveled with his wife, Eileen, and two architect sons, Chien Chung and Li Chung, to Suzhou to sign a contract with the Suzhou municipal government. At a meeting on the afternoon of April 30 he announced to half a dozen top Chinese experts his new building project in the very neighborhood of his ancestral home and solicited their opinions.[53] Among the invited were architects Wu Liangyong, Zhang Kaiji, Qi Kang, and Chen Wei, urban planner Zhou Ganshi, and archeologist Luo Zhewen. Present on the occasion were also mayor of Suzhou Yang Weize and other city leaders.[54]

Ninety-year-old Zhang Kaiji, the designer behind the Diaoyutai State Guest House and other Beijing landmark structures, surprised other local experts by criticizing the city leaders before the meeting began. "These creamy towers are so out of place here," he grumbled. "I don't remember who said it, but a great city depends on its skyline and color code. These towers viewed from afar dampen my spirit. They give one the impression that Suzhou leaders do not have good taste." "You mean this conference center?" Zhou Ganshi gave away Zhang's oblique criticism of the very building in which they were meeting.

Pei arrived on time with his wife, two sons, and city leaders. After greeting the local experts, he came directly to the point, inviting them to offer solutions to his commission's predicaments—the cramped space (less than a hectare between three historic structures) and conflicting demands (to be contemporary and in the traditional Suzhou style).

As a former vice president of the International Union of Architects (IUA) and as Pei's old friend, Wu Liangyong spoke first. "If any other master from abroad was to take up this commission, I would have worries," he said, "for his or her lack of knowledge of China, lack of knowledge of Suzhou, but with I. M. I am put at my ease." Having said this he put forward some practical suggestions. "I. M. ought to have access to all our data about the museum's art holdings and exhibition plans. Any delay in giving such data would be a drag on his design. I have inspected the site. The space is narrow. Some facility could of course be built underground, but with high water table in Suzhou, there would be other problems."

If Wu's suggestions were too general, urban planner Zhou Ganshi

tried to be more specific. "Since the museum's height must be con-
trolled and its area cannot extend beyond its neighbors, the only solution seems to go underground. Not only would the museum need
underground space for auditorium, administration, storage, and restora-
tion lab, but it would need passageways underneath leading to neighboring Prince Zhong's Mansion, Garden of the Humble Administrator, and Grove of Stone Lions. Or there would be traffic headaches in
the future."[55] In reference to the requirement to be both modern and
in the traditional Suzhou style, he suggested using high-tech material
but sticking to the Suzhou color code—black, white, and gray. Luo
Zhewen, an expert on historical Chinese architecture, concurred with
Zhou. Taking his cue from Zhou's recommendations, he stressed, "the
new Suzhou Museum should be modern and in the traditional Suzhou
style, that is, not tall, not large, and not conspicuous, fitting well into its
environment."[56]

When it was Zhang Kaiji's turn to speak, he referred to the Louvre
Pyramid. "To provoke the French pride in their history and culture.
What courage! With convincing result, you've brought honor to Chinese architects. Old as I am I would like to be your student."[57] Zhang
was not trying to flatter Pei. He was alerting him to hurdles ahead and
encouraging him to get over them as he did with the Louvre challenge.

The two younger architects, Qi Kang and Chen Wei, spoke last. Qi
Kang, known for his design of the Nanjing Massacre Memorial Hall,
showed the older masters a drawing he had prepared, which revealed
a museum complex with higher structures at its southwestern corner
and lower structures at its northeastern corner. "Trees can be planted in
the open spaces between the single-story buildings in the northeastern
area," he clarified. "This would make it a garden-style museum." Chen
Wei, a professor of architecture at Southeastern University in Nanjing,
supported Qi Kang's suggestion. Quoting a line from Southern Tang
poet Li Yu, "Ascending the West Tower alone," she pointed out that
the west tower had a special place in the traditional Chinese architecture and landscape gardening.[58] The new Suzhou Museum happened
to be west of Prince Zhong's Mansion and the Garden of the Humble
Administrator. "From a higher point in the museum complex," she
said, "visitors should be able to enjoy a good view of the neighboring
nineteenth-century palace and sixteenth-century World Heritage garden."[59] "Heavily influenced by the aesthetics of landscape painting," as
Li Zehou summarizes, Chinese architecture typically seeks to "bring

the human and natural worlds closer together by 'naturalizing' artificially designed grounds."[60] Qi Kang's garden-style museum idea stemming from this tradition clearly appealed to Pei, who has a reputation for the expansive use of space for gardens and leisure. As Anya Dunaif reminds us, in the early 1950s Pei had already designed Colorado's first skyscraper, Mile High Center, with "only one quarter [for] the building site" and "the remaining acreage . . . for gardens and fountains."[61]

Pei thanked all for their recommendations. He conceded that this would most probably be his last and most challenging commission. "I hope I shall have a plan in six months. By then I shall return to Suzhou. Hope you will all come too." Knowing that Pei liked to compare his various building projects to "daughters," Wu responded, "the new Suzhou Museum, once completed, will be Mr. Pei's youngest and loveliest daughter."[62]

While the BPAT cast and crew were primary collaborators given free hand to influence the production of Miller's *Salesman* in Beijing, the Chinese architects were secondary partners brought in at a select moment to address certain issues. Their optional solutions, as potential cross-cultural interpersonal influence recorded in a witness's report, were to be evaluated and criticized for probable use. In the next six months, therefore, Pei toiled over draft after draft of his design behind closed doors in his sons' midtown Manhattan firm.

As he had promised, in October 2002, Pei, his wife, and two sons returned to Suzhou with a draft plan (figure 16). To make the new Suzhou Museum modern and yet in the traditional Suzhou style, he would keep the city's stucco white walls but replace its curved tile roofs with modern-looking blue-gray granite roofs. With steel and granite roofs it would be easy to open skylights to let in natural light. There would be two wings of exhibition halls connected to each other by hallways. There would also be a spacious central garden with a large pond, a footbridge, a pavilion, and a rock sculpture. Visitors traversing the great octagonal hall, the exhibit halls, and the hallways could all glance at the large garden through their diamond-shaped or hexagonal windows. Not all the buildings would have two stories, only the great octagonal hall and the west wing of exhibit halls, resulting in two structural heights, 52 feet and 20 feet, calling to mind Qi Kang's suggestion at the April 2002 meeting. To expand the museum's space without breaking the height and boundary limits, the museum would have to hide most support facilities—storage, administration, and resto-

Figure 16. Suzhou Museum Plan, 2002. (© 2017 Pei Partnership Architects)

ration lab—and part of the exhibit space underground. Still some old structures west toward Prince Zhong's Mansion would have to go to make way for the project.

On the day before their departure that fall, the Suzhou Bureau for Culture and Media Communications arranged a Kun opera show of *The Peony Pavilion: An Interrupted Dream* for Pei and his team. As a Kun opera fan, Pei acutely appreciated the leading lady, Wang Fang, singing and acting in the manner of Mei Lanfang. It turned chilly when the performance was over. Everyone urged Mr. Pei to return to his hotel room for an overcoat, but he insisted on getting onto the stage to shake hands with the actors.[63] To Pei the Kun opera and Suzhou architecture shared the same sophisticated tone. The opera thus served in a curious way to access Pei's memory and initiate his creative energy. After his return to New York City, he became less satisfied with his initial draft design. To make the new museum lovelier and more expressive, he toiled over additional drafts for another six months. Not only were bamboos added to the central garden and water lilies to its pond, but the rock sculpture was made more intricate and alluring.[64]

Pei's Louvre Pyramid was viewed by some French architects as a potential eyesore before it was accepted as a new Paris icon. His Bank of China Tower in Hong Kong stirred up a spell of fear for bad feng shui that lasted several years. Likewise, after Pei's Suzhou Museum plan was unveiled, a whirlwind of protests swept Suzhou. Among those critical of the plan was deputy chief architect Huang Wei of the Suzhou Bureau for Landscape Gardening. He took issue with the new museum's location. "How can we expand the museum into the west garden of Prince Zhong's Mansion? This is to defile one of Suzhou's treasures, the only well-preserved palace of the short-lived Taiping Heavenly Kingdom (1851–1864)."[65] "Save Prince Zhong's Mansion" and "Save Suzhou's Heritage Site" made headlines in some Nanjing and Shanghai newspapers. Professor Lin Yuanxiang of Shanghai Jiaotong University, a consultant on the National World Heritage Research Committee, was moved to call upon the Suzhou municipal government to reject this plan.[66]

The Suzhou municipal government stood firm with Pei. On September 14, 2003, Mayor Yang Weize spoke to the Singapore media. "No architect is more qualified than Mr. Pei for the design of our new museum. Not only is he a world-renowned master of modern architecture, but he is originally from Suzhou. With perfect knowledge of Suzhou's history and culture, he will do everything within his power to protect our heritage," he assured the journalists.[67] The buildings to be vacated were a former hospital and a former daycare center. The Prince Zhong's Mansion was hastily erected right before the downfall of the Taiping Heavenly Kingdom. In 1877, a wealthy family from Shandong bought its designated west garden and built on it their dynastic temple and shelter for the destitute. In the 1950s these were replaced by the red-brick buildings of the hospital and the daycare center, an eyesore to the surviving Prince Zhong's Mansion.[68] It was after repeated deliberations that the city authorities approved the removal plan. A garden-style museum would become an integral part of the nineteenth-century mansion, whereas the hospital and the daycare center in the 1950s style would forever stand out of place among the historic structures. Thanks to the unfailing support of the Suzhou municipal government, the groundbreaking took place as scheduled in November 2003. In the summer of 2004, during the twenty-eighth session of the World Heritage Committee held in Suzhou, UNESCO World Heritage Center director Francesco Bandarin personally inspected the construction site. To the Xinhua News Agency, he said: "To build a new museum across from Suzhou's World Heritage Sites is a good thing. It shouldn't bring any problem to Suzhou's historic gardens and structures," thus putting an end to the objections of a few local experts.[69]

Two and a half years later, as the project progressed to its final phase, the Peis made a fourth excursion to Suzhou. Pei and his two sons personally selected the trees, shrubs, and rocks used in the museum complex. The rockscape in the central garden had special meaning for Pei. In his favorite Kun opera, *The Peony Pavilion,* the protagonist Du Liniang dreams of strolling in her parents' garden with a handsome young scholar, admiring peonies. Curiously, she becomes lovesick and gradually succumbs to it. Before death she says that she wishes to be buried in the garden with a self-portrait hidden beneath a rock. Three years later, on his visit to the garden the young scholar in Du Liniang's dream discovers Du Liniang's portrait as the rock crumbles. He digs up her grave and brings her back to life. To evoke the setting and the sentiment of the opera, Pei had thinly cut dark-colored rocks shipped in from northern China to be laid by the pond and against a garden wall. When asked why he did not use the local Taihu stone or the limestone he had used in his Fragrant Hill Hotel, he explained that his "aim was to replace with original materials and the skill of local craftsmen, the ancient Chinese landscape paintings in a freshly modern Suzhou style garden."[70]

"To bring the human and natural worlds closer together," Pei, like his Chinese predecessors, used "such ingenious methods as 'borrowing scenes' and 'combining the real with the imaginary.'"[71] As a result, visitors are permitted to stroll at their leisure every now and then in the gardens, which Li Zehou views as spaces "used to produce a sense of clear, harmonious and practical values," and Anya Dunaif, who actually spent an afternoon there, appreciates as "spots for quiet contemplation and achieving harmony with nature."[72]

On October 8, 2006, the Mid-Autumn Festival, a day for the reunion of Chinese families, the new Suzhou Museum finally opened. Pei showed up again with his wife, children, and grandchildren in his ancestral home to celebrate both the Mooncake Day and the birth of his "youngest and loveliest daughter." On that day people from everywhere in the world swarmed to admire the city's newest monument. The 160,000-square-foot museum "has many of the hallmarks of Mr. Pei's earlier designs," observed *New York Times* reporter David Barboza, "his squares, rectangles and pyramids—as well as an expansive use of glass and light. It also has traditional motifs, like a large Chinese garden with an artificial pond, a Chinese footbridge and a wall of thinly sliced rocks that yields an image of a series of mountain peaks against an older, whitewashed garden wall."[73] In the new Suzhou Museum, Pei's very late triumph, we shall find to our amazement what Adorno found in late Beethoven—the evidence of "lateness and newness next to each other by virtue of an 'inexorable clamp that holds together what no less powerfully strives to break apart.'"[74]

Pei has been too modest to claim a breakthrough made at age eighty-nine, but he made one. Think of his earlier successes—the John F. Kennedy Library, the National Gallery of Art East Building, the Grand Louvre, the Bank of China Tower in Hong Kong, and the Shinji Shumeikai Bell Tower in Shiga, Japan (1988–1990). The new Suzhou Museum appears to be dwarfed by them all, but none of the earlier projects can be compared with the Suzhou Museum in architectural integration of the garden into the building envelope. For Pei, who has acknowledged Laozi as an influence on his thinking, building as *yin* (the female half of the Tao) and garden as *yang* (the male half of the Tao) are most suitably integrated into each other.[75] The new Suzhou Museum has proven for the first time the modernity and vivacity of an architectural concept, pointing toward a new type of architecture in the world's second largest economy.

Here all the design details are, in Pound's words, "charged with meaning."[76] Some of its features are not immediately appreciated, though. The octagonal great hall with its eight corners points to eight directions, welcoming visitors from all around the globe. The diamond-shaped and hexagonal windows reveal scenes of bamboos, pines, wisteria, and pond as if depicted in Song dynasty framed albums. The water outdoors and indoors imitates canals and lagoons crisscrossing Suzhou, "the Venice of the East" in Marco Polo's description. The rock sculpture against a whitewashed garden wall at once suggests an abstract landscape painting in Song master Mi Fu's style and the theme of the Kun opera *The Peony Pavilion*.

In 2014, eight years after its opening, architect and critic Rachna Kothari revisited the new Suzhou Museum to reassess its place in contemporary architecture and found "a haven of satisfying, experiential spatiality," a new architectural code in China, "replacing the current frenzy of instant spectacle." In contrast to Pei's earlier triumph, the Grand Louvre, which "asserts itself in counterpoint to the old," she wrote, "the design of the Suzhou Museum aims to establish a new paradigm of contemporary contextualism." Located in a nineteenth-century palace and adjacent to two World Heritage gardens, "the museum draws directly from this rich contextual repository."[77] The new Suzhou Museum with all Pei's designing characteristics has in an ostensible fashion departed radically from his past accomplishments.

Since his retirement in 1990, Pei has accepted only commissions outside the United States. In his eighties and nineties, the "Mandarin of Modernism" (Michael Cannell's phrase) continues to work on projects of consequence. Only in countries other than the United States will he be able to bring out works of consequence. This is a lesson he first learned from the Grand Louvre. After the Grand Louvre, Pei told himself, "Let's learn about the world."[78] He knows that he will face more challenges working in other countries, but he also knows that tackling challenges is a way to initiate the renewal of creativity. The Suzhou government officials' requirements might be excessive. Pei's Chinese colleagues' recommendations might be overambitious. The Kun opera singers might have conveyed too complex a motif for him to inject into his commission. Ironically, however, the stringent challenges worked in Pei's advantage, pushing him to innovate and break new ground. Without the exchanges and without the challenges, there would have been no breakthrough in the new Suzhou Museum. What is Pei's secret to late-life creativity and success then? Isn't it more or less the same as Williams's, Moore's, and Pound's secret to their old-age renewal of early twentieth-century modernism? Certainly they share a sustained interest in interacting with other worlds, exploring alien or forgotten concepts—minimalism, nonmimesis, "wholeness of Heaven and Earth," balance of yin and yang, and so on—and making them new.

"Tedium and Integrity
in Poetry" by
Marianne Moore

The following is a transcription of Moore's lecture as recorded at Mills College in Oakland, California, on October 16, 1957.

Tonight our topic is "Tedium and Integrity." How are we going to express it, a creative principle? It should in any case be the opposite of the uninstructed teaching the lesson, the unnecessary. It should be the initiate making explicit the intangible. Now, what kind of poetry is not tedious? What is tedium? One of my compositions is entitled "Poetry," and I said, "I, too, dislike it." What do I mean by that? I mean that we dislike manner for matter, shadow for substance, and ego for rapture. Then, tedium: Is tedium in art a crime? I would say, rather, a contradiction in terms. I trapped myself when I gave that piece of work the title that I gave it. It gave the impression that I was going to define poetry. I did that again in my, rather disjointedly, commentary called "Marriage." It's just a little anthology that might have been called . . . I don't know what it could be called except that . . . This is habitual, thank you, this is habitual of me, because I did the same thing when in desperation about too awkward a title for something I'd written, I called it "Style." I might have chosen "Symmetry" or "The Principle of Bonds." I recall a lecture by Mrs. Jane Berenson about design, in which she illustrated the statement that design involves an understanding of the diagonal or the principle of bonds. They are not all counterparts to one another, but the principle of conversation is counter to all. In music we have restatement after contrast, and it is only recently that we've had our isometric wholes and feet longer than a leg. And when I deplored poetry, I was objecting to what, in poetry, was tiresome to me. And when I applied the word *style* to a certain kind of dancing that I was commending, I was commending what I liked. And the moral was: it's very profitable, I feel, when we say painting centers much less on seeing the real world than on making of it another world. Maybe I should say that again. Painting centers much less on seeing the real world than on making of it another world. All things visible serve style, he said. Now far from being blight, poetry makes exciting what did not exist until sensibility and imagination created it, I feel. Now the point of this little exegesis is that in referring to what embodies a vision, we should use precise terms and not words which are discrepant. *Discrepant* is not another of those terms, also.

Now, what is integrity? Well, literally, it's uprightness, honesty; it is a thing of which all the parts are there. It has not been touched or diminished but is left whole. It comes from the word *tangle,* "I touch." We think of Dr. Samuel Johnson as a man of integrity. He spoke to the point. Now, Babette Deutsch, in her *Poetry Handbook,* a dictionary of terms that has been published just recently, quotes in the preface as applying to her dictionary what Dr. Johnson said of his. He said, "I cannot hope to satisfy those who are perhaps not inclined to be pleased, since I have not always been able to satisfy myself." Now how is poetry defined in the *Handbook?* Ms. Deutsch says, "Poetry is distinguished by feeling, economy, and resonance of language, by an imaginative power that integrates and intensifies and enhances experience." Now I need to repeat this is all in the *Handbook,* "Poetry often exhibits such formal elements as meter, line, stanza structure." And she quotes William Carlos Williams, "You shall weave for poesy out of such drab trash as this by a metamorphosis, a gaudy sleeve." She also quotes Coleridge, who said, "Meter, worthless or disagreeable by itself, imparts vivacity and spirit to that with which it is combined." For the poet, Babette says, "the poem is a bridge between the world and the self, across which the reader walks for a livelier, wider, or deeper view." I agree with that, and I like this definition of the caesura: "It is a pause not counted in the time." I overestimate all my poems, but I think that it's very poetic indeed to be able to formulate definitions that are compact and that you do not trip over while you're thinking about them. Then she says, or she gives an example of primary and secondary accent as occurring in the same word. "Desolation," Shelley, exactly, "Ah, desolation is a delicate thing." I like that kind of intensity. Now, Ms. Deutsch says, "As Mr. Philip Sidney put it in *The Defense of Poesy,* 'One may be a poet without versing, or versifying, or versify without poetry'"—one of my favorite axioms.

Another book which to me is not tedious is Margaret Lane's *Life* [*sic*] *of Beatrix Potter*—Beatrix Potter who wrote *Peter Rabbit, Squirrel Nutkin,* and others—and I feel that this little book conveys a sense of uncompromising fortitude and inner strength. In what it is said, in what is said of Beatrix Potter, who was a writer, was rarely taken anywhere, and she never went to school. But, as the book says, did not rest as a child, had nothing but a bunch of keys as a plaything. Beatrix Potter had a fascinating grandmother, age seventy-five, to whose conversation she would listen, seated on a crossbar under the table, hidden by the frame. She could surreptitiously listen. But she was exceedingly shy, tongue-tied, and farouche, it's said; on the rare occasions when she found herself in society, her precocious and tenacious memory preserved what she observed, unclouded and unchanged, no leaf too modest, no twig too small for her attention. And she herself, when speaking of Scotland, said, "I cannot remember a time when I did not try to invent pictures and make for myself a fairyland amongst the wildflowers, fungi, animals, woods, and streams." Beatrix and her brother Bertram used to take walks, sometimes as far as an old dollhouse in the foot of the hill, in a stunted wood, where he would ask the caretaker to unlock a particular cover and let him have the little harp that belonged to Mary Queen of Scots. And then there was a column on which was mounted a unicorn's head. So there was no dearth of land, although there was an apparent dearth of anything pleasant or interesting. Also there was a rabbit that was supposed to live in a hutch at the back, and it was generally stretched at ease on the hearth rug. And bats which hung upside down in a parrot cage would come zigzagging across the room and light on one of her fingers. Apparently life consisted of furnished houses, select lodgings, quiet hotels, the barouche, the bath chair, and the promenade. Not quite the setting for art, it would seem, but art doesn't have to have the right setting. Now *Peter Rabbit* was returned, she said, with or without thanks from at least six publishers. So she used savings and published it herself: five inches by four, with one or two sentences on each page, a picture every time you turn the page; one and twopence a copy. Then some ladies came to tea, and she heard from them a curious story of a tailor in Gloucester who left a coat unfinished, cut out but unfinished. And the next day he found it finished, all but one buttonhole, and on a scrap of paper pinned to the fabric, "No more twist." Now in submitting this story of her tailor to the Warrens, 8 Bedford Square, she said, this is really the point of my illustration; she said, "I will go on with it on approval if you are undecided, or for myself if you decline it." Now I consider that the epitome indicative of what a complete writer is.

Beatrix Potter, after earning enough to do it, ran a mixed farm, a small mixed farm, at Sawrey and in time produced these little books, which Margaret Lane says have the shapeliness and texture of perfect lyrics. She says, "Her fidelity to her animal characters is the very strength and sinew of her work. All her little hedgerow, wainscot, and farm animals are conceived in imaginative truth." And in her case, the person and the work, it seems to me, are one.

Now, this whole theme of integrity, for I would like to dispatch tedium for good, was suggested to me by *The Tao of Painting,* edited and with a translation by Mai-mai Sze. It was published by the Bollingen Foundation in 1956, and anything I say that is worth the hearing should be attributed to Ms. Mai-mai Sze. Well, Hsieh Ho, whose six canons of painting were formulated about AD 500, said, "The terms ancient and modern have no meaning in art." And I indeed felt that art is timeless when I saw in the book review section of the *New York Times* last winter, a reproduction of a plum branch, a blossoming branch, entitled "A Breath of Spring."

A shock of felicity is precipitated, I feel, by the sweep of the line, as when in opening a plum, just perchance the fragrance is a blossom. Now Tao, as I'm sure you know, means "way" or "path." As Ms. Sze explains, there is *a* tao and there is *the* Tao. And in Chinese writing, which is pictographic, of course, a tao is a pair of legs, whereas the Tao has legs, arms, and a head—it's a total harmony, from head to foot. Now step-by-step progress requires deliberateness, suggesting that meditation is basic to all living, to all that we do, and that conduct is a thing of inner motivation. As Lieh Tzu said, "To the mind that is still, the whole universe surrenders." Impressive statement: "To the mind that is still, the whole universe surrenders." Now we find exposited in the *Manual,* two important features of Chinese painting: the close relationship between painting and calligraphy. As Ms. Sze, Mai-mai Sze, says, "Writing a Chinese character develops a fine sense of proportion." And a sense of fitness or proportion is prominent in every aspect of Chinese life. This sense of proportion Confucius regarded as one of the five cardinal virtues. Secondly, and this is most valuable I think, the view that painting is not a profession but an extension of the art of living. Usually therefore, painting was an expression of maturity by someone who had lived and experienced things, and a painter was likely to be an astronomer, a musician, a medical man. In acquiring the education prescribed by the Tao of painting, a painter underwent rigorous intellectual discipline, which included training of the memory. So I like this thought, and I believe in it. Authorship in China is integral to education; it's not a separate proficiency to be acquired. It's rather humbling to those of us who spend, devote, a great deal of time to incidental aspects of writing. Chinese philosophy, Ms. Mai-mai Sze observed, might be said to be psychology—a development of the whole personality; and egotism—or what the Buddhists call ignorance—obscures a clear view of the Tao. It is unusual, in my experience at least, to come on a book of verse which has not a tincture of animosity, sarcasm, grievance, or some sense of injury, personal or impersonal—general. And I feel very strongly what Señor Jiménez, the Spanish poet, says in referring to something else to what is not poetry: "There is a profounder profundity" than wistful egocentricity. The *Manual* should serve as a contrast to this, as an ideal that is both universal and practical. Now, the *Manual* demonstrates that painting should be a fusion of that which pertains to heaven, the spirit, and of matter, which pertains to earth, as affected by the painter's insight and skill. And the search for a rational explanation of nature and the universe encouraged the tendency to classification. It became almost a disease; it *could* become a disease when carried to an extreme.

And in China, six canons of painting were formulated, as has been said, about AD 500. The first of these is basic to all and controls all the others, the world of the spirit, *ch'i*. This translation says, in the Cantonese version, it's pronounced "hey." They outdo the English, I think, in mystifying the reader regarding the actual pronunciation of words. And that word *ch'i* suggests exhaling a breath, cognate in meaning to *pneuma* and the Latin *spiritus.*

And the second canon says the brush is the means of creating structure; the ideal takes form. Now, I hope it doesn't sound crazy to some academicians. Is innocence hampered? Spontaneity, the happy result— a happy result was the superb painting of insects, flowers, animals, and birds in Volume II of this treatise. I think the enumeration of the categories, where to find things, how to treat this subject and that, this enumeration really amounts to poetry. They have buds, buds beginning to open, thick leaves that withstand winter, plants with thorns, those with furry leaves, grasshoppers, large grasshoppers, mentioned in that order, crickets, beetles, the praying mantis, small birds fighting while flying, birds upside down, birds shaking off water.

And then the third category, that of verisimilitude, and the fourth, with applying color.

Now, the fifth, about organizing a composition with each element in its rightful place; this applies very closely I think to writing. And one is reminded of André Malraux's statement: "Accidents impair and time transforms, but it is we who choose." That is quite consoling or the opposite: all we have now is illustrations of method and principles to memorize. Drawings, really very beautiful some of them, our "structures of several levels at a distance," angles and nests of roofs and walls and bridges, a lean-to of beanstalks. It says, "If a man has eyes, it's a very beautiful thing, but if a man had eyes all over his body, he would be a monstrosity.... A landscape with people and dwellings in it has life, but too many figures and houses give the effect of a market place." Now this problem of standard and the rightful place indeed applies to writing. Cardinal Newman, oh, in trying to produce this commentary, exactly like Cardinal Newman, in a letter to Mrs. Mosley in 1838. He was trying to explain his attitude to the doctrine of justification. And he said, "I write, I write again, I write a third time, in the course of six months. Then I take the third version; I literally fill the page with corrections, so that another person could not read it. I then write it out fair for the printer and put it by. I take it up; I begin to correct it again—it will not do. So I write it again. I cannot count how many times this process is repeated."

Now perhaps the most important factor in unifying and harmonizing the elements of a picture is space, Ms. Mai-mai Sze says, for herself, not as one of the traditional statements. Space of any kind is regarded not as empty but as filled with meaning. In fact, it is synonymous with the Tao. Hollow trees were not just hollow trees; they are filled with meaning. The space in a wheel, the spaces between the spokes make the wheel, not the spokes or the bars. And it's not a set of walls but the space in a room that is its usefulness.

Now the sixth canon, just to be complete, exhorted the painter, in copying a master, to transmit the essence of the brush and of the master's methods. And I've been studying these selected works of Juan Ramón Jiménez, and I was rather interested in this statement.[1] He said, "Anyone who progresses in one discipline—poetry, for example, religion, art, or science—will inevitably progress in all others, even though not so well versed in others as in his own specialty." I think that's something to think about; I don't know that I believe it.

Now, Chinese painting, thinking, abounds in symbolism, and the circle as a concept of holiness will surely hold a great fascination. Everything must be in relation to the Tao, the center. The Tao is the mark, and the arrow is the soul. And certainly this concept is one of the oldest in Chinese thought and common to all schools. A circle's beginning, its head, and its end, or foot, are the same, unmoving and continually moving. And therefore still life is contrary to the whole concept of Chinese painting. Again, the Tao, the path, lies on the ground and it is still, yet it leads somewhere and so it has movement. So we have an identity of contraries which are not in conflict but are complementary. And then there's a bit again about the yin and yang; that's in my paper, but perhaps you know it, and we haven't time for it. Symbolism, as I said, is a characteristic of Chinese thinking, and as a symbol of the power of Heaven, the dragon, slumbering or winging its way across the heavens, has movement as a main characteristic. At will, it can change, be the size of a silkworm, or swell so large as to fill the heaven and earth, thus representing totality. It has also the gift of invisibility, and of course there are many other symbols, those that we are familiar with, symbols of long life: the peach tree, the pine, and the bamboo as a symbol of elegance. Then there are the four treasures: the brush, ink, the inkstand, and the paper or silk. And that's really fascinating to me; I like that also. The brush may be pointed, rounded, fat, thin, coarse, or fine. Now the illustrations and text of the *Mustard Seed Garden,* the guiding manual of painting, which appeared during the last part of the seventeenth century, by three painters, who were brothers, and their surname was Wang. They were possessed of other names as well, since one may take extra names, courtesy and literary names. This I was thinking: what sensibility, on the part of Ms. Mai-mai Sze, allows it to me, would make this version of the *Manual* enthralling. It's the first concise version in English of the *Manual,* which received its title from the name of a small property near Nanking, the home of the publisher who had built his house and bookstore there, and said, "It occupies only a hillock, hence the name 'mustard seed,' to designate its smallness."

Now I'll read a few poems. Nevertheless, anyone may go out a suitable place. I was asked to read some—no, before I read this, I want to say what I forgot to say last night at Stanford. Pardon me, the editors of the *Sequoia* were really very unusually persevering about my contributing to *Sequoia.* They said they'd be very glad to publish this. They'd heard I was to give a lecture. And I said, well it belonged, it was the property of President White. "Well, we'd be glad to publish it too." "No," I said. And then I thought, and I will say this obligingly, that I thought of this: I was at a party the other night, and a gentleman who seemed to be an expert in every field, we were talking about the Chinese and these symbols, and he said, "O, to be a dragon!" Symbol of the power of Heaven! So I thought there's something.

> If I had, like Solomon . . .
> my wish . . . O to be a dragon,
> of silkworm
> size or immense; at times invisible.
> Felicitous phenomenon!

I don't know if it is a poem, but that's what I sent the girls, and they're using it. Should not be afraid of me, if they didn't like it—I'm used to having more things not liked than liked.

A Face
"I am not treacherous, callous, jealous, superstitious,
superscilious, venomous, or absolutely hideous":
>   studying and studying its expression,
>   exasperated desperation
>   though at no real impasse,
>   would gladly break the glass;[2]

when love of order, ardor, uncircuitous simplicity
[. . .] are all one needs to be![3]
>   Certain faces, a few, one or two—or one
>   face photographed by recollection—
>   to my mind, to my sight,
>   must remain a delight.

Now I have a friend, whose mother attended Mills College and has graduated in 1884, I believe, Josephine Keely, or Josephine Keely Lassell, and I had a little piece addressed to her daughter. I think I'll read this:

The Wood-Weasel

"The Wood-Weasel emerges daintily"—oh I guess I should say, it's an acrostic, and it's very un-public content because each line begins with a small letter and they read upward, and the last name reads upward. But that was discovered by Lord Frankenberg, and he told everybody about it, so I might as well explain it, myself. "The skunk—"' er,

The Wood-Weasel
emerges daintily, the skunk—
don't laugh—in sylvan black and white chipmunk
regalia. The inky thing

adaptively whited with glistening
goat-fur, is wood-warden. In his
ermined well-cuttlefish-inked wool, he is
determination's totem. Out-
lawed? His sweet face and powerful feet go about
in chieftain's coat of Chilcat cloth.
He is his own protection from the moth,

noble little warrior. That
otter-skin on it, the living pole-cat,
smothers anything that stings, Well,—
this same weasel's playful and his weasel
associates are too. Only
Wood-weasels shall associate with me.

The data, the, what do you call it, documentation or what authenticates all this is Dr. Ditmars's *Strange Animals I Have Known,* in which he tells how skunks can eat bees and kill snakes and do most anything, and their long fur protects them from these various enemies, and their accurate paws.

Now somebody that messes with demons was talking about Scarlett Jackson. And I haven't heard this anywhere, but he reviewed one of my books and commended this piece, so it occurred to me that I would do this one. "Bird-Witted." I have to have a little encouragement . . . Well, can't find it. Excuse me. It is called "Bird-Witted"; maybe I've got the wrong page . . . . Yes, thank you, underneath it.

This is—as novelists don't say, this is a true story.

Bird-Witted
With innocent wide penguin eyes, three
    large fledgling mocking-birds below
the pussy-willow tree,
    stand in a row,
wings touching, feebly solemn,
till they see
    their no longer larger
    mother bringing
something which will partially
feed one of them.

Toward the high-keyed intermittent squeak
    of broken carriage-springs, made by

the three similar, meek-
      coated bird's-eye
freckled forms she comes; and when
from the beak
      of one, the still living
      beetle has dropped
out, she picks it up and puts
it in again.

Standing in the shade till they have dressed
      their thickly-filamented, pale
pussy-willow-surfaced
      coats, they spread tail
and wings, showing one by one,
the modest
      white stripe lengthwise on the
      tail and crosswise
underneath the wing, and the
accordion

is closed again. What delightful note
      with rapid unexpected flute-
sounds leaping from the throat
      of the astute
grown bird, comes back to one from
the remote
      unenergetic sun-
      lit air before
the brood was here? How harsh
the bird's voice has become.

A piebald cat observing them,
      is slowly creeping toward the trim
trio on the tree-stem.
      Unused to him
the three make room—uneasy
new problem.
      A dangling foot that missed
      its grasp, is raised
and finds the twig on which it
planned to perch. The

parent darting down, nerved by what chills
    the blood, and by hope rewarded—
of toil—since nothing fills
    squeaking unfed
mouths, wages deadly combat,
and half kills
    with bayonet beak and
    cruel wings, the
intellectual cautious-
ly creeping cat.

And I will say he didn't get one of the baby birds. Now, my favorite, "Silence," I think this will do for my own, and I'll read two fables.

Silence
My father used to say,
"Superior people never make long visits,
have to be shown Longfellow's grave
or the glass flowers at Harvard.
Self-reliant like the cat—
that takes its prey to privacy,
[. . . . .]⁴
they can be robbed of speech
by speech which has delighted them.
The deepest feeling always shows itself in silence;
not in silence, but restraint."
Nor was he insincere in saying, "Make my house your inn."
Inns are not residences.

Well, make me feel a little better about these ventures. Now, my topic, one of them, is "tedium," so I'll read this and one more. Well, "The Scythian Philosopher," and then "The Cat and the Mouse."

Once a philosopher famed for austerity,
Left Scythia that he might taste luxury
And sailed to Greece where he met in his wanderings
A sage like the one Virgil has made memorable—
Who seemed a king or god, remote from mundane things,
Since like the gods he was at peace and all seemed well.
Now a garden enabled his life to expand
And the Scythian found him pruning hook in hand
Lopping here and there what looked unprofitable.

He sundered and slendered, curtailing this and that,
   Careful that not a dead twig be spared;
Then for care to excess, Nature paid a sure reward.
   "But are you not inconsiderate?"
The Scythian inquired. He said, "Is it good
To denude a tree of twigs and leave it scarcely one?
[. . . . .]⁵
   Permit Time to do what needs to be done:
[. . . . .]⁶
The sage said, "Remove sere boughs and when they are gone,
   One has benefited what remain."
The Scythian returned to his bleak shore,
Seized his own pruning hook, was at work hour on hour,
Enjoining upon any in the vicinity
He sheared off whatever was beautiful,⁷
Or that he—Enjoining upon any in the vicinity⁸
   That they work—the whole community.
(There's plenty of those, advisers we have)⁹
He sheared off whatever was beautiful,
Indiscriminately trimmed and cut down,
   Persevering in reduction
   Beneath new moons and full
Till none of his trees could bear.
     In this Scythian
   We have the injudicious man
   Or so-called Stoic, who would restrain
His best emotions along with the depraved—
   Renouncing each innocent thing that he craved.
As for me, such perverted logic is my bane.
Don't smother the fire in my heart which makes life dear;
Do not snuff me out yet, I am not late on my bier.

Now, "The Cat and the Mouse." Now, His Grace the Duke of Burgundy requested of La Fontaine, "Monsieur de La Fontaine, a fable to be called 'The Cat and the Mouse.'" There's nothing so detestable as to write a piece to order, but he seems to have done it.

   Desiring to show a young prince her esteem
     And bow here literarily,
  Fame asks that Cat and Mouse be my theme.
     Cat and Mouse—let me see.

Ought I to portray someone beautiful
And charming, but so sportive and unmerciful
That she tortures the person in captivity
       As cats tease mice they will not free?

Or should I take as my theme the whims of Fate?
Nothing more to the point than demonstrate
How smiling Fortune treats folk contradictorily,
       As cats treat mice they will not free.

[. . . . .]10

But the windings of my thought have imperceptibly
Brought me out where each step I take will be a loss
If I let myself drone on suicidally
And make my Muse a mouse for the young prince to toss,
       Like one the cat pretends to free.

Notes

INTRODUCTION

1. Tyrus Miller, *Late Modernism: Politics, Fiction, and the Arts between the World Wars* (Berkeley: University of California Press, 1999), 5, 10.

2. Anthony Mellors, *Late Modernist Poetics: From Pound to Prynne* (Manchester, UK: Manchester University Press, 2005), 19. See also Robert Ganter, *Late Modernism: Art, Culture, and Politics in Cold War America* (Philadelphia: University of Pennsylvania Press, 2010). In Ganter's book *late modernism* refers to a project of modernism reformulated in the Cold War period (4).

3. The description of modernism is from Michael Levenson, ed., *The Cambridge Companion to Modernism* (Cambridge, UK: Cambridge University Press, 1999), 1; Marjorie Perloff, *21st-Century Modernism* (Oxford: Blackwell, 2002), 3.

4. Christine Froula, "Proust's China," *Modernism/Modernity* 19, no. 2 (2012), 229.

5. On modernism and East Asia (or the Orient), see Sabine Sielke and Christian Kloeckner, eds., *Orient and Orientalisms in US-American Poetry and Poetics* (Frankfurt, Germany: Peter Lang, 2009); Zhaoming Qian, ed., *Modernism and the Orient* (New Orleans, LA: University of New Orleans Press, 2012); and Gao Fen, ed., *Xiandaizhuyi yu dongfang wenhua* (Modernism and oriental culture) (Hangzhou, China: Zhejiang University Press, 2012).

6. See Geneviève Aitken and Marianne Delafond, eds., *La collection d'estampes japonaises de Claude Monet à Giverny* (Paris: La Bibliothèque des Arts, 2003).

7. For reproductions of Kunisada's *Abalone Fishing* in Monet's collection and Monet's *The Pink Skiff*, and a comparison between the two, see Virginia Spate, Gary Hickey, and Claude Monet, *Monet and Japan* (Canberra: National Gallery of Australia, 2001), 135, 104, and 38, respectively.

8. For a reproduction of Hiroshige's *Inside Kameido Tenjin Shrine* in Monet's collection, see Spate, Hickey, and Monet, *Monet and Japan*, 155.

9. For reproductions of two prints in Monet's collection bearing Hayashi's seal (林正忠)—Utamaro's *The Hinodeya Widow* and Hokusai's *Peonies and Butterfly*—see Spate, Hickey, and Monet, *Monet and Japan*, 120 and 131. Hayashi owned Monet's *Rocky Coast and the Lion Rock, Belle-Ile* and *Young Girl in the Garden at Giverny*, both painted in the second half of the 1880s (ibid., 36).

10. See Tadamasa Hayashi, *Histoire de l'art du Japon* (Paris: Maurice de Brunoff, 1901); Tadamasa Hayashi, *Objets d'art du Japon et de la Chine,* 3 vols. (Paris: Les Galeries de MM. Durand-Ruel, 1902).

11. Spate, Hickey, and Monet, *Monet and Japan,* 33.

12. For an example of "one-corner" composition, see Ma Yuan's *Watching the Deer by a Pine-shaded Stream* (gift of Mrs. A. Dean Perry in the Cleveland Museum of Art), reproduced in Zhaoming Qian, *The Modernist Response to Chinese Art: Pound, Moore, Stevens* (Charlottesville: University of Virginia Press, 2003), 102.

13. Monet's set of Hokusai's *One Hundred Views of Mount Fuji* (vols. 1–3) is in the Musée Marmottan. See Aitken and Delafond, eds., *La collection d'estampes japonaises,* 181.

14. Cited in Spate, Hickey, and Monet, *Monet and Japan,* 71.

15. On Southern Song painters' simple colors and fragmentary treatment of nature, see Li Zehou, *The Path of Beauty: A Study of Chinese Aesthetics,* trans. Gong Lizeng (Hong Kong: Oxford University Press, 1994), 192–94.

16. Ronnie Landfield, "Monet and Modernism," http://ronnielandfield.com /monet-and-modernism/.

17. See Ann Temkin and Nora Lawrence, *Claude Monet: Water Lilies* (New York: Museum of Modern Art, 2009).

18. Teresa Larraz, "Monet Face to Face with Abstract Art in Madrid," *Reuters Canada,* February 22, 2010, http://ca.reuters.com/article/idCATRE61L0DH20100222.

19. Clement Greenberg, *Art and Culture: Critical Essays* (Boston: Beacon Press, 1961), 45.

20. Froula, "Proust's China," 229.

21. Perloff, *21st-Century Modernism,* 3.

22. See Edward Said, *On Late Style: Music and Literature against the Grain* (New York: Vintage Books, 2006); Nicholas Delbanco, *Lastingness: The Art of Old Age* (New York: Grand Central Publishing, 2011).

23. Said, *On Late Style,* 43.

24. Fritz Henle, *Casals* (Garden City, NY: American Photographic Book Publishing, 1975), caption to the tenth photograph, n.p.; Delbanco, *Lastingness,* 63, 128.

25. Cited in Jeffrey Kluger, "The Art of Living," *Time,* September 23, 2013, 46.

26. Charles Altieri, *Painterly Abstraction in Modernist American Poetry* (Cambridge, UK: Cambridge University Press, 1989), 7.

27. Tung Wu, *Tales from the Land of Dragons: 1,000 Years of Chinese Painting* (Boston: Museum of Fine Arts, Boston, 1997), 225–26. For a recent discussion of Liang Kai, Muqi, and splash ink technique, see Zhu Liangzhi, *Nanhua Shiliu Guan* (Sixteen views on Chinese literati paintings) (Beijing: Peking University Press, 2013), 286–88.

28. Cristanne Miller, *Cultures of Modernism: Marianne Moore, Mina Loy, and Else Lasker-Schüler* (Ann Arbor: University of Michigan Press, 2007), 149.

29. Zhaoming Qian, *Orientalism and Modernism: The Legacy of China in Pound and Williams* (Durham, NC: Duke University Press, 1995), 2.

30. Hans-Georg Gadamer, *Truth and Method,* trans. Garrett Barden and John Cumming (New York: Seabury Press, 1975), 236.

31. Theodor Adorno, *Aesthetic Theory,* trans. Robert Kenter-Hullot (New York: Continuum, 2002), 28.

32. Ibid., 22.

33. Cited in Ezra Pound, *Gaudier-Brzeska: A Memoir* (New York: New Directions, 1970), 81.

34. Ezra Pound, *Ezra Pound and the Visual Arts,* ed. Harriet Zinnes (New York: New Directions, 1980), 192.

35. Miller, *Cultures of Modernism,* 131.

36. Cited in Kluger, "The Art of Living," 50.

37. Ibid.

38. Perloff, *21st-Century Modernism,* 3.

39. Marjorie Perloff, *The Poetics of Indeterminacy: Rimbaud to Cage* (Princeton, NJ: Princeton University Press, 1981), 151.

40. Hugh Kenner, *A Homemade World: The American Modernist Writers* (Baltimore, MD: Johns Hopkins University Press, 1975), 101.

41. Cited in Paul Mariani, *William Carlos Williams: A New World Naked* (New York: McGraw-Hill, 1981), 751.

42. Ezra Pound and E. E. Cummings, *Pound/Cummings: The Correspondence of Ezra Pound and E. E. Cummings,* ed. Barry Ahearn (Ann Arbor: University of Michigan Press, 1996), 408–10.

43. Robert Lowell visited Pound at St. Elizabeths Hospital in 1947 and 1958. He sent Pound his poems in November 1957. See Paul Mariani, *Lost Puritan: A Life of Robert Lowell* (New York: W.W. Norton, 1994), 156, 259–60, 267. On May 6, 1951, Allen Ginsberg sent Pound two poems, "Ode to the Setting Sun" and an untitled song, seeking advice, to which request Pound does not seem to have responded. For Ginsberg's letter, see "6 May (1951): Allen Ginsberg to Ezra Pound," *The American Reader,* http://theamericanreader.com/6-may-1951-allen-ginsberg-to-ezra-pound/.

44. Ezra Pound, *Selected Prose 1909–1965,* ed. William Cookson (New York: New Directions, 1973), 464.

45. For a discussion of Zukofsky and East Asia, see Richard Parker, "Louis Zukofsky's American Zen," in Qian, ed., *Modernism and the Orient,* 232–48.

46. J. Hillis Miller, *Illustration* (Cambridge, MA: Harvard University Press, 1992), 14–15. For a recent discussion of this topic, see J. Hillis Miller, *An Innocent Abroad: Lectures in China* (Evanston, IL: Northwestern University Press, 2015), 107–14.

47. Ezra Pound, *Ezra Pound's Poetry and Prose Contributions to Periodicals,* eds. Lea Baechler, A. Walton Litz, and James Longenbach (New York: Garland, 1991), 3:99.

48. Cited in Zhaoming Qian, ed., *Ezra Pound's Chinese Friends: Stories in Letters* (Oxford, UK: Oxford University Press, 2008), 106.

49. Marianne Moore, *The Complete Prose,* ed. Patricia C. Willis (New York: Viking, 1986), 255. Further references to this volume will be given parenthetically as *CPr.*

50. Christopher Bush, *Ideographic Modernism: China, Writing, Media* (Oxford, UK: Oxford University Press, 2010), xxx.

51. Ezra Pound, *The Cantos* (New York: New Directions, 1998), 244. Further references to this volume will be given parenthetically as *C.*

52. As Baosun Zeng recalls in her autobiography, *Huiyilu* (Taipei: Longwen, 1989), in April 1928 she visited a former Yifang faculty member, Ms. Madge of Rapallo (98). After moving to Taiwan, Zeng helped found Tunghai University in Taizhong. In April 1957, she traveled to New York City to attend a meeting of the United Nations Committee on Women's Rights. Having learned of her visit, Pound wrote to David Wang: "Do get Miss Tseng's news while she is in N.Y." Wang replied on

May 2, 1957: "Mrs. Pao Swen Tseng has already departed for Formosa." The letters are in the Beinecke Rare Book and Manuscript Library, Yale University. Further references to archival materials in that library will be given parenthetically as Beinecke.

53. In a letter to his father dated May 30, 1928, Pound refers to the source of Canto XLIX as "poems on a set of scenes in Miss Thseng's part of the country." See Qian, ed., *Ezra Pound's Chinese Friends,* 15. In *Huiyilu* Miss Zeng acknowledges having met Pound shortly after Easter in 1928 and "discussed Chinese culture, Chinese poetry, and traditional Chinese ethics" (215).

54. Qian, *The Modernist Response to Chinese Art,* 127.

55. Miller, *Illustration,* 28.

56. *Qi ze* or "seven lakes" occurs in the second paragraph of *Zixu fu* or "*Fu* of Sir Vacuous" by Sima Xiangru (ca. 179–117 BC): "chen wen chu you qi ze, chang jian qi yi" (I have heard of seven lakes in Chu, though I have seen one and not the rest). Chu, as one of the warring state powers in the fourth to third centuries BC, included most of present-day Hubei and Hunan, the provinces north and south of Dongting, China's second largest lake.

57. In Li Bai's "Song of Zhao Yan's Landscape Painting" "seven lakes" occurs juxtaposed with Xiao-Xiang. For a fuller discussion of "seven lakes" in classic Chinese poetry, see Zhaoming Qian, "Why Is Canto XLIX Called the 'Seven Lakes Canto'?" *Paideuma* 43 (2016): 167–174.

58. J. Hillis Miller, *Speech Acts in Literature* (Stanford, CA: Stanford University Press, 2001), 1–5.

59. M. Thomas Inge, "Collaboration and Concepts of Authorship," *PMLA* 116, no. 3 (2001): 629.

60. Richard Badenhausen, *T. S. Eliot and the Art of Collaboration* (Cambridge, UK: Cambridge University Press, 2004).

61. T. S. Eliot, *Selected Prose* (New York: Harcourt Brace, Jovanovich, 1975), 74.

62. Pound, *Gaudier-Brzeska,* 89.

63. Qian, *The Modernist Response to Chinese Art,* 223.

64. The letter is in the Rauner Special Collections Library, Dartmouth College. Further references to materials in that library, courtesy of Dartmouth College Library, will be given parenthetically as Dartmouth.

65. Jack Stillinger, *Multiple Authorship and the Myth of Solitary Genius* (New York: Oxford University Press, 1991), 20.

66. The letter is in the Marianne Moore Collection of the Rosenbach Museum and Library, Philadelphia. Further references to materials in the Rosenbach Museum and Library will be given parenthetically as Rosenbach.

67. The letter is in the private collection of Josephine Fang. Further references to materials in that collection will be given parenthetically as JFC.

68. Cited in Jill Rubalcaba, *I. M. Pei: Architect of Time, Place, and Purpose* (New York: Marshall Cavendish, 2011), 47.

ONE. Williams, Wang, and "The Cassia Tree"

1. Ezra Pound, *Cathay: The Centennial Edition,* ed. Zhaoming Qian (New York: New Directions, 2015), 25.

2. Cited in T. S. Eliot, "Ezra Pound: His Metric and Poetry," in *To Criticize the Critic* (New York: Farrar, Straus, and Giroux, 1965), 180.

3. The letter is in the *Poetry* magazine collection at the University of Chicago's Joseph Regenstein Library.

4. Ezra Pound and William Carlos Williams, *Pound/Williams: Selected Letters of Ezra Pound and William Carlos Williams,* ed. Hugh Witemeyer (New York: New Directions, 1996), 22.

5. Williams's copies of Herbert Giles's *A History of Chinese Literature* and Arthur Waley's *A Hundred and Seventy Chinese Poems* and *More Poems from the Chinese* are kept at the Fairleigh Dickinson University Florham-Madison Campus Library.

6. William Carlos Williams, *The Collected Poems of William Carlos Williams, Volume I, 1909–1939,* eds. A. Walton Litz and Christopher MacGowan (New York: New Directions, 1986), 173. Further references to the volume will be given parenthetically as *CP1.*

7. About the discovery of "To the Shade of Po Chü-i," see Dennis M. Read, "Three Unpublished Poems by William Carlos Williams," *American Literature* 58 (1986): 422–26.

8. Qian, *Orientalism and Modernism,* 144.

9. Perloff, *The Poetics of Indeterminacy,* 152, 153.

10. William Carlos Williams, *Paterson,* ed. Christopher MacGowan (New York: New Directions, 1992), 78.

11. William Carlos Williams, *The Collected Poems of William Carlos Williams, Volume II, 1939–1962,* ed. Christopher MacGowan (New York: New Directions, 1988), 287. Further references to the volume will be given parenthetically as *CP2.*

12. Williams to John C. Thirlwall, June 13, 1955, in William Carlos Williams, *Selected Letters,* ed. John C. Thirlwall (New York: New Directions, 1957), 334.

13. The letter is cited in Mariani, *William Carlos Williams,* 689.

14. Wang Fenggao (1858–1933) was on the Board of Trustees of Guanghua University in the 1920s. In 1938–46 Guanghua relocated its operations to Chengdu, Sichuan province. Its Chengdu campus has become the present-day Southwestern University of Finance and Economics, and its Shanghai campus has become the present-day Donghua University.

15. For selected letters between Ezra Pound and David Wang, 1955–58, see Qian, ed., *Ezra Pound's Chinese Friends,* 172–95.

16. Among the selections in this anthology are eight of David Wang's original poems ("Dynamo," "Quartet for Gary Snyder," "Miracle in Honolulu," "Rivers on Fire," "Portrait of a Failure," "The Rub," "Cool Cat," and "The Lapse"), excerpts from Carlos Bulosan's *America Is in the Heart,* and John Okada's *No-No Boy;* David Hsin-fu Wand, *Asian-American Heritage: An Anthology of Prose and Poetry* (New York: Washington Square Press, 1974).

17. See Hugh Witemeyer, "The Strange Progress of David Hsin-fu Wand," *Paideuma* 15, nos. 2 and 3 (1986): 191–209.

18. Helen Vendler, *The Breaking of Style* (Cambridge, MA: Harvard University Press, 1995), 1.

19. David Wang to Ezra Pound, January 24, 1958 (Beinecke).

20. Ezra Pound to Iris Barry, August 24, 1916, in Pound, *Selected Letters 1907–1941,* ed. D. D. Paige (New York: New Directions, 1971), 93.

21. See reproduction of the page with Williams's autograph in Qian, *Orientalism and Modernism,* 121.

22. Herbert A. Giles, *A History of Chinese Literature* (New York: Appleton, 1901), 144–46.

23. William Carlos Williams, *I Wanted to Write a Poem: The Autobiography of the Works of a Poet,* ed. Edith Heal (Boston: Beacon Press, 1958), 65–66.

24. Marjorie Perloff, *The Dance of the Intellect: Studies in the Poetry of the Pound Tradition* (1985; repr. Evanston, IL: Northwestern University Press, 1996), 89.

25. Ibid.

26. Ibid., 103.

27. Ibid., 104.

28. Wai-lim Yip, ed. and trans., *Chinese Poetry: An Anthology of Major Modes and Genres* (Durham, NC: Duke University Press, 1997), 10–11.

29. In a letter of May 7, 1958, Wang informs Williams of his decision to "leave for California" (Beinecke). Enclosed are several cantos from his "Grandfather" poem. In a reply dated May 20, 1958, Williams thanks Wang for explaining the yin/yang principle in Chinese poetry before discussing the "Grandfather" cantos. Regarding Wang's plan to move to the West Coast Williams writes: "Come in and see us on your way to California and read us more of your grandfather poem" (Dartmouth). Nowhere in the May 7, 1958, letter does Wang mention the yin/yang principle. Nor does he in any other letters to Williams (Beinecke). The yin/yang reference is presumably to Wang's meeting with Williams on January 17, 1958—his explanation of the "deep woods/light, sunset/sunrise" contrasts in Wang Wei's stop-short poems. There is no way to find out if Wang might have discussed the yin/yang idea with Williams between February and May 1958 on another visit to Rutherford or in a telephone conversation. A telephone conversation would be extratextual rather than textual. In *Speech Acts in Literature,* J. Hillis Miller uses the example of a telephone conversation in Marcel Proust's *À la recherche du temps perdu* to show the difference between talking face to face and talking over the phone: over the phone Marcel's grandmother was to Marcel a different person speaking in her voice "without the accompaniment of her face and features" (193). Over the phone, Wang would also seem a different person to Williams.

30. Stephen Field, "'The Cassia Tree': A Chinese Micropoem," *William Carlos Williams Review* 18 (1992): 34–49.

31. "The Grandfather Cycle" is a long, unfinished poem of 101 cantos, of which only the first fifteen have been published. For these fifteen cantos, see *The Human Voice* 2, no. 1 (1966): 31–36.

32. Pound, *Cathay: The Centennial Edition,* 56.

33. Williams was in correspondence with Sheri Martinelli. In a letter to Wang dated May 20, 1958, Williams wrote: "Yes, I heard from Sheri. She spoke in her letter of some other famous lover . . ." (Dartmouth).

TWO. Modernist Minimalism Reinitiated in Rutherford

1. Peter Schmidt, *William Carlos Williams, the Arts, and Literary Tradition* (Baton Rouge: Louisiana State University Press, 1988), 243.

2. Ibid., 244.

3. Jonathan Mayhew, "William Carlos Williams and the Free Verse Line," in Carroll F. Terrell, ed., *William Carlos Williams: Man and Poet* (Orono, ME: National Poetry Foundation, 1983), 298.

4. Cited in *CP2,* 508.

5. There are other poems in English made up of quatrains similar to stop-short. William Blake's "Sick Rose," for example, resembles a double stop-short. Emily Dickinson's poem "Wild Nights—Wild Nights!" consists of three stop-short quatrains. But it is doubtful that any poets before Williams imitated the Chinese stop-short or double stop-short.

6. Henry Sayre, *The Visual Text of William Carlos Williams* (Urbana: University of Illinois Press, 1983), 78. The emphasis is in the original.

7. Cited in *CP2,* 510.

8. Cited in *CP2,* 510.

9. Ibid.

10. Sayre, *The Visual Text of William Carlos Williams,* 142.

11. Eliot, *Selected Prose,* 48.

12. Perloff, *The Poetics of Indeterminacy,* 118.

13. Arthur Waley, *More Translations from the Chinese* (New York: Alfred A. Knopf, 1919), 84.

14. William Carlos Williams, "Two New Books by Kenneth Rexroth," in *Something to Say: William Carlos Williams on Younger Poets,* ed. James Breslin (New York: New Directions, 1985), 241.

15. Ibid., 242–43.

16. See Qian, *Orientalism and Modernism,* 132–33.

17. Waley, *More Translations from the Chinese,* 45.

18. See *CP2,* 504.

19. Ovid, *Metamorphoses,* ed. and trans. Frank Justus Miller (Cambridge, MA: Harvard University Press, 1966–68), 217–18.

20. Robert Lawson-Peebles, "William Carlos Williams' *Pictures from Brueghel,*" *Word & Image* 2 (1986): 19.

21. Gustav Glück, *Pieter Brueghel the Elder* (New York: Braziller, 1952), 30 and 31.

22. James A. W. Heffernan, *Museum of Words: The Poetics of Ekphrasis from Homer to Ashbery* (Chicago: University of Chicago Press, 1993), 157.

23. Cited in Mariani, *William Carlos Williams,* 571.

24. Cited in Fun Yu-lan, *A History of Chinese Philosophy,* trans. Derk Bodde (Princeton, NJ: Princeton University Press, 1952–53), 2:467.

25. Eliot, *Selected Prose,* 40.

26. As Jeanne Heuving argues, the Pound of *The Cantos* and the Eliot of *The Waste Land* are primarily concerned with "establishing their authority and identity through mirroring others." See Jeanne Heuving, *Omissions Are Not Accidents: Gender in the Art of Marianne Moore* (Detroit, MI: Wayne State University Press, 1992), 31.

27. Cited in Mariani, *William Carlos Williams,* 735.

28. William Carlos Williams, "Charles Olson's Maximus, Book II," in *Something to Say,* 227.

29. William Carlos Williams, "Contribution to a Symposium on the Beats," in *Something to Say,* 261.

30. Ibid.

31. Cited in Mariani, *William Carlos Williams,* 751.

32. William Carlos Williams, "Howl for Carl Solomon," in *Something to Say,* 225.

THREE. Moore, Sze, and the Tao

1. For a detailed discussion of Moore's interest in Chinese art and aesthetic, see Qian, *The Modernist Response to Chinese Art,* 22–43, 64–80, 111–22, and 167–92. See also Cynthia Stamy, *Marianne Moore and China: Orientalism and a Writing of America* (New York: Oxford University Press, 1999).

2. Linda Leavell, *Marianne Moore and the Visual Arts: Prismatic Color* (Baton Rouge: Louisiana State University Press, 1995), 157n42.

3. For a transcript of the sound recording of "Tedium and Integrity in Poetry," see the appendix. Further references to this lecture will be given parenthetically as "Tedium and Integrity."

4. Mai-mai Sze, *The Tao of Painting: A Study of the Ritual Disposition of Chinese Painting* (New York: Bollingen Foundation, 1956), 31. Further references to the volume will be given parenthetically as *The Tao of Painting.*

5. Charles Q. Wu renders this opening line as: "Ways may be spoken of as *dao,* but they are not the eternal *Dao*"; Charles Q. Wu, trans., *Thus Spoke Laozi: Dao De Jing: A New Translation with Commentaries* (Honolulu: University of Hawaii Press in association with Beijing Foreign Language Teaching & Research Press, 2016), 3.

6. Cf. chapter 3, line 8, of the *Dao De Jing,* in Wu, *Thus Spoke Laozi:* "Keep their minds empty" (10). According to a second century AD edition of the *Dao De Jing* by He Shang Gong, the line is also meant to encourage rulers' self-cultivation. "Thus," observes Wu, "to empty the mind could mean to 'clear the mind of all desires and worries'" (11).

7. Cristanne Miller, *Marianne Moore: Questions of Authority* (Cambridge, MA: Harvard University Press, 1993), 26.

8. On unorthodox readings of Xie He's six canons, see Qian Zhongshu, *Limited Views: Essays on Ideas and Letters,* trans. Ronald C. Egan (Cambridge, MA: Harvard University Press, 1998), 97–104. For the original comment, see Qian Zhongshu, *Guanzhuibian* (Limited views), vol. 4 (1979; repr., Beijing: SDX Joint Publishing, 2001), 2109–2127.

9. Qian, *Limited Views,* 98.

10. Ibid., 97.

11. Herbert A. Giles, *An Introduction to the History of Chinese Pictorial Art* (London: Bernard Quaritch, 1918), 28.

12. Laurence Binyon, *The Flight of the Dragon: An Essay on the Theory and Practice of Art in China and Japan Based on Original Sources* (London: Murray, 1911), 11.

13. Ibid., 15.

14. Pound, *Ezra Pound's Poetry and Prose,* 3:99.

15. See Mai-mai Sze, *China* (Cleveland, OH: Western Reserve University Press, 1944).

16. See Mai-mai Sze, *Echo of a Cry: A Story Which Began in China* (New York: Harcourt, Brace and Co., 1945).

17. See Mai-mai Sze, *Silent Children: A Novel* (New York: Harcourt, Brace and Co., 1948).

18. My thanks to Janice Braun of Mills College for this contextual information.

19. Marianne Moore, "O, to Be a Dragon," *Sequoia* 3, no. 1 (1957): 20.

20. Marianne Moore, *The Complete Poems* (New York: Viking, 1981), 177. Further references to this volume will be given parenthetically as *CPo*.

21. In Perloff's *21st-Century Modernism,* Susan Howe's and Charles Bernstein's millennium poems serve as major illustrations of twenty-first-century modernism (164–72, 172–80).

22. Marjorie Perloff, *Unoriginal Genius: Poetry by Other Means in the New Century* (Chicago: University of Chicago Press, 2010), 4, 22–23.

23. Marianne Moore, *Selected Letters,* eds. Bonnie Costello, Celeste Goodridge, and Cristanne Miller (New York: Knopf, 1997), 194, 197.

24. Miller, *Marianne Moore,* 43.

25. Ibid.

26. Qian, *The Modernist Response to Chinese Art,* 184.

27. Cf. chapter 4, line 1, of the *Dao De Jing,* in Wu, *Thus Spoke Laozi*: "*Dao* is an empty vessel" (13). The remaining quotations are restatements of chapter 11 of the *Dao De Jing,* in Wu's *Thus Spoke Laozi*: "Thirty spokes converge at the hub: / Where there is nothing / There lies what makes the cart useful. // Mix clay to make a vessel: / Where there is nothing / There lies what makes the vessel useful. // Chisel doors and windows to make a house: / Where there is nothing / There lies what makes the house useful" (27). The ideas are cited in Sze, *The Tao of Painting,* 17.

28. For discussions of these poems, see Qian, *The Modernist Response to Chinese Art,* 184–91.

29. Marianne Moore, *The Poems of Marianne Moore,* ed. Grace Schulman (New York: Penguin Books, 2003), xvii–xviii.

30. For a fuller discussion of Moore's revisions of "Poetry," see Andrew J. Kappel, "Complete with Omissions: The Text of Marianne Moore's *Complete Poems,*" in George Bornstein, ed., *Representing Modernist Texts: Editing as Interpretation* (Ann Arbor: University of Michigan Press, 1991), 125–56.

31. See Pound, *Gaudier-Brzeska,* 89.

32. Altieri, *Painterly Abstraction,* 266–67.

33. According to Linda Leavell, "we / do not admire what / we cannot understand" is a quotation from Mrs. Mary Warner Moore. See Leavell, *Holding on Upside Down: The Life and Work of Marianne Moore* (New York: Farrar, Straus and Giroux, 2013), 170. See also Wu, *Thus Spoke Laozi,* 57.

34. Kappel, "Complete with Omissions," 154.

35. Ezra Pound, *Literary Essays,* ed. T. S. Eliot (New York: New Directions, 1968), 23.

36. Altieri, *Painterly Abstraction,* 268.

37. Cf. chapter 37, lines 1–2, of the *Dao De Jing,* in Wu's *Thus Spoke Laozi*: "*Dao* in its eternity does nothing. / Yet nothing is not done" (84).

FOUR. Sze's "Permanent Gifts" and Moore's Last Achievement

1. About the American poet Randall Jarrell, see Marianne Moore, "Randall Jarrell" in the September 1967 *Atlantic Monthly,* reprinted in *CPr,* 612–16. About the American artist Robert Andrew Parker, see Marianne Moore, "Robert Andrew Parker," in the April 1958 *Arts,* reprinted in *CPr,* 500–502.

2. Irene Sharaff, along with Renié Conley and Vitorio Nino Novarese, garnered

the 1963 Academy Award for Best Costume Design for *Cleopatra,* starring Elizabeth Taylor and Richard Burton.

3. The January 1964 letter from Moore to Sze has not survived.

4. Mai-mai Sze and Irene Sharaff bequeathed to the New York Society Library their collection of books with some of Sze's newspaper clippings and one of Sze's letters in them. According to Erin Schreiner, special collections librarian at the New York Society Library, the Sharaff/Sze collection includes no correspondence between Moore and Sze. In a letter to the author in June 2004, Sze's sister, Alice Sze Wang, confirms that Sze's relatives kept none of Mai-mai Sze's papers.

5. "The Elephant and the Mouse," *Times Literary Supplement,* August 16, 1963, 626.

6. See Marianne Moore to Ezra Pound, January 9, 1919, in Moore, *Selected Letters,* 122.

7. See Leavell, *Holding on Upside Down,* 378. "The Paper Nautilus" is in Moore's 1941 volume *What Are Years (CPo,* 121–22).

8. China has two kinds of ancient plucked string instruments, the *guqin* for the cultured and the *guzheng* for both the more and less cultured. The *guqin* has five or seven strings whereas the *guzheng* has thirteen, eighteen, or twenty-one strings.

9. *The Yellow-River* (1684–87), a handscroll said to be painted by Zhou Zhi and Li Hanmei under the auspices of Qing dynasty emperor Kangxi (1654–1722), is kept at the Taipei Palace Museum. In the poem there is no hyphen in "Yellow River" and the line ends with a hyphen.

10. See chapter 3, note 12.

11. W. B. Yeats, *The Collected Works of W. B. Yeats, Volume IV, Early Essays,* eds. Richard Finneran and George Bornstein (New York: Scribner, 2007), 169.

12. Barry Ahearn, *William Carlos Williams and Alterity: The Early Poetry* (Cambridge, UK: Cambridge University Press, 1994), 109.

13. "The Elephant and the Mouse," 626.

14. Ibid.

15. Bernard F. Engel, *Marianne Moore* (Boston: Twayne, 1989), 134,

16. Ruth Carrington, "Marianne Moore's Metaphorical Giraffe," in *Marianne Moore: Woman and Poet,* ed. Patricia C. Willis (Onono, ME: National Poetry Foundation, 1990), 149.

17. Ibid.

18. Ibid.

19. Moore, *Selected Letters,* 501.

20. Ibid., 502.

21. Marianne Moore's *Idiosyncrasy and Technique* was published by the University of California Press in 1958.

22. Engel, *Marianne Moore,* 134.

23. Ibid.

24. Carrington, "Marianne Moore's Metaphorical Giraffe," 152.

25. Eliot, *Selected Prose,* 40.

26. Gertrude Stein, *Writings, Volume 2: 1932–1946* (New York: Library of America, 1998), 356.

27. Perloff, *21st-Century Modernism,* 47.

28. For discussions of Baosun Zeng's contribution to Pound's Canto XLIX, see

Qian, ed., *Ezra Pound's Chinese Friends,* 9–17; and Qian, "Why Is Canto XLIX Called the 'Seven Lakes Canto'?"

29. Leavell, *Holding on Upside Down,* 386.

30. Elizabeth Gregory, ed., *The Critical Response to Marianne Moore* (Westport, CT: Praeger, 2003), 230.

31. Leavell, *Holding on Upside Down,* 380.

32. John Ashbery, *Selected Prose,* ed. Eugene Richie (Ann Arbor: University of Michigan Press, 2005), 83.

33. Ibid., 85.

34. Ibid., 108–09; T. S. Eliot, "Introduction," *Selected Poems of Marianne Moore* (New York: MacMillan, 1935), xiii.

35. Ashbery, *Selected Prose,* 86.

FIVE. Fang as Pound's Teacher of Naxi Pictographs

1. Pound and Cummings, *Pound/Cummings,* 408.

2. Pound, *Selected Prose,* 464.

3. See Ezra Pound, "Two Cantos [From Canto CXV and Canto CXVI]," *Paris Review* 28 (Summer/Fall 1962): 13–16.

4. See Ezra Pound, "Sections from New Cantos: From CX, From CXII, Unassigned, From CXV," *Agenda* 3, no. 3 (December 1963/January 1964): 1–3. Only one word in the *Agenda* version of "From Canto CX" has been emended for its final text: "spirits" in "many spirits are at the foot of / Hsiang Shan" is changed to "springs" (*C,* 804).

5. Peter Stoicheff, "The Cantos: Drafts and Fragments of Cantos CX–CXVII," in *The Ezra Pound Encyclopedia,* eds. Demetres Tryphonopoulos and Stephen Adams (Westport, CT: Greenwood, 2005), 49.

6. Stephen Sicari, "Pound after Pisa: 1945–1972," in *Ezra Pound in Context,* ed. Ira B. Nadel (Cambridge, UK: Cambridge University Press, 2010), 464.

7. Ronald Bush, "Late Cantos LXXII–CXVII," in *The Cambridge Companion to Ezra Pound,* ed. Ira B. Nadel (Cambridge, UK: Cambridge University Press, 1999), 133, 130.

8. Peter Makin, *Pound's Cantos* (Baltimore: Johns Hopkins University Press, 1992), 290.

9. Ibid.

10. The Beinecke Library of Yale University keeps a summer 1959 typescript of "From Canto CXV," with two lines from Canto XIII: "the flowers of the apricot blow from the East to the West / I have tried to keep them from falling." The word "blossoms" in Canto XIII is changed to "flowers," and the word "And" before "I" is omitted (*C,* 60). These lines are not in the final text of "From Canto CXV." See also Ronald Bush, "'Unstill Ever Turning': The Composition of Ezra Pound's *Drafts & Fragments,*" *Text* 7 (1994): 406–408.

11. See Carroll F. Terrell, *A Companion to the Cantos of Ezra Pound* (Berkeley: University of California Press, 1993), 674, 713.

12. Fredrick Jameson, *The Political Unconsciousness: Narrative as a Socially Symbolic Act* (Ithaca, NY: Cornell University Press, 1981), 9.

13. Neither the Arnold Arboretum Horticultural Library in Boston, nor the

Hunt Institute for Botanical Documentation, a research division of Carnegie Mellon University, keeps catalogued or uncatalogued correspondence between Joseph F. Rock and Ezra Pound. The Joseph F. Rock Herbarium at the University of Hawai'i has no archive of Joseph F. Rock papers. Thanks to Sheila Connor, archivist at the Arnold Arboretum Library, J. Dustin Williams, archivist and research scholar of the Hunt Institute for Botanical Documentation, and Michael Thomas, collections manager of the Joseph F. Rock Herbarium, for confirming the above. I am grateful to Emily Mitchell Wallace for sharing Rock's letter of January 3, 1956, to Pound, discovered among the Ezra Pound Papers of the Beinecke Library of Yale University.

14. The card is in the Lilly Library, Indiana University. Further references to archival materials in that library will be given parenthetically as Lilly. Pound's interest in the *Yi jing* hexagrams began perhaps in the mid-1950s when he wrote in Canto CII: "50 more years on The Changes" (*Cantos*, 749), alluding to Confucius. "If many years were added to me, I would give fifty to the study of the Book of Changes, and might therefore manage to avoid great mistakes." In 1962–72, according to Pound's companion Olga Rudge, Pound and Rudge made hexagrams together every day, "usually in the morning, first thing after breakfast" (Beinecke).

15. The backs of the two greeting cards from the Fangs to the Pounds at the Beinecke Library of Yale University *are* labeled, in Mary de Rachewiltz's hand, "*Not* Achilles Fang" (Beinecke).

16. In 1937–38, due to Japanese intrusion into northern China, Peking University and Tsinghua University in Beijing and Nankai University in Tianjin merged to form Changsha Temporary University in Changsha and later National Southwestern Associated University in Kunmin. After the war, the three prestigious universities moved back to Beijing and Tianjin, respectively.

17. Dorothy Pound's 1959 letter to the Fangs is in the Josephine Fang Collection. Further references to letters and autograph note in this collection will be given parenthetically as JFC.

18. The trade edition of Pound's translation of the Confucian odes, *Shih-ching: The Classic Anthology Defined by Confucius,* was published by Harvard University Press in 1954. Pound's manuscript for a projected bilingual edition of the Confucian odes with a Chinese seal text and a sound key remains unedited and is held at the Beinecke Library of Yale University. For exchanges between Pound and Achilles Fang about the bilingual edition of *Shih-ching,* see Qian, ed., *Ezra Pound's Chinese Friends,* 146–51.

19. See Joseph Rock, *Ancient Na-khi Kingdom of Southwest China* (Cambridge, MA: Harvard University Press, 1947), 1:48–62.

20. Carroll Terrell, "Na-khi Documents I: The Landscape of Paradise," *Paideuma* 3, no. 1 (1974): 93.

21. Paul Fang's two grandchildren, Jason and Shelley Fang, visited the Stone Drum that summer. Paul Fang did not go with them because "there would have been too much walking for him" (Josephine Fang to the author, May 27, 2015).

22. Pound relied on Ernest Fenollosa's Chinese poetry notebooks to make *Cathay* (1915). He depended on M. G. Pauthier's *Doctrine de Confucius: Les quatre livres de philosophie morale et politique de la Chine* to compose Canto XIII and translate *Ta Hio* (1928). He used J. A. M. de Moyriac de Mailla's *Histoire générale de la Chine* as a guide

when drafting the Chinese history cantos. He used James Legge's *The Four Books* as a guide when doing his late Confucian translations.

23. In recent years Naxi and Chinese bilingual education has been encouraged in Lijiang. When in Lijiang in May 2014, I saw Naxi pictographs on road signs, shop signs, and in advertising on buses everywhere.

24. According to Fang Guoyu, *Naxi Xiangxing Wenzi Pu* (A dictionary of Naxi pictographs), 91, the Naxi pictograph for the moon has the crescent moon's inner curve turned upward. Pound's has it turned downward toward the lower left.

25. See Joseph Rock, "The ²Muan ¹Bpö Ceremony or the Sacrifice to Heaven as Practiced by the ¹Na-²khi," *Monumenta Serica: Journal of Oriental Studies of the Catholic University of Peking* 13 (1948): 67–68. See also Joseph Rock, "The Romance of ²K'a-²mä-¹gyu-³mi-²gkyi, A ¹Na-²khi Tribal Love Story," *Bulletin de l'Ecole Francaise d'Extreme-Orient* 39 (1939): 9–10.

26. Pound, *Literary Essays*, 5, 23.

27. Rock, "The ²Muan ¹Bpö Ceremony," 1–3.

28. See Terrell, "Na-khi Documents I," 94.

29. See Rock, "The Romance of ²K'a-²mä-¹gyu-³mi-²gkyi," 9.

30. R. H. Mathews, *Mathews' Chinese-English Dictionary* (Cambridge, MA: Harvard University Press, 1944).

31. See Humphrey Carpenter, *A Serious Character: A Life of Ezra Pound* (Boston: Houghton Mifflin, 1988), 797–98.

32. See Rock, "The Romance of ²K'a-²mä-¹gyu-³mi-²gkyi," 53.

33. Ibid.

34. In her e-mail to the author on September 22, 2004, Mary de Rachewiltz writes: "There's no sign of P. H. Fang in any books here. The Muan Bpo [here] has EP's initials on cover. The various books & articles by J. Rock were given to Boris by Peter Goullart who was in [Lijiang] with Rock."

35. According to Joseph Rock, "The ²Muan ¹Bpö Ceremony," each of the three factions of the Naxi in Lijiang performs the ²Muan ¹bpo on a different date, one on the ninth day of the first moon, one on the seventh day of the first moon, and one on the third day of the first moon (11).

36. Interview with Paul Fang, August 18, 2003.

37. Rock, "The ²Muan ¹Bpö Ceremony," 13, 42.

38. See F. W. Baller, trans., *The Sacred Edict: With a Translation of the Colloquial Rendering* (Shanghai: American Presbyterian Mission Press, 1892; repr. 1907).

39. Ho Tso-wei, a Naxi dongba (priest) "well versed in ¹Na-²khi literature," assisted Rock in the preparation of "The ²Muan ¹Bpö Ceremony." See Rock, "The ²Muan ¹Bpö Ceremony," 3 and 12.

40. Ibid., 12.

41. The manuscript in Rock's possession is entitled "²Mùan-³llü ³dsu ²gkv ²szi = to do as in the days of ²Mùan-³llü-¹ddu-²ndzi." See ibid., 10. For translations of the four prayers, see ibid., 17–21.

42. Terrell, *A Companion to the Cantos of Ezra Pound,* 658.

43. Rock, "The ²Muan ¹Bpö Ceremony," 35, 38.

44. In a letter to Peter Goullart on September 10, 1962, Paul Fang refers to Grand Lama Shenlou Hutuktu, who appears in Goullart's *Forgotten Kingdom:* "I remember him [Shenlou Hutuktu] well. He was a good friend of my grandfather. We visited his

monastery, and at the death of my grandfather he stayed in our house for two months to help with the preparations for the funeral" (JFC).

45. See Kay Larson, *Where the Heart Beats: John Cage, Zen Buddhism, and the Inner Life of Artists* (New York: Penguin Books, 2012), 240–252, 277; and Spate, Hickey, and Monet, *Monet and Japan*, 37. The Noh enthusiast, "nameless" to Yeats, was either Torahiko Gun or Sugano Nijuichi, both Michio Itō's classmates from Gakushuin. See Ian Carruthers, trans., "A Translation of Fifteen Pages of Itō Michio's Autobiography, Utsukushiku naru kyoshitsu," *Canadian Journal of Irish Studies* 2 (1976): 35.

46. Apparently not all cross-cultural interpersonal influence can be recovered. A January 1964 letter from Marianne Moore to Mai-mai Sze might contain clues of cross-cultural interpersonal influence on her final work (see chapter 4). With the loss of that letter, proof for any such influence is lost.

47. Curtis Bradford, *Yeats at Work* (Carbondale: Southern Illinois University Press, 1965), 211.

48. Yeats, *The Collected Works*, 165.

49. See Pound, *Gaudier-Brzeska*, 88–89.

50. Geoffrey Hartman, *The Fatal Question of Culture* (New York: Columbia University Press, 1997), 83.

51. See Rock, "The ²Muan ¹Bpö Ceremony," 38, 101; "The Romance of ²Ka-²mä-¹gyu-³mi-²gkyi," 52, 84. According to Fang Guoyu, *Naxi Xiangxing Wenzi Pu* (91), the moon pictograph meaning "the moon" or "month" is pronounced "le" or "heme" or "he" or "hemetsi."

SIX. Naxi Rites and Vortex in Pound's Final Cantos

1. Rock, "The Romance of ²K'a-²mä-¹gyu-³mi-²gkyi," 3.

2. For a full discussion of Pound's Malatesta cantos (Cantos VIII–XI), their production, transmission, and reception, see Lawrence Rainey, *Ezra Pound and Monument of Culture: Text, History, and the Malatesta Cantos* (Chicago: University of Chicago Press, 1991).

3. Perloff, *The Poetics of Indeterminacy*, 181, 183, 184.

4. Rock, "The Romance of ²K'a-²mä-¹gyu-³mi-²gkyi," 20n2.

5. Ibid., 42.

6. Perloff, *The Poetics of Indeterminacy*, 182.

7. Ibid., 184.

8. John Peck, "Landscape as Ceremony in the Later Cantos: From the Roads of France to Rock's World," *Agenda* 2 (1971): 50–60.

9. Emily Mitchell Wallace, "'Why Not Spirits?'—'The Universe Is Alive': Ezra Pound, Joseph Rock, the Na Khi, and Plotinus," in Zhaoming Qian, ed., *Ezra Pound and China* (Ann Arbor: University of Michigan Press, 2003), 246.

10. Ibid.

11. See Bush, "Unstill, Ever Turning," 403.

12. See Bush, "Late Cantos," 127.

13. Wallace, "'Why Not Spirits?'" 252.

14. Hilda Doolittle (H.D.), *End to Torment: A Memoir of Ezra Pound*, ed. Norman Holmes Pearson and Michael King (New York: New Directions, 1979), 12–15.

15. Rock, "The Romance of ²K'a-²mä-¹gyu-³mi-²gkyi," 5.

16. Doolittle, *End to Torment*, 12.

17. Cited in William McNaughton, "A Report on the 16th Biennial International Conference on Ezra Pound, Brantôme, France, 18–22 July 1995," *Paideuma* 27, no. 1 (1998), 130.

18. Peter Goullart, *Forgotten Kingdom* (London: Murray, 1955), 180–182.

19. Ibid., 84.

20. Wallace, "'Why Not Spirits?'" 220; Goullart, *Forgotten Kingdom,* 142.

21. Goullart, *Forgotten Kingdom,* 142.

22. Ezra Pound, *The Spirit of Romance* (New York: New Directions, 1968), 92.

23. Ezra Pound, *Poems & Translations,* ed. Richard Sieburth (New York: Library of America, 2003), 14.

24. Goullart, *Forgotten Kingdom,* 158.

25. Bush, "Late Cantos," 126.

26. Both letters are kept at the Hunt Institute for Botanical Documentation, a research division of Carnegie Mellon University. In his letter on January 29, 1962, sent from Merano, Italy, Goullart wrote: "Ezra Pound and Prince Boris de Rachewiltz send you their best wishes. They and I hope that your new appointment will be in Munich so either you could come down here for a short holiday or, perhaps, I could come up to Munich, especially after the publication of my book there in March." Rock does not seem to have responded to either letters. He died in Honolulu on December 7, 1962. Thanks to Hunt Institute archivist J. Dustin Williams for calling my attention to the two early 1962 letters from Goullart to Rock.

27. In 1960 Paul Fang was sent to the Institut Fourier in Grenoble, France, to be a U.S. federal government research fellow. That year he and Josephine sent a family photograph Christmas card to Rock, expressing their wish for "a visit from you." The card is kept at the Hunt Institute for Botanical Documentation at Carnegie Mellon University.

28. Bush, "Late Cantos," 126; Ezra Pound, "An Interview [by Donald Hall]," *Paris Review* 28 (Summer/Fall 1962): 47.

29. Bush, "Late Cantos," 126.

30. Doolittle, *End to Torment,* 15.

31. Bush, "Late Cantos," 130.

32. Doolittle, *End to Torment,* 15, 14.

33. The caption reads: "Na-khi Women of the Village of Nv-lv-kö: The first two (from the left) are unmarried, the third is married. Girls usually wear Chinese caps on festive occasions, otherwise a simple cloth is worn on the head with the hair (braids) wound outside. Married women wear their hair in a knob on the top of the head around which a cloth is wound to keep it in place, another cloth is then placed over it as in the picture." Plates 74 and 75, and this photograph (plate 76) illustrate a passage in chapter 4, "Li-chiang Snow Range and Territory South of the Yangtze Loop," section 3, "The Northern Edge of the Li-chiang Plain": "The Chinese name of the hamlet is Wen-hua-ts'un 文華村. Formerly it was known as San-chia-ts'un 三家村, as originally only three families lived there. To-day there are eighteen. The most northerly village on this part of the plain, situated at the actual foot of the snow range at an elevation of 9,400 feet, is Nv-lv-k'ö, consisting of about 100 families." There is not a single word about Naxi women's costume in this passage in Rock, *Ancient Na-khi Kingdom,* I:218.

34. Letter to the author, June 16, 2005.

35. Rock, "The ²Muan ¹Bpö Ceremony," 22, 24–25.

36. See ibid., 65: "There are the many springs which issue at the foot of the Hsiang Shan, or Elephant Mountain, immediately north of Li-chiang. A Lung-wang Miao 龍王廟, or Dragon King Temple, has been built there with a large pond with sacred fish. The springs are called ²Ngu-¹lu ¹gyi, and their waters flow through the city of Li-chiang as the Yü ho玉河 or Jade stream."

37. Ibid., 68.

38. David Levi Strauss, "Approaching *80 Flowers*," in *Code of Signals: Recent Writings in Poetics*, ed. Michael Palmer (Berkeley, CA: North Atlantic Books, 1983), 86.

39. Pound, *Literary Essays*, 3.

40. Ibid.; Pound, *Gaudier-Brzeska*, 92.

41. Pound, *Literary Essays*, 3.

42. "Rag-bag" is a word from Pound's "Three Cantos of a Poem of Some Length" in *Poems & Translations*, 318: "the 'modern world' / Needs such a rag-bag to stuff all its thought in."

CODA

1. Ryōkan Taigu (1758–1831) was a Japanese Zen monk, an artist and calligrapher. Zukofsky's *I's (pronounced eyes)* and *"A"*-14 explore Zen ideas implicit in "(Ryokan's Scroll)." Ryōkan's Scroll was reproduced on the cover of the original publication of *I's (pronounced eyes)* by Trobar Press, but mistakenly printed upside-down. It was a scroll of a poem by Ryōkan in his own beautiful running style calligraphy. Cid Corman who owned the scroll loaned it to Zokofsky in 1959. See Parker, "Louis Zukofsky's American Zen."

2. Gary Snyder, *Mountains and Rivers without End* (Berkeley, CA: Counterpoint, 2008), ix.

3. See Anthony Hunt, *Genesis, Structure, and Meaning in Gary Snyder's Mountains and Rivers without End* (Reno: University of Nevada Press, 2004), especially 57–60. See also Tan Qionglin, "Shinaide changshi 'shanhe wujin' zhong de 'Ku' jiegou jiqi yiyun" ("Ku" and its poetic role in Gary Snyder's *Mountains and Rivers without End*), *Foreign Literature Review* 3 (2011): 204–15. Among those who consider late Snyder a modernist are Robert Kern in *Orientalism, Modernism, and the American Poem* (Cambridge, UK: Cambridge University Press, 1996) and Josephine Park in *Apparitions of Asia: Modernist Form and Asian Poetics* (New York: Oxford University Press, 2008).

4. See Tony Lopez, "The Orient in Later Modernist English Poetry," in Qian, ed., *Modernism and the Orient*, 255–60; Marjorie Perloff, *21st-Century Modernism*, 190–95.

5. Christopher Innes, "Modernism in Drama," in Levenson, ed., *The Cambridge Companion to Modernism*, 141.

6. Matthew C. Roudané, "*Death of a Salesman* and the Poetics of Arthur Miller," in *The Cambridge Companion to Arthur Miller*, ed. Christopher Bigsby (Cambridge, UK: Cambridge University Press, 1997), 75.

7. Norris Houghton, "Understanding Willy," *New York Times*, June 24, 1984.

8. See Arthur Miller, *Salesman in Beijing* (London: Methuen, 1984), 7.

9. Arthur Miller, *Death of a Salesman* (New York: Penguin Books, 1976), 12.

10. See Ludwig Wittgenstein, *Philosophical Investigations*, trans. G. E. M. Anscombe (New York: Macmillan, 1958), proposition 215.

11. Marcel Duchamp, *Notes,* ed. and trans. Paul Matisse (Boston: G. K. Hall, 1983), no. 45.

12. See Miller, *Salesman in Beijing,* 6.

13. Miller, *Death of a Salesman,* 28.

14. Ibid., 11, 27.

15. Miller, *Salesman in Beijing,* 110.

16. Fang Kunlin, "The Coordination of Stage Lighting and Sound Effects for Art Creation," *Entertainment Technology* 1 (2008): 65.

17. Henry Y. H. Zhao, *Towards a Modern Zen Theatre: Gao Xingjian and Chinese Experimentalism* (London: School of Oriental and African Studies, 2000), 69.

18. Miller, *Salesman in Beijing,* 211–12.

19. See Ou Rong and Qian Zhaoming, "*Death of a Salesman* in Beijing Revisited," *The Arthur Miller Journal* 2 (2013): 66.

20. Miller, *Salesman in Beijing,* 28.

21. Ibid., 240.

22. Inge Morath and Arthur Miller, *Chinese Encounters* (New York: Farrar, Straus, and Giroux, 1979), 71, 74.

23. Ibid., 74.

24. Morath and Miller, *Chinese Encounters,* 74; Miller, *Salesman in Beijing,* 107.

25. Miller, *Salesman in Beijing,* 107.

26. Ibid., 114.

27. Ibid., 150–51.

28. Ibid., 151.

29. Xiaomei Chen, *Occidentalism: A Theory of Counter-discourse in Post-Mao China,* 2nd ed. (Lanham, MD: Rowman & Littlefield, 2002), 113. See also Bertolt Brecht, *Brecht on Theatre: The Development of an Aesthetic,* ed. and trans. John Willett (New York: Hill and Wang, 1964), 94–95, 99; Stark Young, "Ambassador in Art," *The New Republic,* April 6, 1932, 206–8, and Min Tian, *Mei Lanfang and the Twentieth-Century International Stage: Chinese Theatre Placed and Displaced* (New York: Palgrave, 2012), 175–213.

30. Georges Banu, "Mei Lanfang: A Case against and a Model for the Occidental Stage," trans. Ella Wiswell and Jane Gibson, *Asian Theatre Journal* 3, no. 2 (1986): 154.

31. Innes, "Modernism in Drama," 134–35.

32. W. B. Yeats, *Explorations* (London: Macmillan, 1962), 258. About Yeats and the Japanese dancer Michio Itō, see Helen Caldwell, *Michio Ito: The Dancer and His Dances* (Berkeley: University of California Press, 1977).

33. Brecht, *Brecht on Theatre,* 91.

34. Ibid., 99.

35. Ibid., 95.

36. Stein, *Writings Volume 2,* 315.

37. *Death of a Salesman,* directed by Volker Schlöndorff, with a documentary by Christian Blockwood on the stage-to-screen process and a close-up look at the collaboration of Arthur Miller, Dustin Hoffman, and Volker Schlöndorff (1985; Chatsworth, CA: Image Entertainment, 1985), DVD.

38. Marilyn Ferdinand, "Death of Salesman (1985)," *Ferdy on Films,* http://www.ferdyonfilms.com/2009/death-of-a-salesman-1985/499/.

39. Scott Brown, "Mike Nichols's Staggering New *Death of a Salesman* Goes Back to the Source," *Vulture* 15 (March 2012), http://www.vulture.com/2012/03/mike -nichols-new-death-of-a-salesman-review.html.

40. Cited in William Barillas, *The Midwestern Pastoral: Place and Landscape in Literature of the American Heartland* (Athens, OH: Ohio University Press, 2006), 49. Frank Wright's estate Taliesin is in Spring Green, Wisconsin. The original Taliesin (1911) was burnt in 1914. The rebuilt Taliesin II was partially burnt in 1925. In his junior year at MIT (1938) Pei drove to Spring Green to inspect Taliesin III, completed the previous year.

41. Cited in Rubalcaba, *I. M. Pei,* 12.

42. See Gero von Boehm and I. M. Pei, *Conversations with I. M. Pei: Light Is the Key* (New York: Prestel, 2000), 37–38.

43. Cited in Louise Chipley Slavicek, *I. M. Pei* (New York: Chelsea House, 2010), 56–57.

44. Michael Cannell, *I. M. Pei: Mandarin of Modernism* (New York: Carol Southern Books, 1995), 281.

45. Miller, *Illustration,* 14–15.

46. Cited in Cannell, *I. M. Pei,* 84.

47. Cited in Rubalcaba, *I. M. Pei,* 47.

48. See Slavicek, *I. M. Pei,* 99.

49. Robert Ivy, "Suzhou Museum," *Architectural Record,* April 2008, China issue, http://archrecord.construction.com/ar_china/BWAR/0804/0804_suzhou/0804 _suzhou.asp.

50. Cited in Cannell, *I. M. Pei,* 352.

51. Boehm and Pei, *Conversations,* 61.

52. Wang Jun, *Bei Yuming zhaokai dashihui* (Pei meeting local masters), May 1, 2002, http://www.hutong.net/html-882/. Chien Chung Pei and Li Chung Pei (both present at the meeting) were kind enough to read my summary of the report, providing corrections of factual inaccuracies.

53. The Suzhou Museum has proved to be not Pei's last project. Shortly after its completion he took up the project of the Museum of Islamic Art in Doha, Qatar, and completed it in 2008.

54. In 2015 Yang Weize was put under investigation for corruption, which led to the charges of his bribery crimes committed in 2005–14 when he was party chief of neighboring cities Wuxi and Nanjing.

55. Wang Jun, *Bei Yuming zhaokai dashihui.*

56. Ibid.

57. Ibid.

58. The reference is to the first line of *Xiang Jian Huan* or "To the Melody: Joyful Reunion" by Li Yu (937–978).

59. Wang Jun, *Bei Yuming zhaokai dashihui.*

60. Li Zehou, *The Path of Beauty,* 64.

61. Anya Dunaif, "Discovering the Aesthetics of Suzhou and Architect I. M. Pei," November 7, 2013, http://kidspiritonline.com/2013/11/discovering-the-aesthetics -of-suzhou-andarchitect-i-m-pei/.

62. According to Wang Jun, *Bei Yuming zhaokai dashihui,* at the April 2002 meeting, Wu Liangyong recalled an earlier meeting with Pei where a colleague asked Pei

to name one of his projects as his personal favorite. Pei compared the difficulty in doing this to the difficulty in naming one of one's daughters as his or her favorite. "Should you insist on my naming one," Pei eventually yielded, "I would name my current project, the Grand Loure." From this mid-1980s response, Wu concluded, "the new Suzhou Museum, once completed, will be Mr. Pei's youngest and loveliest daughter."

63. See Ma Jie, *Jianzhuxue he lishi wenhua chuancheng de wanmei jiehe* (Perfect integration of architecture and cultural heritage: An interview with I. M. Pei), October 23, 2006, http://www.backchina.com/forum/20080426/info-659467-1-1.html. Kun opera originated in Kunshan near Suzhou in the sixteenth century. Mei Lanfang is remembered not only as a great Beijing opera performer but also as a Kun opera performer, especially for his portrayal of Du Liniang in *The Peony Pavilion*, a masterpiece by playwright Tang Xianzu (1550–1616).

64. Scenes 8 and 15 of the opera respectively have allusions to a bamboo grove and to lotus flowers. See Tang Xianzu, *Mudan Ting (The Peony Pavilion)* (Shanghai: Classic Literature Press, 1958), 35, 74. As lotus grows only in deep water, water lilies have been used instead in the shallow Suzhou Museum pond.

65. For a report on Huang Wei's argument, see *Suzhou bowuguan xinguan shifou pohuai shiyi?* (Will the new Suzhou Museum bring any damage to World Heritage Sites?), August 18, 2003, http://www.huaxia.com/zt/whbl/2003-17/00097801.html.

66. "Beizhi yingxiang wenhua yichan, Bei Yuming fengdao zhi zuo yinfa zhenglun" (Accused of affecting cultural heritage, Pei's last commission arouses dispute), *China News*, September 15, 2003, http://www.chinanews.com/n/2003-09-15/26/346612.html.

67. Ibid.

68. See Zhao Guiyue, *Gao Fumin, yige wenhua guanyuan de youyuan jingmeng* (Gao Guimin, a cultural official's "interrupted dream"), *Southern People's Stories*, November 17, 2014, http://www.nfpeople.com/story_view.php?id=6090.

69. Chang Ailin and Li Can, *Shiyi zhongxin zhuren: Baohu yichan bushi jiandan dongjie zhoubian tudi* (World Heritage Center director: To protect heritage is not to freeze its surroundings), July 6, 2004, http://www.china.com.cn/chinese/zhuanti/28ycdh/603712.htm.

70. See Zhang Xin, *Suzhou Museum* (London: Great Wall Publishers, 2007), 34.

71. Li, *The Path of Beauty*, 64.

72. Ibid., 60; Dunaif, "Discovering the Aesthetics of Suzhou."

73. David Barboza, "I. M. Pei in China, Revisiting Roots," *New York Times*, October 9, 2006, http://www.nytimes.com/2006/10/09/arts/design/09pei.html?_r=0.

74. Theodor W. Adorno, *Essays on Music*, ed. Richard Leppert, with new translations by Susan Gillespie (Berkeley: University of California Press, 2002), 186. See also Said, *On Late Style*, 17.

75. See Cannell, *I. M. Pei*, 291.

76. Pound, *Literary Essays*, 23.

77. Rachna Kothari, "Elemental Experience: Pei's Suzhou Museum Revisited," *Building of the Week*, October 23, 2014, http://www.uncubemagazine.com/blog/14750609.

78. Barboza, "I. M. Pei in China."

APPENDIX

1. *The Selected Writings of Juan Ramon Jiménez,* ed. Eugenio Florit, trans. H. R. Hays (New York: Farrar, Straus, and Cudahy, 1957). For Moore's review of the book, see *CPr,* 497–99.

2. The version in the *Complete Poems* has "mirror" instead of "glass."

3. Five words from the *Complete Poems* version—"with an expression of inquiry" (141)—are missing.

4. Two lines from the *Complete Poems* version—"the mouse's limp tail hanging like a shoelace from its mouth—/ they sometimes enjoy solitude" (91)—are omitted.

5. A line from *The Fables of La Fontaine* version—"Lay down your pruning hook; your onslaught is too rude" (306)—is missing.

6. A line from *The Fables of La Fontaine* version—"Dead wood will soon be adrift on the Styx' dark flood" (306)—is missing.

7. This duplicated line is not in *The Fables of La Fontaine* version.

8. This duplicated line is not in *The Fables of La Fontaine* version.

9. This line is not in *The Fables of La Fontaine* version.

10. Five lines from *The Fables of La Fontaine* version—"Or should some king, a great one, be my simile, / At whose word even Fortune's wheel stands still, / Undeterred by all sorts of hostility, / Who makes sport of the mightiest if he will, / As cats toss mice they will not free" (284)—are omitted.

Index